Utilitarian Logic
and Politics

Utilitarian Logic and Politics

James Mill's 'Essay on Government', Macaulay's critique and the ensuing debate

EDITED AND INTRODUCED
BY
JACK LIVELY
AND
JOHN REES

1978

CLARENDON PRESS · OXFORD

Oxford University Press, Walton Street, Oxford OX2 6DP

London Glasgow New York Toronto
Delhi Bombay Calcutta Madras Karachi
Kuala Lumpur Singapore Hong Kong Tokyo
Nairobi Dar es Salaam Cape Town
Melbourne Auckland
and associated companies in
Beirut Berlin Ibadan Mexico City Nicosia

Oxford is a trade mark of Oxford University Press

Published in the United States
by Oxford University Press, New York

ISBN 0 19 827471 8

First published 1978
New as Paperback 1984

Printed in Great Britain by
Cox & Wyman Ltd
London, Fakenham and Reading

Contents

I

Introduction

1. THE DEBATE ON THE 'ESSAY ON GOVERNMENT'

BORN in 1773, James Mill in 1802 took the trail, familiar enough to a poor Scot, to London. It took some time to achieve the fame and fortune he sought, fame coming with the publication of his *History of India* in 1817 and fortune with his appointment to a post in India House in 1819. In the intervening years, he had supported himself and his family by literary hackwork. Nevertheless, these years cover two of the most important aspects of his life, his education of his son, John Stuart, and the beginning of his long association with Jeremy Bentham. Bentham and the elder Mill met in 1808 and, with periods of coolness, they enjoyed a close association until Bentham's death, being for many years close neighbours in London.

Mill became an unreserved disciple of Bentham and an ardent propagator of his ideas, but the influence was not just the one way, for it was after their association had begun that Bentham moved to a Radical, democratic position in politics. Previously, he had been relatively uninterested in purely constitutional problems and hostile to the democratic ideas of the French Revolution. He was concerned primarily with legal reform, and accepted without questioning the possibility of persuading the British aristocratic leadership to undertake legal reconstruction on utilitarian principles. Chagrin over the failure of his Panopticon scheme is one explanation of the deflation of these early hopes;[1] but his move to political Radicalism, culminating in the publication of his *Plan of Parliamentary Reform, in the Form of a Catechism* in 1817, was no doubt stimulated in part by the influence of Mill.[2]

Mill not only prompted the merger of utilitarian and radical ideas; he was also the most powerful and influential advocate of the new doctrine. According to John Stuart Mill, although Bentham was 'a much greater name in history' than his father, James Mill was the more important in diffusing the creed and 'gave the distinguishing character to the Benthamic or

---

[1] Bentham spent a good deal of his time between 1791 and 1803 vainly pressing the government to undertake the building of a panopticon, an ideal prison, devised by him and his brother Samuel—see Leslie Stephen: *The English Utilitarians* (1900), vol. i, pp. 193–206. For the effect of this failure, see the footnotes in Bentham: *Works* (ed. J. Bowring 1843), vol. i, p. 3 and vol. iii, p. 468.

[2] See Elie Halévy: *The Growth of Philosophic Radicalism* (1949), pp. 255–8.

utilitarian propagandism of that time'.[3] The creation of an ideol-
ogical school (the 'Utilitarians', or 'Benthamites' or 'philosophic
Radicals'), bound together by a common intellectual style and
to a lesser degree by a common political programme, was very
much his personal achievement. Nothing contributed more to
the definition of this new ideology, and nothing illustrates better
the alliance of Utilitarianism and Radicalism, than the articles
which Mill contributed to the Supplement to the fifth edition of
the *Encyclopaedia Britannica* which appeared in parts between
1815 and 1824. Above all, the article on Government, which
first appeared in 1820 and was republished several times during
the decade,[4] was taken to be central to the Benthamite credo.
The substance if not the tone of Macaulay's sneer that the sect
took it to be 'perfect and unanswerable' was confirmed by
John Stuart Mill's recollection that the essay 'was regarded
probably by all of us as a masterpiece of political wisdom'.[5]

James Mill himself claimed that the essay would be uncontro-
versial. Writing to Napier, the editor of the Supplement, in
September 1819, he remarked, 'You need be under no alarm
about my article *Government*. I shall say nothing capable of
alarming even a Whig . . .'[6] The essay goes some way towards
meeting this promise to the editor. The Whig language of
'checks on power' is used as much as the Benthamite language of
utility, and the essay ends with an encomium on the middle
class. None the less, there was sufficient to alarm 'even a Whig'—
the rejection of the idea of balance of power, the criticism of the
representation of interests and, above all, the recommendation
of universal male suffrage. Even before Mill wrote, the ideolo-
gical battle-lines between Whig and Benthamite had been laid
down with an attack on Bentham's *Plan of Parliamentary Reform*
by Sir James Mackintosh in the *Edinburgh Review*. An explicit
Benthamite reply to Mackintosh was made in 1821 by George
Grote, the future historian of Greece,[7] and Mill's article itself,
behind its affectation of impartiality, can be seen as yet another
reply. Although there was much Whig criticism during the 1820s

---

[3] John Stuart Mill: *Autobiography* (World's Classics 1952), pp. 85–6.
[4] See Note on the texts, below, p. 51.
[5] See below p. 99: John Stuart Mill: *Autobiography* (World's Classics 1952),
p. 87.
[6] A. Bain: *James Mill, a Biography* (1882), p. 188.
[7] [G. Grote]: *Statement of the Question of Parliamentary Reform* (1821).

of the demands of Radical reformers, a direct response to the 'Essay on Government' had to await Macaulay's article in the March 1829 issue of the *Edinburgh Review*.

Macaulay was in many ways a natural choice for Napier, now the *Edinburgh*'s editor, to make as reviewer of Mill's 'Essay'. Macaulay, who was elected to a Fellowship at Trinity, Cambridge in 1824, had met with the young Cambridge Benthamites through his friend Charles Austin; he had been an Edinburgh Reviewer since 1825; and, with Parliamentary ambitions, he was anxious to make a reputation in public affairs. [8] Above all, his views reflected a general Whig ambivalence towards Benthamite ideas, combining an admiration for Bentham's legal philosophy (shared by many Whig reformers) with a distrust of both the general intellectual style of the Utilitarians and their advocacy of Radical reform of Parliament.

As inevitable as an attack on the 'Essay' from the *Edinburgh Review* was a reply from the *Westminster Review*. Founded by Bentham in 1824, the *Westminster Review* was intended, and for a time served, as the Utilitarian answer to the Whig and Tory organs, the *Edinburgh* and the *Quarterly*. The first suggestion was that Bentham should answer Macaulay's article but in the event the reply was written by Perronet Thompson, who incorporated in his article a condensation of a paper provided by Bentham on the history of his own ideas. [9] This was the start of a debate which stretched over into 1830 and produced two further articles from Macaulay and two further replies from the *Westminster*.

The general contemporary verdict on the debate, even amongst Benthamites themselves, was that the Utilitarian cause suffered considerable damage. [10] What was thought to have been damaged was both a philosophic and a political position, both the general Utilitarian approach to social theorizing and Utilitarian arguments for Radical reform. This

[8] It was, in fact, his articles on Mill that prompted Lord Lansdowne in February 1830 to offer his support in the election to the vacant seat at Calne. See George Otto Trevelyan: *Life and Letters of Lord Macaulay* (Popular Edition, 1889), p. 101.

[9] See G. L. Nesbitt: *Benthamite Reviewing* (New York, 1934), pp. 139–43. Macaulay wrote his first reply to the *Westminster* under the impression that Bentham had written the article, but acknowledges his mistake in an addendum: see below, pp. 177–8.

[10] Francis Place collected notices of the *Westminster Review* articles, which were without exception unfavourable. See Place Collection B.L. Add. MSS. 35145 fos. 97, 98, 99, 101, 103, 104.

ambiguity about the nature of Mill's 'Essay' and the debate to which it gave rise has persisted into modern scholarship. Was the debate a serious engagement in political theory or a tactical skirmish in the political conflict between Whigs and Radicals? Was Mill's 'Essay' a philosophic or a propagandist exercise?

To ask this question of James Mill's article is to risk incurring the charge of naïvely supposing that political philosophers do not have political objectives. Yet when judgements on Mill's political motives are sometimes combined with criticism of his mode of argument this would seem to point to a distinction between the *method* and *purpose* of the essay. Thus R. H. S. Crossman calls it 'one of the ablest and most perverse pieces of argument in the English language'; and its perversity lies less in its being a piece of 'special pleading for the middle classes' than in the manner of reasoning employed—'cold, dogmatic, and devoid of all understanding of human nature'.[11] Here Crossman echoes Macaulay's complaint that 'Mr. Mill has chosen to look at only one-half of human nature', a complaint which was taken up and elaborated by J. S. Mill in the sixth book (chapter VIII) of his *Logic*. But the younger Mill thought that his father could have defended himself by saying: 'I was not writing a scientific treatise on politics. I was writing an argument for parliamentary reform.'[12] And this view of the essay on Government has had its influence. Hamburger, for instance, is sure that the essay's purpose was primarily polemical, that it was 'written as a reform tract at a time when reformist opinions were anything but popular'. Mill had therefore to be 'cautious in his choice of words'. Even so, Hamburger admits that what was written mainly as a tract could nevertheless rest on a particular theoretical position, and singles out Macaulay for having done much 'to create the impression that Mill intended the 'Essay' primarily as a theoretical treatise'.[13]

Now, it is not our purpose here to take sides in this debate, to

---

[11] *Government and the Governed* (3rd edn., 1947), pp. 150 and 153–4.

[12] *Autobiography* (World's Classics, 1952), p. 134.

[13] Joseph Hamburger, 'James Mill on Universal Suffrage and the Middle Class', *Journal of Politics*, vol. 24 (1962), pp. 169–70. See also Joseph Hamburger: *Intellectuals in Politics* (1965), chap. 2. S. R. Letwin's verdict, '. . . he wrote what looks very much like a scientific treatise on politics, rather than a proposal for parliamentary reform', is a recent example of what Hamburger takes to be Macaulay's view (*The Pursuit of Certainty* (1965), p. 200).

decide whether Mill's essay was principally a propagandist tract or a contribution to political theory. And it may be that Macaulay's own aim was, mainly or in part, to put a brake on the agitation for parliamentary reform. His purpose, so he said, was 'not so much to attack or defend any particular system of polity, as to expose the vices of a kind of reasoning utterly unfit for moral and political discussions'. Yet Leslie Stephen has claimed that what gave the appearance of a purely methodological criticism was prompted by the fear that the middle class would lose its 'moral authority' if the franchise were extended to the masses. Macaulay's 'real thought', says Stephen, may be inferred from the speech he made in 1842 on the Chartist demand for universal suffrage:

If the chartists acted upon their avowed principles, they would enforce 'one vast spoliation' [so Macaulay argued] ... What Macaulay professes to deduce from Mill's principles he really holds himself, and he holds it because he argues, as indeed everybody has to argue, pretty much on Mill's method. He does not really remain in the purely sceptical position which would correspond to his version of 'Baconian induction'. He argues, just as Mill would have argued, from general rules about human nature. Selfish and ignorant people will, he thinks, be naturally inclined to plunder; therefore, if they have power, they will plunder.[14]

Let us grant that both Mill and Macaulay wished to make an impact on the debate over parliamentary reform. Even if their primary purpose was thus 'polemical' the manner in which they presented their cases raises interesting problems in political philosophy and it is on these that we shall concentrate our attention. In particular, we shall examine two major issues raised by the debate, the nature of a science of politics and the theoretical basis for representative and democratic institutions.

2. THE SCIENCE OF POLITICS

Government is necessary, says Mill, because labour is required to provide the means for life and happiness. If nature supplied all the objects of desire there would be no conflict among men. Since men would, without restraints, attempt to take from each other what they desire, only a system of law and order can

[14] Leslie Stephen: *The English Utilitarians* (1900), vol. ii, pp. 96–7.

prevent mutual plunder and ensure to each the fruits of his labour. But government is composed of men, hence they are tempted to, and are in a strong position to, plunder their subjects. How to restrain them? By ensuring a correspondence of interests between rulers and ruled. There must be representatives with a controlling power over the executive, elected on a much wider franchise than in the Britain of 1820 and limited in the duration of office—such are the principal institutional measures best designed to create a checking body which would (*could*) not oppress the community whose interests it existed to protect.

This, in very brief outline, is Mill's argument. But the reader of his essay will not have failed to notice the important role which certain assumptions about human nature play in it. Early on we meet the assertion that the 'science of government' is, or should be, based on 'the whole science of human nature' and there are several passages in which the 'laws' or 'principles' of human nature are invoked. Now, what Mill appeals to—the 'science' of human nature—is not something we could eliminate from the essay as so much philosophical window-dressing or 'scientific' dross, for there would be nothing distinctive about the argument, nor indeed would it hang coherently together, if these 'foundations' were taken away. Perhaps 'foundations' is the wrong word here, since it might be read to imply that the argument could somehow be detached from its foundations; in Mill's case, we submit, they are clearly interwoven and non-detachable. Consider, for instance, the way he dismisses the three traditional forms of government—monarchy, aristocracy, and democracy—as inadequate methods of protecting a community's interests, and notice in particular the part dealing with monarchy at the end of this section (pp. 59–61). What rules out monarchy serves also to rule out any other form of government in which the interests of the power-holders are not identical with those of the community, for 'those principles of human nature' which point to the necessity of government at all show also that under these forms of government the rulers will oppress their subjects. Clearly what Mill refers to as 'the principles of human nature' are a necessary component of the thesis he wishes to maintain. We should, therefore, be well-advised to accept him at his own word when he says that the whole chain

of reasoning in the essay depends on the principle that 'the acts
of men will be conformable to their interests' and that this
principle in turn rests on a 'strong foundation', namely, 'that the
acts of men follow their will; that their will follows their desires;
and that their desires are generated by their apprehensions of
good or evil; in other words, by their interests' (p. 88). One
might ask, what are men's 'interests' in this context? For Mill
'the lot of every human being is determined by his pains and
pleasures' (pp. 55–6); the desires of men are 'directed to pleasure and relief from pain as *ends*, and to wealth and power as the
principal means . . .' (p. 69). It would seem, therefore, that to
speak of men's 'interests' is either simply a way of talking about
the optimum pleasure/pain balance or is a reference to the
means whereby that optimum is secured. And it would also
seem to follow that if it is the proper end of government 'to
increase to the utmost the pleasures, and diminish to the utmost
the pains, which men derive from one another' (p. 56), then a
government which actually sought to attain, and perhaps even
succeeded in achieving, that end would be promoting the
public interest, and there would be an identity of interests
between rulers and ruled.

Taken together these several contentions are crucially
important for Mill and in this sense they do constitute 'foundations'; certainly they enter into and determine, and hence are
inseparable from, the case he makes for representative government. Whether or not they amount to a 'strong foundation'
must be decided in the light of what has been said by the critics
and those who have come to Mill's aid, foremost among whom
must be counted Macaulay and the author(s) of the articles in
the *Westminster Review*; though we must not forget that Mill
wrote in his own defence in the *Fragment on Mackintosh* and that
his son discussed, and was much influenced by, the controversy.

For the political or social philosopher the most important
issues raised by Macaulay's attack on Mill's essay and the
exchanges with the *Westminster Review* derive from the charge
that Mill's procedure is *a priori* and from the discussion of the
principle of utility. Let us begin with the former and observe
just how Macaulay spells out the charge. Mill's mode of argument, he says, is *a priori* in that 'certain propensities of human
nature are assumed; and from these premises the whole science

of politics is synthetically deduced.' And he cites examples from quite different spheres of the same method of reasoning, so he claims, before the time of Bacon and Galileo: deducing how to treat fever from the nature of heat, and proving by logical argument that the planets cannot move independently because the heavens are incorruptible and nature abhors a vacuum (Macaulay's way of stating a well-known Aristotelian thesis). As in the natural sciences, so in such a subject as Government and Politics, *a priori* reasoning is inappropriate: we must use the method of induction. It is, he insists, 'utterly impossible to deduce the science of government from the principles of human nature'; and this, he declares, is the fundamental objection to Mill's essay. There is only one proposition about human conduct which is absolutely true and that is a mere truism, namely, that men always act from self-interest—here Macaulay's criticism overlaps with his case against the principle of utility—and from that proposition nothing of an empirical sort to do with Politics can be deduced.

Now it might appear that this last point cannot be reconciled with Macaulay's further complaint that not only does Mill reason *a priori* in matters where such reasoning is out of place but the principles from which the whole chain of deduction moves are *false*, and they are false because Mill 'has chosen to look only at one-half of human nature, and to reason on the motives which impel men to oppress and despoil others, as if they were the only motives by which men could possibly be influenced'. Macaulay says that the Utilitarians assert the proposition that 'men always act from self-interest' as if it were an important thing to maintain, and he seems to want to include Mill among the culprits. But since he claims that the proposition amounts to no more than declaring 'whatever is, is', or that men do what they do, then how can it be *false*? Well, the dilemma into which we seem to have put Macaulay is neatly averted by his confronting Mill with a similar kind of dilemma. Either Mill must stick to the empty truism; or narrow the meaning of the notion, 'acting from self-interest', so as to render it a testable hypothesis. And he accuses Mill of trying to have it both ways, by resorting to 'one simple trick of legerdemain'; i.e. on the one hand he attempts to insure himself against refutation by adhering to an irrefutable maxim, on the other hand he argues as if men have no interest except to injure and oppress others for their own gain. In thus narrowing the notion of self-interest Mill turns his basic principle into a factual assertion which is false, 'and all the doctrines consequent upon it are false likewise' (pp. 125–6).

Macaulay says it is false because it cannot be reconciled with what he states to be undeniable facts about human conduct. Some of the desires of men lead them to injure, others to confer benefit on, their neighbours. There is no single general rule in regard to the motives which influence human actions that holds in all cases. Even in respect of a particular individual whom we may know we cannot say, for instance, whether the desire of approbation will always be a stronger motive than the desire of wealth, and vice versa. When applied to men generally the many factors involved combine to 'produce infinite shades of variety' and hence the possibility of arriving at generalizations of universal validity. Moreover, Macaulay contends, Mill's account of the means through which men seek to maximize pleasure, namely, power and wealth, is incomplete and one-sided, for it fails to recognize, in the essay on Government at least, the important part played by the desire for the good opinion of others. The *Westminster Review* declares that absolute rulers care nothing for the good opinion of their subjects, yet elsewhere, in his essay on Education, Mill says that 'the most despotical masters of human destiny' would have agreed with Frederick of Prussia in acknowledging that they wanted 'to occupy a large space in the admiration of mankind'. Now it is true that Mill qualifies his doctrine by an occasional resort to the expression, 'and nothing checks', but once we allow for such checks as the desire of approbation and posthumous fame, the principles of human nature from which his chain of reasoning moves lose their deceptive simplicity.

Macaulay follows up his charge that Mill employs a purely *a priori* mode of argument in matters where such a procedure is inappropriate, and from premises which fail to square with the facts, with the claim that even were his assumptions true Mill goes on to draw conclusions which are flagrantly at odds with his own premises. What Macaulay probably regarded as the most effective count in this particular indictment relates to the well-known passage in which Mill praises the virtues of the middle class, and attributes to them an influence which Macaulay and several later commentators have found to be incompatible with the stark postulates that Mill himself insists constitute the foundation of the whole essay. How, on Mill's premisses could the mass of the people accept the leading role of the middle class? If one says that it is in their interest to do so then the thesis that men always act in their own interest is fatally undermined. Yet if, contrary to their own interest, they nevertheless succumb to middle-class domination, their behaviour is equally inexplicable on Mill's terms. The Marxist would of course cut through the debate with the claim that classes may be deceived, in the short run, as to where their true interests lie, and there are signs in the *Westminster Review* articles of a similar type of view, namely, that ignorance can obscure from a man, and perhaps from a class, what is to his, or their, real advantage. Macaulay however is content to argue his case within the limits set by Mill's stated assumptions.

We ought now to consider what significance Macaulay's criticism of Mill could have beyond impugning a particular set of premisses. And we should notice that Macaulay seems at times to challenge not only the specific postulates adopted by Mill but *a priori* reasoning as such, at least in the study of human affairs, including Politics. How far did he intend to take this objection? After all, it is one thing to say that it is impossible to deduce the 'science of government' from the principles of human nature—whether Mill's principles or any other set—and quite another to rule out *a priori* reasoning completely. Indeed Macaulay himself resorts to *a priori* reasoning in his assault on Mill's theory. If men always pursue their own interests, why should women be excluded from the franchise, why should the mass of people accept middle-class tutelage? Clearly Macaulay's own critical thrusts frequently assume an *a priori* twist. We should, therefore, look more closely at this matter and also attempt to establish just what kind of procedure and manner of inquiry Macaulay recommends in place of Mill's faulty method.

When Macaulay says that we cannot deduce the 'science of government' from the principles of human nature his target is not just Mill; anyone who attempts to do the *sort* of thing Mill did would be in error. This does not mean, however, that Macaulay denied we could acquire any kind of general empirical knowledge about government. Where then does the difference lie? What distinguishes Macaulay's inductive procedure, which appears to aim at empirical generalizations about political life, from the method employed by Mill? Unfortunately, the answer to this question is not a straightforward one, partly because Macaulay does not elaborate the occasional flashes of insight of which he was undoubtedly capable. Hence we are left somewhat in the dark as to what he thought the inductive method could achieve in the project of constructing a 'science of government'. And we should certainly not take his use of the term 'science' as a sign that he was concerned to champion the cause of social *science*, as it would be understood nowadays, against the sceptics; that he was in the same camp to which Mill is commonly assigned, except that he believed his own methods were more scientific. His remarks about Bacon and induction could well create that impression, and they do complicate the picture, but the main trend of his thought lies decidedly in the other direction.

A fundamental error in Mill's method, as Macaulay sees it, is the attempt to treat human affairs along the same lines as geometry. This is the main burden of the *a priori* charge, and it is one that J. S. Mill took very much to heart. Macaulay tries to bring out the nature of the error in at least two ways. Firstly, he points to the complexity and variety of social life which resists summary in the form of precise and simple axioms. 'Man differs from man', he says, 'generation from generation; nation from nation. Education, station, sex, age, accidental associations, produce infinite shades of variety' (p. 127). Consequently it is not possible to discover any generalizations with empirical content which hold absolutely of human conduct. Secondly, he claims that the concepts and notions in terms of which we describe and evaluate human actions are not capable of being defined with the precision characteristic of mathematics. When men 'begin to talk of power, happiness, misery, pain, pleasure, motives, objects of desire, as they talk of lines and numbers, there is no end to the contradictions and absurdities into which they fall'. What Macaulay is saying here is that given the definitions of line, angle, square, and so forth, or given the way we use numbers, one can proceed to draw conclusions which are deductively related to the original axioms or postulates. But concepts like 'pleasure' or 'power' cannot yield to this treatment because they lack a rigidly specific meaning; they are neither like the axioms and postulates of logic or mathematics, nor do they operate like the concepts of natural science. When, therefore, these concepts are incorporated in general propositions which purport to say something universally true of human nature, what ensues is a theory that can be faulted on both grounds. The accusing finger is levelled at Mill but the charge has much wider application.

We might be tempted to suppose that Macaulay's remarks about concepts like 'power' and 'pleasure' were made as if all the distinctions and refinements of modern analytical philosophy were at his disposal. We are familiar nowadays with the objections to making, say, 'power' an 'operational' term with precise empirical indicators. The difficulty, it is argued, stems from the range of 'power' words, stretching from 'domination' to 'influence' and embracing that very elusive idea, 'authority'. Macaulay however does show himself to be sensitive to some of these distinctions, sufficiently so to support his claim that notions like 'power' cannot serve either a Euclidean or a Newtonian purpose. Consider, for instance, the way he insists that, when we compare the power of two persons or two groups, there should be a 'common measure' (p. 109). In the case of, say, lifting weights there is no problem in judging who is the most 'powerful'. But when we are confronted with two different *kinds* of power there is 'no criterion of equality'. It would be as absurd to say that the power of a comedian was greater or less than that of a boxer as to ask 'whether Bonaparte was stronger than an elephant' (p. 110). Let not the air of frivolity about these examples blind us to Macaulay's ability to see that in specifying 'wealth' and 'power' as the principal means to the end we all desire, an optimum of pain and pleasure, Mill was on shaky ground in taking for granted that the concept of 'power' was unproblematic. A brief look at what Mill says about 'power' will help to show the relevance of the point Macaulay is making.

In the essay on Government, 'power' and 'wealth' are specified as the principal means to the end, 'pleasure'. Later, in the *Analysis of the Phenomena of the Human Mind*, Mill adds 'dignity', with the caution that 'Dignity is a word of much more vague signification, than Wealth, or Power.'[15] As to 'power', Mill says

[15] Op. cit. (ed. J. S. Mill, 1869), vol. ii, p. 209.

in the essay that it means 'security for the conformity between the will of one man and the acts of other men'; in the *Analysis* that 'a man's Power means the readiness of other men to obey him'. Admittedly these are offered as very loose characterizations, and as such tend to confirm Macaulay's claim that terms which can only be defined in this way are not like 'lines and numbers'. But the cost of making the definitions tighter, in order to produce an 'operational' concept, is the risk of omitting important features in the 'power' spectrum. The 'readiness' with which men obey may be due to, say, the threat of punishment, charismatic leadership, respect for traditional forms of authority, or a belief in the rightness of the order. Rulers vary in the degree to which their 'power' rests on any one or a combination of these factors. The impossibility of assigning a fixed percentage to each of the ingredients in the mixture, even if we could determine what the mixture is in any specific situation, goes to fortify Macaulay's claim that in dealing with 'power' we cannot reason as with 'lines and numbers'.

'The bitterest and ablest attack ever publicly made on him was that which was the immediate cause of the introduction of Mr. Macaulay into public life'. So wrote J. S. Mill in the preface to the 1869 edition of his father's *Analysis of the Phenomena of the Human Mind*.[16] It was indeed an able attack, so much so that one is left wondering what could have been said in reply. But reply there was, both from the *Westminster Review* and from Mill himself. The defence was a lengthy one and we must concentrate on the essentials.

The central criticism of the alleged purely *a priori* nature of Mill's argument was met by the flat assertion that it was in fact based on *experience*; that, so far as politics and government are concerned, the basic premiss of the essay was a prudent and reasonable position to adopt; and that Macaulay's attack was vitiated by its failure to take account of the crucial 'saving clause', namely, 'and nothing checks'. These are all points worth examining in some detail.

In considering how men should be governed, from what else should we draw deductions than from the nature of man?, asks the *Westminster Review* (p. 133). Is it not a true and widely-held belief that government itself exists to prevent men from

[16] ibid., vol. i, p. xvii.

injuring one another; and would this belief make any sense if, were there no restraints, men were not generally inclined to do harm to others for their own interests? It may be admitted that 'there are partial exceptions to the rule, that all men use power as badly as they dare' (p. 135). But would it not be as absurd to rely on the exceptions as to treat wolves on any other assumption than that they are dangerous creatures? James Mill would seem to have gone along with this line of defence, for he quotes Hume approvingly:

Political writers have established it as a maxim, that, in contriving any system of government, and fixing the several checks and controls of the constitution, every man ought to be supposed a knave, and to have no other end, in all his actions, than private interest . . . It is, therefore, a just political maxim, that every man must be supposed a knave; though at the same time, it appears somewhat strange, that a maxim should be true in politics which is false in fact. But to satisfy us on this head, we may consider, that men are generally more honest in their private than in their public capacity, and will go greater lengths to serve a party, than when their own private interest is alone concerned. Honour is a great check upon mankind; but when a considerable body of men act together, this check is in a great measure removed; since a man is sure to be approved of by his own party for what promotes the common interest; and he soon learns to despise the clamours of adversaries.[17]

After quoting Blackstone to the same effect, Mill goes on to remark: 'And though it may perhaps be true of certain individuals out of a multitude, that they are not habitually governed by their own interest; yet, as is truly remarked by Mr. Hume, it may be affirmed of all bodies of men, that they are guided by the principle of interest invariably.'[18]

We should note in passing that in taking this line of defence Mill had the full support of Bentham. In his *Plan of Parliamentary Reform* (1817) he had asserted that the sole clue to political conduct is *interest*. To know how a man will act, he said, look to the state of his interests; pay no attention to 'professions or protestations'. And, in an interesting rider, he went on to say that this is even more true of large bodies of men than of single individuals.[19] This was no chance observation on

---

[17] *Fragment on Mackintosh*, pp. 280–1.   [18] ibid., p. 284.
[19] Bentham: *Works* (ed. Bowring), vol. iii, pp. 526–7.

Bentham's part, for later, in the *Constitutional Code* (1830), although he insists that a study of history and a knowledge of human nature show that 'self-regarding interest is predominant over all other interests put together', he draws a distinction between bodies of men and private individuals and allows that in the case of the latter there may be 'inducements, any one of which may suffice to cause a single man to make sacrifice of his private interest to the universal interest', and among the examples he cites are 'desire of reputation' and 'pleasure of sympathy for the people.'[20]

We must defer discussion of the implications of all this for Mill's original thesis and turn for the moment to the claim that the premises of Mill's essay were derived from 'history' and 'experience'. In his first reply to the *Westminster Review* Macaulay had asked how Mill had arrived at the principles of human nature from which he supposed he could deduce the science of government. The *Westminster Review* answers: by experience. But, insists Macaulay, 'What is the extent of this experience?' (p. 167). Does the 'experience' include man's *political* behaviour? Principles of human nature which do not take into consideration the way men behave in politics are bound to be defective; reliable knowledge of human nature, 'instead of being prior in order to our knowledge of the science of government, will be posterior to it' (pp. 167–8). Yet Mill and his supporters are emphatic that they have taken the whole of human nature into account. This suggests that we need to go deeper than the simple level of affirmation and denial in order to bring out fully the nature of the Utilitarian argument, which Macaulay's method of criticism, for all its virtues, does not wholly suceed in doing.

When the Utilitarians distinguish between the actions of men in their private and public capacities and go on to admit that, as private persons, men do not always act out of self-interest, this constitutes in effect a denial of Macaulay's suggestion that their basic premiss is merely 'an identical proposition'; for it implies that there are criteria for judging whether or not a man is pursuing his own interest. In this sense Mill's laws of human nature could be said to have empirical content or to be based on 'experience'. And when Mill says that history provides evidence

[20] ibid., vol. ix, pp. 102–3.

to support his premisses this again would seem to reinforce the claim that the laws of human nature are empirical generalizations or, at least, are empirically supported. But the appeal to 'experience' can assume different forms, and it is important to see what the difference is. We could say, for instance, that 'experience' warrants a number of general assertions like, 'falling off a tall building will result in death or severe injury', or 'stones thrown off a tall building fall down to the ground' or 'the prospect of large pecuniary gain often induces men to commit crimes' and so on. There would be no great harm in referring to assertions of this sort (let us leave aside the question of when we should want to make them!) as 'empirical generalizations' provided that we realize it required no research to produce them, and that, unlike the laws of science, they are couched in imprecise language and contain none of the qualifications which it would be necessary to introduce if we wanted to make assertions of a rigorously factual nature. A man can fall off a tall building with a parachute and come to no harm, or he could fall into a safety net; and the crucial word 'often', as well as the failure to specify the nature of the crime, renders our last example almost useless even as a common-sense maxim. Now, Newton's laws of gravitation might be loosely described as 'empirical generalizations', and could be said to be based on 'experience', but it would be a mistake to assimilate them to the common-sense assertions we have just cited. We certainly could not say of them that they just emerged in the ordinary course of living, as we might do of the latter.

The Utilitarians, at least in the writings assembled in this collection, seem to have wanted to accord to their laws of human nature a scientific status and yet also to offer them as prudential maxims, i.e. it is wise to assume that in politics men will, unless checked, abuse their positions of power. Mill, for example, both invokes Hume's 'just political maxim' and formulates 'a grand governing law of human nature' (p. 63). And when, in relation to absolute monarchy, the example of Denmark strikes him as anomalous and so 'the surface of history affords . . . no certain principle of decision', he abandons the evidence of history, 'the outside of the facts', in favour of the laws of human nature (pp. 62–3). The reader will notice how quick Macaulay was to seize on the Denmark example. But in this context it is even more interesting to see how the *Westminster Review* (pp. 182–3), when discussing the very same example, likens Mill's procedure to that involved in an appeal to the laws which govern falling bodies. Since there are kings of Denmark as well as Caligulas, the writer explains, then the 'facts are not such that the causes are determinable by simple inspection', hence 'it is necessary to go deeper, and look for some more complex causes that may account for the whole'. The facts concerning the behaviour of material objects are not, from the *outside* at any rate, self-consistent. Not all bodies fall to the earth. But there are laws which explain the apparent conflict in the evidence and they can be expressed by saying that the tendency to fall is sometimes 'overpowered by another force'. In the same way we can postulate that absolute monarchy tends to produce misrule unless there are checks to prevent it. It is Mill's contention, of course, that the behaviour of absolute monarchs is only a special case of human behaviour and it is therefore subject to those same principles of human nature which form the basis of the whole chain of reasoning in the essay. The structure of the argument is succinctly manifested in this passage of the essay:

If Government is founded upon this, as a law of human nature, that a man, if able, will take from others any thing which they have and he desires, it is sufficiently evident that when a man is called a King, it does not change his nature; so that when he has got power to enable him to take from every man what he pleases, he will take whatever he pleases. To suppose that he will not, is to affirm that Government is unnecessary; and that human beings will abstain from injuring one another of their own accord (p. 61).

There are, therefore, several major components in the Utilitarian argument, as stated by James Mill and his defender in the *Westminster Review*, the combined effect of which makes their position a complex one. It may be that the complexity passes over, at certain points, into inconsistency, so that what appears to be a clear, if over-simple, thesis turns out to have its gaps and ambiguities. Let us try, first of all, to identify the principal elements in the argument.

(*a*) Mill's essay proclaims, and is itself an example of, the belief that the best, or at least a profitable, way to approach matters of government and politics is to start from and/or appeal to the laws of human nature.

(*b*) The laws of human nature are based upon or are supported by empirical evidence. History and our knowledge of human nature over its entire range serve both to suggest and to confirm these laws.

(*c*) The laws of human nature are laws in the same sense as laws in natural science, e.g. the law relating to falling bodies.

(*d*) In regard to individual behaviour the laws of human nature do not hold absolutely. This raises the possibility that what are stated to be 'laws' are in fact assertions of a probabilistic kind or 'statistical laws'.

(*e*) There are certain prudential maxims relating to political life which it is safe to rely on and folly to ignore. Among these is the proposition that men in groups, organizations, and parties 'are guided by the principle of interest invariably'.

The first of these propositions might be taken to imply that the study of politics is, or should be, 'scientific'; that what is said about political matters could be wholly empirical; that there is, or should be, nothing else to political inquiry than the formulation and following out of the implications of the laws of human nature. (This is not the place to enter the controversy whether the work of the natural scientist can properly be described in these terms.) But we do not intend to attribute such a view to Mill. His appeal to the laws of human nature is conducted on the assumption that rulers should not oppress their subjects, that oppression, at least when it is the mass or the majority of the people who suffer, is wrong. We do not wish to interpret Mill as saying that the evil nature of oppression is a 'wholly empirical' matter, that it can somehow be deduced from the facts about human nature. More cautiously, we do not think it *necessary* to interpret him this way. It is true that there are passages in Bentham and Mill which have, quite plausibly, been construed to affirm a special kind of ethical naturalism; that is to say, moral judgements are treated as if they are a species of factual statements; in particular, that to say something is wrong is to estimate its effects in terms of the pain/pleasure calculus. We shall not enter into this question just here, and such as we do want to say about the problem will be deferred until we deal with Macaulay's remarks on the principle of utility. It is enough for the present that we do not wish to attribute to Mill what seems an unduly restrictive scope to political inquiry, i.e. that it is

'wholly empirical'. For quite apart from the fact/value problem there is the role that philosophical analysis can play in
elucidating the central political concepts. Bentham frequently
engaged in this activity, as when he offered an account of the
nature of law or criticized the notion of natural rights; and the
reader will notice that the *Westminster Review* makes big claims
for the clarificatory value of the principle of utility in elucidating concepts like justice, liberty, and rights (pp. 141–2). We
think it unnecessary to assume that Mill would want to describe
intellectual inquiry of this sort as either 'scientific' or 'wholly
empirical'.

With regard to the second proposition, we have already made
the point that statements which would commonly be thought as
'empirical' or based on 'experience' do not fall into a single and
uniform category. It is sometimes said that a defining characteristic of empirical assertions is that factual evidence can actually
be cited to support them, or that, if the evidence is not available,
we could describe the sort of evidence which would serve either
to confirm or refute them. It has also been said that we arrive at
the beliefs which empirical assertions express *inductively*, and
Macaulay would seem to champion this view. Strictly, however,
his position may have been less far-reaching and he might only
have wanted to say that within the range of beliefs we would
designate as empirical there is a class of statements whose
generation and justification is inductive and that among these
are the propositions of science. The matter has to be put in this
more guarded way, and Macaulay given the benefit of the
doubt, precisely because it is a highly variegated range and the
requirement of inductive proof would seem to be out of place
both in respect of the origin and the grounds of many empirical
assertions. Consider, for instance, the varied assortment of
beliefs involved in putting an anti-freeze solution into the
radiator of one's car. These range from the 'common-sense
knowledge' that it gets much colder in Britain in winter, and
sometimes freezes, to the specialized scientific knowledge
required to produce an effective solution. The entire complex of
beliefs might loosely be called 'empirical'—apart from the value
judgement which makes the protection of the radiator a desired
goal. But the call for evidence or inductive proof clearly makes
more sense in some cases rather than in others. Would it not be

strange to insist on evidence or inductive proof for the belief that it
gets much colder, and sometimes freezes, in winter? (Of course, if
the demand were made the evidence could easily be supplied.)
On the other hand it would be prudent to check the facts if
one had recently settled in, say, south Devon and were told that
anti-freeze was unnecessary there. Now it follows from what we
have been saying that, given Mill's and the *Westminster Review*'s
rejection of Macaulay's charge that Mill's fundamental premisses
are non-empirical, much is left open and indeterminate as to
the character of those premisses. Macaulay insists that they have
not been established inductively and are therefore suspect.
Or, to be more exact, that they are either non-empirical or false;
and they are false because 'they have not been formed by a
sufficiently copious induction' (p. 168). But is this a reasonable
demand on Macaulay's part?

The immediate issue that concerns us is whether generalizations should only be made after a 'copious induction' has been
carried out. If a generalization or proposed law flies in the face
of a substantial body of evidence than Macaulay would seem
entitled to say it is false. If it is couched in such elusive terms as
to render it untestable, then that could also make it unaccep-
table. We shall come to these questions presently. Let us consider first Macaulay's positive requirement of a 'copious
induction'.

It might be thought that Macaulay recommends the method
of induction especially for Politics because he took the view that
human activities are radically different from the behaviour of
physical objects and the results of centuries of inquiry into
political life had yielded nothing comparable to the achieve-
ments of the natural sciences. In fact, however, he thinks
induction is the correct method in *any* branch of empirical
study. We should, he says, reason from the phenomena up to the
principles. Through observation we build up a body of evidence
and arrive at a theory which is securely based on the facts.
This is the 'method which, in every experimental science to
which it has been applied, has signally increased the power and
the knowledge of our species' (p. 128). It is true that he allows a
theory to be modified or even abandoned by further observation, but from his account it is clear that we come to theories in
the first place through an accumulation of facts. Hence his

advice that we inquire into the constitutions 'of all those communities in which . . . the blessings of good government are enjoyed' in order to discover what they have in common and what differentiates them from those constitutions where the government is bad. To proceed thus, he claims, is to adopt the same method as that proposed by Bacon for tracking the principle of heat.

Fortunately for the student of politics the number of constitutions in the world at any one time is, for research purposes, of manageable extent. There need be no gap between the number of instances examined, assuming that one knew what to look for, and the number of constitutions that are or have been in existence. Constitutions, however, come and go and there is always the danger that future experience will upset a generalization based on the evidence of past and present. Even so, the gap between all *observed* instances and *all* instances of 'good government' would seem to require no great inductive leap, certainly nothing like the one demanded by the size of the gap between the observed instances of heat and any universal generalization of a law-like character proposed about hot bodies. Macaulay's advice would run into much greater difficulty if it were a question of determining the nature of all human actions; whether, for example, they should be explained in terms of the pain/pleasure calculus. And if it were objected that this would be an impossible task in any case because the criterion specified is far too elastic, the same might be said about Macaulay's 'blessings of good government'.

Macaulay's advocacy of the method of induction is, however, open to a more important criticism, namely, that induction is not the method of science. There are, to be sure, voices urging that science has no method at all, but the well-known and less extreme position taken up by Sir Karl Popper brings some weighty charges against inductivism. We can only deal here in a brief and simplified way with part of the complex of issues that have been discussed under the heading of 'induction' and shall confine ourselves to the relatively specific question of whether, as Macaulay claims, inductive procedure is responsible for the successes of science. The answer, in short, is that it cannot be; for the history of science contains many examples of hypotheses being put forward, and then adopted by the scientific community, before the massive accumulation of data called for by the inductivist account. Observation and experiment are carried out not by persons with blank minds who refrain from judgement until all the 'facts' are in, but by scientists facing problems and equipped with an intricate set of beliefs, concepts, and expectations, sometimes prepared to take an imaginative leap in order to solve those problems. When Macaulay, intending to make a point against Mill, says that '*Experience* can never be divided, or even appear to be divided, except with reference to some hypothesis', he speaks in an anti-inductivist strain. A stray utterance, it might be said, since he seems to have been unaware of its implications for the theory of induction he stoutly championed.

If, then, an hypothesis may be held 'in advance of the evidence', what are the grounds for its acceptance? According to an influential modern school of thought the grounds are given by its ability to survive tests. No matter how copious the induction, positive confirmation can never confer absolute certainty on an hypothesis (by hypothesis here we mean what is offered as a candidate for a scientific law); falsification, on the other hand, is decisive for its rejection. But so long as it has withstood attempts to falsify it and it accords with the data it purports to cover, then it fulfils all the demands we can justifiably make of the scientific hypothesis. A basic requirement, therefore, is that it should be testable and this is taken to be the principle of demarcation which separates science from non-science. Do Mill's laws of human nature satisfy these conditions, less exacting conditions it may be thought, than those specified by Macaulay? The answer implicit in Macaulay's bill of indictment must surely be that they do not, for in so far as the laws are testable they go against the facts about human conduct and political life which he adduces. And the distinction between private and public conduct, drawn by the Utilitarians themselves, would seem to constitute a powerful fortification of this conclusion. Macaulay's insistence on a 'copious induction' can therefore be turned into a more modest requirement, namely, that the laws of human nature should cover all the known and relevant facts and that they be framed in terms specific enough for them to be checked against these facts. Much of what Macaulay actually says fits this requirement and his commitment to the method of induction serves only to obscure and weaken the force of his criticism.

We must stress once again that our treatment of these matters cries out for amplification, qualification, and refinement. In particular, it would be a seriously misleading description of the present state in philosophy of science to represent it as one of consensus, far less of universal agreement, on the issues we have just been discussing. Among the subjects of current controversy is the question of 'testability'. We have already emphasized the relevance of this idea for a critical assessment of Mill's premisses and pointed to its importance in contemporary writings in the philosophy of science (including the social sciences). But it is an idea which has not gone unchallenged, and one of its most radical critics has argued that the history of science contains many examples of hypotheses and theories being advanced, and then adopted by the scientific community, which fail to measure up to Popper's standard of falsifiability. He claims that if the typically empiricist thesis that theories be consistent with the facts were applied with absolute rigour it would put an end to scientific discovery.[21] It would be outside the scope of our introduction to enter into the details of this controversy, but it is our view that if the attempt were made to defend Mill by refusing to admit, or by minimizing, the need for factual support, and by denying the relevance of the falsifiability test, then the consequences for the Utilitarian position would be extremely awkward. Such a tactic would, in the first place run counter to their insistent claim that history, 'experience' and our 'knowledge' of human nature combine to provide empirical support for Mill's basic premisses. Further, it would give rise to the obvious question: what are to count as reasons for accepting or rejecting those premisses? And it would be open to a defender of Macaulay, given that factual evidence is to be at a discount, simply to reject Mill's and offer his own set of premisses. He would feel especially free to do this in light of the Utilitarian admission that not all individual actions are performed out of self-interest, though how the Utilitarians would be able to establish that there were any exceptions to a 'law of human nature' if empirical evidence is either out of court or of little significance must undoubtedly strike him as mysterious.

[21] Paul K. Feyerabend: *Against Method* (1975).

It might be objected at this point that we have put too much weight on Mill's use of the term 'law' in the expression 'laws of human nature'. There are places where he talks of 'principles' of human nature as an alternative to, and with the same force as, 'laws'. His intention, therefore, could well have been to signify something much looser than the concept of a scientific law. He might have been thinking of something like a prudential maxim; or he might have been pointing to a common tendency in human, especially political, conduct; or even, perhaps, drawing our attention to the importance of such concepts as 'power' and 'self-interest' in the understanding of political behaviour. Now if it is true that Mill's meaning can be stated in one or other of these alternatives then our remarks would indeed have to be seriously qualified. But even if we were to concede the case entirely, empirical evidence would still be highly relevant to each of these possible versions. We have, incidentally, already allowed for them in the sketch we drew of the structure of the Utilitarian argument. Whether or not we should make the concession cannot be decided before we take a closer look at Mill's use of 'law' and the problems associated with it.

Some of the best-known studies of the English Utilitarians have asserted, as if it were obvious and unproblematic, that Bentham and his successors aspired to create a science of society similar to physics. Perhaps the most influential version of this thesis appears in Halévy's *The Growth of Philosophic Radicalism*: 'What is known as Utilitarianism, or Philosophic Radicalism, can be defined as nothing but an attempt to apply the principles of Newton to the affairs of politics and of morals.'[22] A few years earlier Leslie Stephen had written: 'Bentham hoped for no less an achievement than to become the Newton of the moral world.[23]

That James Mill shared this aspiration would seem to be the only inference one could draw from the testimony of his son. In the preface to his father's *Analysis of the Phenomena of the Human Mind* J. S. Mill says:

... the task which was proposed to himself by the author of the present treatise ... is an attempt to reach the simplest elements which by their combination generate the manifold complexity of our mental states, and to assign the laws of those elements, and the elementary laws of their combination, from which laws the subordinate

[22] op. cit., p. 6.   [23] *The English Utilitarians*, vol. i, p. 179.

ones which govern the compound states are consequences and corollaries. The conception of the problem did not, of course, originate with the author; he merely applied to mental science the idea of scientific inquiry which had been matured by the successful pursuit, for many generations, of the knowledge of external nature.[24]

It is natural to suppose that John Stuart was in a better position than anyone else to say what his father's assumptions were, but there is very little evidence in James Mill's own writings to suggest that he was anything like as self-conscious as his son about the 'logic of the moral sciences'. True, he refers to the 'science' and 'laws' of human nature in the essay on Government, and he frequently uses the term 'law' in his works on economics and psychology. Moreover, in one of his early economic writings he had this to say about Adam Smith:

... Dr. Smith reared the study to the dignity of a Science. He explained the real sources of wealth, which till his time had been so grossly misunderstood; and conferred as great a benefit upon Political Economy, as was conferred on Astronomy by those philosophers who first confuted the perplexed doctrine of the cycles and epicycles, and established the simple principles of the Copernican system.[25]

Yet in one of his latest writings, in which he discusses the nature of political economy as a *science*, the account of 'science' which Mill offers, that it provides knowledge and an explanation of the whole of a subject, is very rudimentary. It scarcely suggests that he had devoted much thought to the relation between economics and, say, physics. And when we consider the various laws he cites in economics, politics, and psychology important differences immediately become evident: differences in respect of the generality of the laws and their precision (or lack of it). The contrast with the laws of the natural sciences is even greater. An example from economics will serve as a partial illustration of what we have in mind.

Mill's *Elements of Political Economy* followed in the classical tradition of Smith and Ricardo and divided the subject into four major segments: production, distribution, exchange, and consumption. The activity studied in each of these divisions was

---

[24] op. cit., vol. i, pp. ix–x.
[25] *Selected Economic Writings* (ed. Donald Winch, 1966), pp. 24–5.

governed by laws which it was the task of the economist to discover and formulate. Some of these laws are either expressions
of, or are closely connected with, what might be called 'natural
facts', e.g. that soil and climate favour particular areas of land
for certain forms of agriculture. The law of rent is bound up with
variations in the fertility of land and the rising demand for land
caused by an increase in population. As Ricardo himself put it:
'If all land had the same properties, if it were unlimited in quantity, and uniform in quality, no charge could be made for its
use, unless where it possessed peculiar advantages of situation.'[26]

But though the practice of charging rent depends on the
presence of certain necessary conditions they do not amount to
sufficient conditions, for it is a practice which goes with particular forms of property ownership. There have been, and are
now, societies where the law of rent has no application. Indeed
it has often been said that the laws of classical economics, in so
far as they are valid laws at all, relate only to a specific type of
social order; and that even within this restricted scope they
assume ideal conditions which never, or rarely, obtain in real life,
e.g. perfect information, complete mobility of resources and
rational choice. Mill had this sort of criticism levelled at him by
one of his fellow-economists. Commenting on the *Elements*,
McCulloch said: 'Those secondary principles and modifying
circumstances, which exert so powerful an influence over general principles are wholly, or almost wholly, overlooked by
Mill . . . The Science is very far from having arrived at the
perfection Mr. Mill supposed.'[27]

There is, however, a way of attempting to meet this last
charge which points to a fundamental question about Mill's
laws of human nature. Laws, it is claimed, can have an explanatory value despite the fact that they embody concepts and
involve postulates which abstract from reality. Scientists make
use of the concept of an 'ideal gas' or a 'frictionless machine';
the economist, likewise, operates with the idea of a perfectly
competitive market or 'the economic man'. Furthermore, it is
one of the features of a scientific law, so it is argued, that it
expresses, or purports to express, a regularity that underlies
some other less fundamental regularity or regularities, i.e., one

[26] D. Ricardo: *Principles of Political Economy* (Everyman edn.), p. 35.
[27] James Mill: *Selected Economic Writings* (ed. Donald Winch, 1966), pp. 188-9.

that can be used to analyse and explain these other regularities. Leaving aside the question whether this line of defence gets over the problem of the 'social relativity' of Mill's economic laws, a question which does not arise over the 'ideal gas' or the 'frictionless machine'—at least not in the same way—is it one that can serve to elucidate and support his conception of the laws of human nature? Given the fact that history supplies apparently conflicting evidence, that there are Caligulas as well as Kings of Denmark, is there some fundamental law (or set of laws) of human behaviour which operates at a deeper level and offers an explanation of all the phenomena? Both Mill and the *Westminster Review* seem, at times, to have thought that there is.

If we follow up this suggestion we could put Mill's laws on to four different levels, the fourth level being the most general and fundamental. The scheme would run roughly as follows:

   (i)   Rulers, unless restrained, will oppress their subjects;

  (ii) Every man, if he has the power and nothing checks, will take from others the objects of desire;

 (iii) Men's actions are governed by their interests;

 (iv) Laws of the association of ideas.[28]

[28] The order in which we have put these laws corresponds to our reading of Mill. But there are difficulties in sustaining the order. In stating the laws of association Mill assumes the truth of psychological hedonism, yet the generalization which asserts this doctrine (proposition iii) appears to be derived from, or explained by, a more fundamental set of laws which nevertheless depend on it.

The theory of the association of ideas rests on a philosophical thesis, i.e. the empiricist claim that all mental phenomena can be analysed into impressions and ideas, which are the ultimate and irreducible constituents of the human mind. There is an order and sequence in these simple 'feelings' (as Mill called them in his article on Education), hence the contention that there are laws of association. But two factors are decisive in determining the order and sequence—custom, and pain and pleasure. That pain and pleasure do exercise this control over mental phenomena would, therefore, need to be established independently of the laws of association (see W. H. Burston; *James Mill on Philosophy and Education*, chap. VI).

Of the laws of association cited by Mill, the following would seem to be amongst the most important:

(*a*) The general law of the association of ideas—'Our ideas spring up, or exist, in the order in which the sensations existed, of which they are the copies' (*Analysis*, vol. i, p. 78);

(*b*) 'The causes of strength in association seem all to be resolvable into two; the vividness of the associated feelings; and the frequency of the association' (ibid., p. 83);

(*c*) 'Where two or more ideas have been often repeated together, and the association has become very strong, they sometimes spring up in such close combination as not to be distinguishable' (ibid., p. 90).

In one important respect this scheme corresponds to J. S
Mill's more carefully worked-out position, namely, that
empirical generalizations about human behaviour lack a scientific character unless they can be shown to be deducible from
the basic laws of mind. A more thoroughgoing reductionist
would maintain that the laws of mind are themselves, in principle, derivable from physiology and, ultimately, from physics;
and this would seem to be the logic of mind/brain identity
theories. But to follow up these suggestions would take us well
outside our terms of reference, and there are no signs that either
John Stuart or his father aspired to move in that direction.

In the explanatory model we have attributed to James Mill
it would follow from proposition (ii) that, since they are men,
rulers will try to oppress their subjects—unless it could be
shown that on becoming rulers men's behaviour is modified or
transformed. Then, of course, proposition (ii) would have to be
amended in order to express this fact, for as it stands it purports
to state what *all* men do. But Mill denies that it stands in need
of amendment, so, assuming its validity, we could say that it is
related to proposition (i) in the same sort of way that Newton's
first law of motion is related to the behaviour of projectiles or
the lurching of human bodies in a train which had been
brought to a sudden halt. Similarly, proposition (iii) covers a
wider range of phenomena than proposition (ii) whilst the laws
refered to in proposition (iv) provide the ultimate explanation
of why the actions of men are always directed to promoting
their own interests.

We have already reviewed the objections made by Macaulay
to the first three propositions and we find it difficult to resist the
conclusion that his criticisms are very cogent. But there are one
or two points which can be taken further. In contrast to the
laws of physics, and even to some in economics, the first three of
Mill's laws are imprecisely formulated. Macaulay argued that
they were either false or so loosely framed that one could not
determine what would count against them. We noticed, too,
that it was urged against Macaulay that he had overlooked
the force of the crucial qualification—'and nothing checks'.
Yet it is doubtful that the notion of 'checks' helps matters,
which is not to say that it has no place at all in political theory.
Scientists have specific criteria for measuring 'checks' in the

case of, say, Newton's first law of motion. Vague though it may sound to say that 'a body continues in a state of uniform motion in a right line unless it is compelled to change that state by forces impressed upon it', its status as a law is ensured by the ability to supply exact requirements for the 'checking' forces. Mill's first two laws (in the scheme set out above) both incorporate the idea of 'checks' and *look* something like Newton's, but in Mill's case the criteria are lacking. If fear of public opinion or revolution, or desire of posthumous fame, are examples of 'checks' on rulers, Mill did not supply us with the rules for estimating their counteracting power in different types of situation.

No less important are the considerations advanced by J. S. Mill in his criticism of the 'interest-philosophy of the Bentham school'. Almost all rulers, he claims, are influenced to some extent, and some rulers to a very great extent, by a 'sense of duty' or by 'feelings of philanthropy'. Further, he insists, it is true of all rulers that:

... the character and course of their actions is largely influenced (independently of personal calculation) by the habitual sentiments and feelings, the general modes of thinking and acting, which prevail throughout the community of which they are members, as well as by the feelings, habits and modes of thought which characterise the particular class in that community to which they themselves belong. (p. 255)

What J. S. Mill says here applies to men in both their private and public roles. Are we to regard these factors as part of the 'internal' constitution of social man or as 'external' checks to the natural, predatory creature? Either way, they present formidable problems for Mill's laws. The actual wording used in the formulation and elucidation of those laws assumes that man is already a social animal, but the idea of 'checks' either renders the laws nugatory or else requires that they apply to a 'natural man' who is outside, or prior to, human social relations.

However cogent these objections to James Mill's position are taken to be, they do not affect the contention that specifically constitutional checks, of the sort that go with representative government, are vitally necessary in order to restrain the actions of rulers. For as J. S. Mill put it: Although the actions of rulers are by no means wholly determined by their selfish interests, it is chiefly as a security against those selfish interests that constitutional checks are required . . . (p. 257).

The conclusion to which we are led must therefore be that if it was James Mill's aim to create a science of man, of which the science of Politics would be part, his laws of human nature fall well short of fulfilling the conditions of scientific laws. Were they offered as probabilistic or statistical laws they might be said to supply a solid empirical base for prudential maxims, but it is a mistake to suppose that precepts of this sort must be backed by statistical evidence. Bentham and James Mill, as we have noted, allow that not all human actions are selfish, but they make no attempt to fix a percentage. Nor is it possible to see how this could be done. Hume's maxim, quoted by Mill in the *Fragment*, is more like 'A stitch in time saves nine' or 'Look before you leap', than the warning doctors give about the risks from smoking cigarettes. Nothing like the research findings about the relationship between smoking and disease supports any of the prudential maxims we have cited, which is far from saying they are worthless.[29]

John Stuart's attitude to the 'Essay on Government' was one of almost unqualified admiration. In the years before the onset

[29] The distinction between 'laws of strictly universal form' and 'probabilistic laws' is commonly made in philosophy of science. Since there are very few laws of the former kind (many would say that there are none) in the social sciences, the generalizations which sociologists and political scientists produce are typically of a probabilistic sort, though there are many examples of the latter to be found in the natural sciences. From what Bentham and James Mill say about the difference between the actions of men as political actors and as private persons it could be inferred that Mill's 'first law' purports to be 'strictly universal' and the 'second law' probabilistic. There, could, therefore, be no straightforward deduction of the first from the second, i.e. without auxiliary hypotheses designed to show how men, on entering political life, become subordinate exclusively to considerations of interest.

The debate over the explanatory status of probabilistic laws has frequently turned on the claim made by Carl Hempel that they constitute a necessary component of explanations in history and the social sciences. Against Hempel, Michael Scriven has argued that historians typically invoke 'truisms', which he assigns to the category of 'normic statements'. Whether Mill's laws should be regarded as probabilistic or as examples of historical 'truisms', and how these are to be differentiated, are questions which would need a far more detailed examination than we can give them here. See Carl Hempel: 'Explanations in Science and History', in *The Philosophy of Science*, ed. P. H. Nidditch, 1968; and Michael Scriven, 'Truisms as the Grounds for Historical Explanations', in *Theories of History*: edited by P. Gardiner, 1959. A good idea of the issues raised in the debate over historical explanation can be gained from the collection, *The Philosophy of History*, ed. P. Gardiner, 1974.

of his 'mental crisis' in 1826, his only reservation related to his father's claim that women could, without damage to their interests, be safely excluded from the suffrage. Later, however, on the appearance of Macaulay's criticism, he came to think that, although 'Macaulay's conception of the logic of politics was erroneous', the premises from which his father had argued 'were really too narrow, and included but a small number of the general truths, on which, in politics, the important consequences depend'. Exactly why he considered those premises too narrow he explains in detail in the sixth book of the *Logic*. None the less there was a core of truth in his father's theory of government which he was anxious to extract and separate from the faulty mode of reasoning designed to demonstrate its truth. This was the belief that a necessary safeguard for good government is responsibility on the part of the rulers to the ruled by means of a system of representation. In both the *Logic* and his later work, *Considerations on Representative Government*, this belief is accepted and restated. But it is important to notice that he refuses to employ the language of even the modified position taken up by James Mill in the *Fragment on Mackintosh*. There the elder Mill sought to defend his essay against Macaulay's attack and though he no longer appeals to the science of government or invokes the laws of human nature, and prefers to rely on Hume's maxim, he is of the opinion that 'it may be affirmed of all bodies of men, that they are guided by the principle of interest invariably'. The rigidly dogmatic premises have, however, become less narrow and the sharp lines of definition decidedly blurred. He now talks of the 'leading' objects of human desire and the 'principal' influence in determining a man's actions. His list of human motives is expanded from power and wealth to include dignity, ease, and escape from degradation; and it is the 'bulk' of men's actions which is 'determined by consideration of these objects'. What gives its distinguishing mark to the essay on Government has largely disappeared and it is almost tempting to conclude that he moved close to sharing the verdict of his son when he said that 'there was truth in several of his (i.e. Macaulay's) strictures on my father's treatment of the subject . . . there was really something more fundamentally erroneous in my father's conception of philosophical method, as applicable to politics, than I had hitherto supposed there was'.

3. UTILITARIAN POLITICS

THE large issues in the philosophy of the social sciences raised by the debate on Mill's 'Essay' did not, of course, emerge in a political vacuum. For Macaulay, as for Mill, the point of a science of politics is to instruct us in what we should do politically, and, given the political concerns of their time, the natural focus of their argument is on the nature and justification of representative and democratic institutions. Nor is the debate without more narrowly political implications. The 'Essay' was written in 1819 when the demand for the reform of Parliament, dormant since the late 1790s, had revived and was moving back on to the public and even parliamentary agenda. Macaulay's attack was not mounted until 1829, but it came at a point of political instability when a Whig administration and Whig measures of reform (which no doubt would fall far short of Radical hopes) seemed imminent. The debate does then form part of the political battle over reform and sets out two partisan positions on the purpose and desirable extent of changes in the electoral system.

Disillusionment with the Glorious Constitution and demands for the reform of representation grew in the period between the late 1760s and the war with revolutionary France. Sparked off by the affair of Wilkes and the Middlesex election and revived by Lord North's mismanagement of the American war, the reform movement gained considerable public and parliamentary support during the early 1780s. By the end of the century, much of this respectable support had dissipated. The development of the French Revolution associated British reform with republicanism, terror, and French ideas at the same time that reform demands were being taken up by incipient working-class movements. The resultant unpopularity of radical views, together with their active repression, was sufficient virtually to silence the demands until 1815. The end of the Napoleonic wars and the consequent economic distress brought widespread popular agitation that produced only negative results, namely the suspension of *Habeas Corpus* and the repressive Six Acts of 1819. Between 1817 and 1819, Burdett brought forward in Parliament three motions for reform which had been fashioned by Bentham, but without serious Whig support these all failed. Emphasizing the differences between Whig and

Radical, Russell later in 1819 proposed, equally unsuccessfully, a moderate measure calling for the transfer of seats from corrupt boroughs to unenfranchised large cities. This was to be the pattern for further reform proposals introduced periodically by Russell throughout the following decade. By 1830, when the Whigs finally achieved power, this timidity was overcome. With widespread disaffection in the country and mounting pressure for change from the 'middling' classes, both party advantage and political necessity prompted the espousal of much more extensive measures.

This move towards more comprehensive proposals might seem to have brought the Whigs close to the Radical standpoint. Yet one profound difference of objective remained. However big the Whigs' leap in the dark in 1831, and however willing the Radicals might be to accept a limited extension of the franchise as an interim payment, ideas on the dangers and desirability of universal suffrage divided the two groups sharply. Bentham had put this as an unambiguous objective of the Benthamites in his *Reform Catechism*, and more ambiguously the commitment is repeated by James Mill in the 'Essay'. It is obscured by his panegyric on the 'middle rank' of society, a panegyric whose glowing terms were to be echoed in the debates on the Reform Bill by speakers such as Brougham. But, whereas Brougham's purpose was to justify a limited extension of the franchise, Mill's was to argue that under universal suffrage the wisdom of the middle rank would be a decisive electoral influence. This difference of objective is clear enough in Macaulay's critique of the 'Essay'. Although he is careful to insist that he is merely following out the implications of Mill's assumptions on human nature, his warning that placing power in the hands of the propertyless would create a serious threat to the stability of property was a commonplace of Whig as well as Tory rhetoric, and certainly his audience would have taken the prediction as more than mere hypothesis. The warning was to be repeated by Macaulay in speeches on the Reform Bills which emphasized the Whig intention, not to enfranchise the propertyless, but to give greater political protection to property by enfranchising new forms of property.[30]

[30] See particularly *Hansard*, vol. ii (Third Series), pp. 1191–201; vol. iv (Third Series), pp. 774–82.

These differences were to be obscured at least temporarily during the Reform Bill crisis. The Benthamite Radicals gave strong support to the Whig measure, support intended as much to prevent Whig backsliding as to prompt Tory acquiescence.[31] Yet differences over ultimate objectives remained, and were illustrated in disagreements about the nature of a representative system and about what reform of representation was intended and expected to achieve.

It is tempting to invest the movement for parliamentary reform with an intellectual coherence it did not possess and to see the Great Reform Act as both the culmination of constant demands which had ebbed and flowed since the mid-eighteenth century and as the first small step towards the twentieth-century achievement of full universal suffrage. In truth, it was not at the time seen as the second—for Whigs it was a final settlement—and there were marked changes up to 1830 in the objectives of parliamentary reformers.

Early reform demands were aimed at reducing the influence of the crown and restoring a constitutional balance which had been, it was claimed, disturbed by the 'unconstitutional' practices of George III and his ministers. One means towards these ends was seen in Economical Reform, cutting down crown patronage which could be used to influence both electors and M.P.s. The restoration of a constitutional balance was also sought through extension of the suffrage, abolition of rotten boroughs, additions to the representation of counties—all intended to create, or restore, an 'independent' House of Commons, independent that is of the crown and the administration. In the 1780s and 1790s, however, another element crept into the debate. The dominant complaint came to be about the influence of peers in elections and the general interference of the House of Lords in the proceedings of the Commons. In part the grounds for the complaint was again that such influence disrupted the balance of the constitution, but increasingly, and particularly amongst rudimentary working-class radical organizations, the burden of complaint moved from constitutional to economic sins. In one crude attempt to link economic distress to constitutional malpractice, distress was

---

[31] See Joseph Hamburger: *James Mill and the Art of Revolution* (1963), chapters 2 and 6.

blamed on excessive taxation, and this in turn on the peers'
ability to milk the Treasury by demanding places, pensions,
and sinecures in return for their parliamentary influence. More
portentous was the charge that the domination of the landed
interest biased legislation and prevented the proper representation and satisfaction of the needs of other and newer groups and
interests.

This last was to be the major theme of Whig arguments for
reform when they revived in the 1820s. Society had progressed,
new forms of property had emerged. The political structure
must adapt itself to these socio-economic changes and must do
so peaceably if violence was to be avoided. Macaulay himself
stressed the point in the Reform Bill debates. '. . . Government
and society are cause and effect—they react on each other . . .
The whole of history shows that all great revolutions have been
produced by a disproportion between society and its institutions; for while society has grown, its institutions have not kept
pace and accommodated themselves to its improvements.'[32] The
balance of interests must be achieved in Parliament and could
be achieved only if the House of Commons represented a
plurality of local, professional, economic, and class interests.

This notion of the representative body as a mirror of social
pluralism was the consistent defence of Whig reform proposals.
It was also the basis for opposition to them. Tories, in the main,
accepted this view of representation, arguing only that the
abolition of rotten boroughs, the enfranchisement of unrepresented towns, the extension of the suffrage to new classes, would
not in fact result in the desired plurality of representation.
The Manchester cotton industry would not be represented by
a Manchester member elected by £10 householders, but by
Manchester cotton manufacturers sitting for close boroughs.
The working-class radical associations re-emerging in the late
twenties also shared these pluralist assumptions. Their repeat-
edly stated objective was 'labour representation'—by which they
meant labouring men sitting as M.P.s—and the prime reason
for their opposing the Great Reform Bill was that it ignored and
even, by the abolition of the pot-walloper boroughs, curtailed
the representation of working-class interests.

Between these positions, agreement on the fundamental

[32] *Hansard*, vol. iv (Third Series), p. 776.

nature of a representative system underlay sharp and emotionally powerful disagreements on programmes. On the electoral system, on the effects that changes in the electoral structure would have on the balance of interests, on what was the feasible and desirable distribution of political influence between socio-economic groups, there was conflict and argument. But the range of shared assumptions was nevertheless wide. The electoral system should be devised, and particularly the suffrage distributed, to produce a desirable composition in the Commons; the Commons should represent all the variety of interests in society; and the 'interests' to be represented were primarily widespread social and economic groups rather than, as on older views of representation, local communities.

The Utilitarian Radicals stood outside this consensus. James Mill attacked the idea of functional representation directly in the 'Essay', significantly choosing as the object of his attack a defence of it by a Tory, Lord Liverpool. The attack could equally as well have been mounted on a Whig, and indeed George Grote's reply to Mackintosh included a sharp attack on the idea of the representation of interests. Mill's own critique of the idea is thin. He argues simply that, if the constituencies electing functional representatives are small, then the electorate so constituted will have a common interest in exploiting the unrepresented which would override their separate group ambitions (pp. 83–6). A more substantial critique, implicit in the whole argument of the 'Essay', was put directly by Grote. There could, he said, be only three species of interest in a society, 'first, the interest of any one man: that of a group: or of the whole community'. Since it is impossible to construct a governing body securing at the same time the interests of more than one group, it was clear that these three types of interest were mutually exclusive and that 'a governing body which would promote the universal interest must inevitably discard all inclination to the separate interest of any class whatever.'[33] This was the crux of the disagreement. For Tory and Whig alike, the general interest was an amalgam of group interests, and a representative system could further the general interest to the degree that it allowed for the representation of group demands and facilitated their compromise. For the Utilitarian, the general interest did

---

[33] *Statement of the Question of Parliamentary Reform* (1821), pp. 51–2, 62.

not consist in a balance between actual group wants but was an objective criterion of government policy and legislation, definable through the utility principle; and the achievement of a representative democracy would be to ensure that it became the actual standard of legislation and government policy.

The questioning of this assumption that the reign of democracy would be the reign of the utility principle is one of the main objectives of Macaulay's attack on the 'Essay'. The ensuing debate highlights many ambiguities in the relation between the utility principle and democratic ideas and, further still, in the connections between the psychological assumptions and the moral theory of the Utilitarians.

Bentham was a late convert to the radical cause. He had elaborated the main lines of his utilitarian philosophy well before he committed himself to parliamentary reform. Always a practical theorist, he nevertheless virtually ignored the constitutional problem in his early writings, concentrating his efforts on legal and penal reform. What were the essential elements in this utilitarian theory? The first was the assumption of psychological egosim, that men act to optimize their own interests, defined in terms of happiness, or alternatively in terms of pleasure–achievement and pain–avoidance. The second was that the moral worth of actions is dependent on their effects on the interest of the community, defined as the greatest happiness of the greatest number. The third was that this utility principle is also the standard on which legislative rules should be based. The last was that, at least in some areas, government action is necessary to reconcile men's egoistic drives with the communal interest. In some spheres, notably in most exchange relations, men's pursuit of their own self-interest automatically contributes to the general good and a 'natural harmony of interests' prevails, but in others an artificial identity has to be created by the calculated use of legislative sanctions (and to a lesser degree of rewards) to induce men to conform to ends defined by the utility principle.

This theory raises many familiar but none the less complex problems. Can a person's interests be identified with the maximization of his happiness or his want-satisfaction? Are particular actions or alternatively classes of actions to be the elements in any utility calculation? Can the utilities of different persons be compared and can in consequence the utilities of different persons be aggregated? Is the hedonist psychology compatible with the utilitarian ethic? We cannot follow through all these questions here,[34] but it is important to notice that at least the last two problems were posed in a particularly acute form with the association of utilitarianism and democray.

Before his conversion, Bentham, firmly within eighteenth-century traditions of enlightened despotism, had assumed the possibility of persuading the aristocratic political leadership to undertake legal reconstruction on Utilitarian principles. After his disillusionment over the Panopticon scheme, he abandoned this earlier optimism and argued, in a manner more in keeping with the psychological assumptions of his utilitarian theory, that rulers are necessarily governed by egoistic motives and a monarchy or an aristocracy must inevitably follow partial and sinister interests.[35] This assertion of the dangerous egoism of rulers forms the ground for the whole argument of Mill's 'Essay'. To hope that power-holders will, without inducement, refrain from using it for their own satisfaction is simply to affirm that men will voluntarily refrain from injuring one another or, in other words, that government is unnecessary (p. 58).

How then was the interest of the community to be made the actual end of government? The answer in Bentham's words was through 'Democratical ascendancy, or Ascendancy of the people.'[36] This is a major theme of Mill's 'Essay' too. If one or few men hold political power, government will serve a 'sinister' personal or group interest. Only if the whole community can check government through a representative democracy will the general interest become the actual end of government. Mill states this as self-evident, but, given the meaning which Benthamites attached to 'the general interest', it is by no means so. The conclusion might follow if 'the greatest happiness of the greatest number' was identical to 'the greatest happiness of the majority'. For, if the majority are rational egoists and the majority decide on the composition and direction of government, then government will attend to the interests of the major-

---

[34] The last question is examined more closely in the Appendix.

[35] J. Bentham: *Plan of Parliamentary Reform, in the Form of a Catechism* (1817), pp. 7–8.

[36] Ibid., p. 15.

ity. This was not, however, what Bentham meant by the utility principle. He had abandoned Priestley's formula that the happiness of 'the majority of the members of any state' should be the standard of state action.[37] For Bentham, the utility principle was an aggregative principle. No calculation of general utility could exclude the interests of any persons within the community nor could it weigh the consideration given to particular persons or groups. At the same time, the principle does not guarantee the maximization of the interests of every member of the public, nor even does it necessarily guarantee that the individual interests of the majority are maximized. As A. J. Ayer has pointed out, the right action for Bentham is that which produces the greatest aggregate of happiness no matter how few enjoy the pleasures or how many suffer the comparative pains.[38]

The problem remains, how can the general interest in Utilitarian terms be achieved through the democratic mechanism if men act on the self-interested motives the Utilitarians impute to them? The difficulty is paralleled in Utilitarian ethical theory. If men must pursue their own happiness and if they ought also to follow an ethical rule (general utility) which might militate against their interests, how are men to act morally? As early as 1804 the Whig Jeffrey had noticed the inconsistency in a review in the *Edinburgh* of Bentham's *Traités de Législation civile et pénale*. The language may be imprecise but the argument foreshadows much subsequent criticism of utilitarian ethics. 'Those actions are bad according to Mr. Bentham, that produce more evil than good: but actions are performed by individuals; and all the good may be to the individual and all the evil to the community.'[39]

This ethical ambiguity assumed a political dimension once the Benthamites moved to the position that legislation, which, Bentham had argued, is the major means of reconciling the egoistic drives of individuals with the interests of the community as a whole, should be controlled by those whom it was intended to restrain. Macaulay's attack upon Mill emphasizes this connection between the ambiguities of Benthamite democratic and

---

[37] *Essay on the First Principles of Government* (1768), p. 17.
[38] A. J. Ayer: 'The Principle of Utility' in *Jeremy Bentham and the Law* (1948), ed. G. W. Keeton and G. Schwarzenberger, p. 250.
[39] *Edinburgh Review*, vol. iv, p. 14.

ethical theory. Admittedly men follow their own happiness or interest—this is merely a restatement of the truism that men will satisfy their desires so far as they are able (p. 125). If the satisfaction of this personal interest happens to coincide with the general happiness they will follow the utility principle, while if they consider their own interests to be contrary to those of the community at large they will ignore it. If the Utilitarians are urging their fellows to pursue their own happiness, they are preaching to the converted, but, if they are pressing men to pursue the general happiness regardless of their own, they are advising what is *ex hypothesi* psychologically impossible (p. 213).

The *Westminster Review* was thus faced with an attack not just on Mill's radicalism but on the Utilitarian position generally. It attempts to answer Macaulay by arguing that a man can maximize his own happiness by following the utility principle. Bentham had shown, or at least cleared the ground for demonstration, 'that the greatest happiness of one individual was in the long run to be obtained by pursuing the greatest happiness of the aggregate' (p. 187). So the plain imperative that Macaulay had challenged the Utilitarians to produce could be either, 'Pursue the rule which is best for the general happiness', since this will eventually lead to your own; or 'Pursue your own happiness *aright*. The precept is not Do what you may *think* for your own happiness; but Do thus and thus, and it will *be* for your happiness' (p. 190). The task of the Benthamites was to explain the 'thus and thus', to show men the difference between their real and their apparent interests and to persuade them to follow the second, not by demanding of them behaviour contrary to their essential nature, but by pointing out a rational pattern of self-interest.

In this light, the *Review* claims, there is no incoherence in supposing that egoists can be morally concerned persons and socially concerned voters. The individual must pursue his own interests—this is a psychological imperative. But, since his final interest is inseparable from the good of his society, he will surrender his immediate desires to the needs of the community. This is a considerable distance from Mill's original premise that 'a man, if able, will take from others anything which they have and he desires.' And Macaulay attacks it as a complete contradiction of the theme of the 'Essay'.

If . . . government and laws are to be constituted on the supposition
on which Mr. Mill's Essay is founded, that all individuals will,
whenever they have power over others put into their hands, act in
opposition to the general happiness, then government and laws must
be constituted on the supposition that no individual believes, or ever
will believe, his own happiness to be identical with the happiness of
society. (p. 215)

Nor would the attempt by the *Westminster* to restore coherence
to the argument by distinguishing between real and apparent
interests serve as a guide to the likely behaviour of a democratic
electorate. It is, Macaulay asserts to the contrary, impossible to
deduce any person's actions from what might be decided objec-
tively to be his real interest; his actions are certainly related to
what he takes his interest to be, but this is not necessarily the
same thing (p. 125).

The cutting edge of this argument lay in Macaulay's application of it to the security of the property system. Under universal
suffrage, it would be a numerical majority, a poor majority,
who would govern. If Mill's psychological premises are correct,
this majority, following its immediate interests, would seek to dis-
possess the rich minority and would not be deterred by any fears
of remote ill consequences (p. 119). If, as Mill claimed, an aristocracy, no matter how rich, will use its power to exploit others, how
can it be supposed that a necessarily more ignorant and deprived
poor majority will desist from spoliation because of calculations of
long-term interests? (p. 121). More tentatively, Macaulay goes
further than this. All men have some desires that lead them to
injure, others that lead them to benefit, their fellows. If there is
in the community one class actuated principally by the first set
of motives and another by the second, political power should
clearly be vested in the latter. It could plausibly be argued that
there are often two such classes, the poor who resent inequalities
of wealth constituting the first and 'people of some property',
more sensitive about their personal reputations, the second
(pp. 107–8). While Macaulay reaches these conclusions cautiously, and re-emphasizes later that they are simply deductions
from Mill's premises, he was providing theoretical support for
the very widespread fear that radical reform of the franchise
would undermine the security of property.

There was of course no question for Benthamites that security of property was necessary to the general utility. Bentham, in considering the ends of government, had placed security as the primary object of law and argued that where security and equality conflict, equality must yield.[40] And Mill at the start of the 'Essay' defines the basic end of government as ensuring to each the fruits of his labour—which meant of course securing his property (p. 57). Nor was Bentham, in his early writings, under any illusion that the security of property could be sustained by general appreciation of its utility. The law alone, accomplishing what the 'natural sentiments' cannot, forces men 'to bow their heads under the yoke of foresight'. The legislator needs 'a vigilance always sustained, a power always in action' to protect property from a 'crowd of indefatigable enemies'.[41]

Macaulay's argument therefore touched Benthamites on a raw nerve. In the furore caused by Macaulay's articles, the Radical M.P., Hume, wrote to Francis Place on this question. If, he asked, twenty-nine men out of a body of thirty agreed that it would benefit them to eat the thirtieth, would this then be justified? Place's answer typifies the response to the dilemma posed by Macaulay. If it could be shown that the eating of the thirtieth man would increase the general happiness, there could be no doubt that he should be sacrificed. But no such proof was possible and so the twenty-nine would not come to any such such decision.[42] The actions of rational men can be deduced from their real interests and, since their real interests are bound up with the general utility, their actions can be deduced from the requirements of general utility. This simplistic solution of the problem was the theme of Bentham's unpublished pamphlet 'Radicalism Not Dangerous', written in 1819. In this, he examined the egalitarian schemes circulating at the time and rejected them on grounds of social utility, dismissing as self-contradictory the objection that despite this a democracy might try to realize such schemes.[43]

The *Westminster*'s answers to Macaulay for the most part repeat these bald assertions. Two specific points are made—

[40] *The Theory of Legislation* (ed. C. K. Ogden, 1931), pp. 109–20.

[41] ibid., p. 110.

[42] Hume to Place (19 Oct. 1829) and Place to Hume (25 Oct. 1829) in B.L. *Add. MSS.* 35, 145, fos. 105, 109–14.

[43] *Works* (ed. Bowring), vol. iii, pp. 599–622.

—that there is no historical evidence for the assumption that the poor will plunder the rich, and that the equalization of property would destroy the hopes, shared by all, of being rich (pp. 137, 186). Otherwise, the *Review* simply resorts to the assertion that the preservation of the existing distribution of property was in the interests of the poor and that the poor would not in consequence disturb it.

Although the *Review* does not provide it, a substantial theoretical defence of this proposition of an identity of interests between rich and poor, capital and labour, had already been elaborated by James Mill in his theory of the wages fund. Fundamental to his theory was the Malthusian law that population when unchecked increases at a rate more rapid than the increase in food supply and that in consequence numbers tend constantly to outrun the means of subsistence.[44] From this proposition, Ricardo drew his 'iron law of wages'. Labour has, like all other marketable commodities, both a natural and a market price. Its natural price is that which allows labourers to subsist and perpetuate their race without either increase or diminution, while its market price is determined by supply and demand, the number of labourers on one side and the capital available for employing them on the other. The market price tends constantly towards the natural price. Any rise in actual wage rates quickly brings an increase of population and so in the labour supply and the demand for necessities; and, if the market price falls below the natural rate, privation and starvation will reduce population and so bring up the market price of labour. The only ways in which distress can be averted are the restriction of population or the accumulation of capital, and the second affords only temporary relief since the increased demand for agricultural produce will stimulate the cultivation of marginal lands and so raise the price of such products.[45] Mill, in his *Elements of Political Economy*, developed this argument, stressing even more emphatically the absolute dependence of labour on capital accumulation. In primitive societies, he argued, men had no need of special skills or instruments, but with increasing division of labour, large accumulations of wealth are necessary to finance large-scale industrial production. Although originally

[44] R. Malthus: *Principles of Population*, ch. i.
[45] D. Ricardo: *Principles of Political Economy*, ch. v, sections 35–8.

both fixed and circulating capital derived from labour, in contemporary society it had emerged as an independent element of production, labour being the other.[46] It has even become the primary element. Since the means of production, the materials used in production and the wages paid to productive labour all make calls on capital resources, the productive industry and the amount of employment in a country must vary in proportion to its capital.[47] So the very subsistence of labour depended on the accumulation of capital and, if capital's rate of increase was slower than that of population, wages would inevitably fall to a starvation level.[48]

Given their conviction that political economy was a science as compelling in its laws and as certain in its practical applications as any physical science, the Utilitarians could therefore assert with absolute confidence that the interests of the poor did not diverge from those of the rich and that the preservation of a highly unequal distribution of property was in the interests of the majority. This of course was not the point at issue in Macaulay's warnings about property. He was not disputing this identity of interests but questioning the assumption that the majority would act on a rational calculation of long-term interests.

In the 'Essay', Mill had himself faced the objection that the people are not capable of acting according to their interests. To demonstrate its invalidity, he appeals for once to an historical parallel. Before the Reformation, the Bible had been refused to the people on the grounds that they would draw wrong opinions from it, but experience has shown that these fears were unfounded. However, assuming that the objection is valid, the choice lies between government by a minority pursuing misrule by design and government by a majority pursuing misrule only when they misjudged their interests (pp. 89–92). The calmness of this acceptance of the possibility of popular misjudgement could hardly be sustained when what was at risk was the stability of property. And, during the 1820s, the likelihood of such a misjudgement seemed to be growing. The socialist ideas of thinkers such as Owen, Hall, Thompson, and Gray, and the egalitarian ideas of Hodgskin, challenged the justice of vast inequalities of

---

[46] *Elements of Political Economy* (2nd ed., 1824), pp. 8–19.
[47] ibid., pp. 21–4.   [48] ibid., pp. 43–5.

wealth; and the inference was drawn by many that these distri-
butive injustices were perpetuated by a class monopoly of
political power and would only be removed when the poor
majority had a decisive political influence.

Mill's response to the spread of such ideas is revealing. Writing to Brougham in 1832, he expressed concern over the
diffusion of 'nonsense . . . about the right of the labourer to the
whole produce of the country' and urged Brougham to press for
the abolition of the stamp tax on newspapers which prevented
any reputable competition to the 'illicit cheap publications'
propagating anti-property ideas. If working men could hear the
full argument, most would realize that their own interests were
bound up with the security of property.[49] The answer to the
dilemma posed by Macaulay, that men act not on their real
interests but on what they take their interests to be, lay in
education, often the last (and perhaps the best) refuge of the
social reformer.

The Utilitarian view of education was fundamentally didactic
and authoritarian.[50] The aim of education is to inculcate those
social and moral truths which will enable men to grasp and
pursue their long-term interests. In his 'Essay on Education',
Mill lays down three educational objectives—intelligence,
temperance, and benevolence. Intelligence enables men rationally to perceive the means necessary to their own felicity; temperance consists in a command over immediate appetites and
the ability to restrain them when they conflict with long-term
interests; and benevolence springs from the recognition of
mutual interdependence of men in their quest for happiness. So,
while education is aimed primarily at showing men how to
maximize their own interests, in doing so it teaches them to
respect the interests of others. As the economic sphere is the one
in which men can most significantly affect the happiness of
others, education must be concerned crucially with instilling
respect for the economic claims of others.[51]

Such instruction in enlightened self-interest is not difficult,
claimed Mill: 'every man possessed of reason, is accustomed to

[49] Mill to Brougham (3 Sept. 1832) in A. Bain: *James Mill* (1882), pp. 364–5.

[50] Bentham's architectural design for his ideal school, the Chrestomathic school,
was similar to his design for the Panopticon, his ideal prison.

[51] 'Essay on Education', pp. 15–16, 34 in the seven-essay collection (1824–5)—see
Note on the Texts pp. 51–2.

weigh evidence and to be guided and determined by its pre-ponderance. When various conclusions are, with their evidence, presented with equal care and with equal skill, there is a moral certainty, though some few may be misguided, that the greater number will judge right.'[52]

This clarity of judgement can be directed with ease towards the realization of social and moral truths. It is always possible to teach men to respect the general good by the demonstration of a few simple and general propositions. In consequence, it is seldom difficult to get the people to see what is 'really good' for them, so long as no attempt is made to confuse and delude them.[53] John Austin, the Utilitarian jurist, shared this optimism, asserting that little was needed to grasp the momentous truths of political economy, since they were 'deducible from plain principles, by short and obvious inferences'. Nor did he fail to point out the social benefit such instruction would bring. It was only the ignorant poor who regarded inequality of property as 'an arrangement upheld by the few at the *cost* of the many'. Once the poor understood that capital is a creator of wealth and is the fund out of which labour is paid, they would appreciate 'that violations of property are mischievous to *themselves* . . . They would see that they are deeply interested in the *security* of property'.[54]

At this point, the wheel of the Benthamite argument had turned full circle. Bentham's initial expectation had been that the reign of utility would be inaugurated by an enlightened aristocracy, the Benthamites' final hope was that it would be inaugurated by an enlightened democracy. The Benthamite creed was based on two convictions, that the actions of men can be predicted in terms of their interests and that both moral and legislative codes should aim at maximizing the total aggregate of interest achievement in the community. In some areas, neither moral nor legislative rules are relevant since the individual's pursuit of his self-interest automatically furthers the general good. Moral or legislative regulation is required where universal pursuit of self-interest does not produce the greatest happiness of the greatest number. If we accept Bentham's

---

[52] 'Essay on the Liberty of the Press', ibid., p. 22.
[53] *Fragment on Mackintosh* (1835), p. 149.
[54] *The Province of Jurisprudence Determined* (1832), pp. 69–72.

psychological axioms, his view that general utility as he defines it is a social value that subsumes all other social values and his assumption that some sort of measurement and aggregation of utility values is possible, we can see that a consistent and coherent theory of law is possible. The science of legislation consists in defining those patterns of behaviour contributive to the general utility and drawing up a schedule of sanctions sufficient to deter rational egoists from departing from those patterns. Bentham was a practical legal reformer rather than a moral philosopher and, as an ethical theory, the coherence of his doctrine is less evident. The inconsistencies of the Utilitarian position were brought up by Macaulay and have often been canvassed since; essentially, they are that there is an inconsistency between Bentham's egoistic psychological axioms and his ethical injunctions, between his claim that a man must seek his own happiness and that he ought to promote the general happiness.

The beliefs that the utility principle constitute an incontestable standard for governmental action and that an exact science of politics can be constructed and utilized in realizing this principle continued to dominate Utilitarian thinking after its association with political radicalism. Indeed, democracy was embraced only because it was seen as instrumental, a means towards a utilitarian end. Bentham became a democrat only when he was convinced that democracy was (at least in this country) the sole form of government in which rulers would be obliged to respect social utility (and thus embark on his programme of legal reform). Where Utilitarians believed they could control government without representative institutions, they were unsympathetic to them. Mill, who, as Examiner for the East India Company, had considerable influence in the government of India, resolutely opposed in 1831 the idea of the establishment of any sort of representative legislature there. He recommended, rather, a legislative council consisting of a lawyer, a native expert in Indian affairs, the Company's bureaucrats and 'a person thoroughly versed in the philosophy of man and government', in other words a Utilitarian.[55] That Mill was instrumental in the appointment of Macaulay to this last position has been taken, and was taken by Macaulay himself, to

[55] Mill's evidence to the Select Committee on the East India Company (1831) in *Parliamentary Papers* (1831–2), vol. ix, p. 46 (Qu. 348), p. 49 (Qu. 364).

demonstrate Mill's personal magnanimity. It also illustrates the Benthamites' order of priorities for, despite his assault on the democratic commitments of the Utilitarians, Macaulay remained an adherent of Benthamite legal philosophy.[56] He was careful, in attacking the *Westminster* article he believed had been written by Bentham, to distinguish between Bentham's 'feeble and sophistical' reasonings on moral and political questions and his merited position as 'the father of the philosophy of Jurisprudence' (pp. 153-4).

This judgement of a representative system in instrumental terms separated the Benthamites from other Radicals, those for instance who pressed for universal suffrage on grounds of rights, either natural or historical. It did not divide them from Whigs and Tories, who believed too that the electoral system should be devised to achieve a desired representative body. Here the coincidence of views ended. Whigs and Tories sought an assembly representing all the varied interests of the community (or at the least all property interests). Such an assembly would both force government towards its proper task and enable it better to perform it, the task being the compromise of the conflicting and continually changing demands of social groups. What *was* a satisfactory compromise could not be determined *a priori*, but could be discovered only through the political process itself. For the Utilitarians, in contrast, the proper ends of legislation and policy could be deduced from the utility principle. The problem was how to make those proper ends, definable through utilitarian calculation, the actual ends of government, and the answer lay in representative democracy. The Utilitarians were therefore democrats in the hope that democratic processes would express a broad uniformity of purpose directed at a single communal interest. Some general parallels with Rousseau's theory of democracy are clear; the point of democracy is to instate a 'general will', general in being both a will common to all and a will directed towards communal rather than individual ends.

Macaulay brought into the open the inconsistency between these expectations and the psychological assumptions on which Mill based his critique of non-democratic forms of government.

---

[56] One of Macaulay's main tasks was to draw up a Penal Code for India on Benthamite lines. See L. Stephen: *The English Utilitarians* (1900), vol. ii, p. 36.

He showed too how close are the ambiguities in the Benthamites' constitutional theory to those in their ethical theory. For
the question, 'Why should an egoist take the general interest as a
standard of action if no sanctions persuade him to it?', is as
applicable to the voter as to the moral actor.

The Utilitarian answer, made all the more urgent by
Macaulay's connecting of the question to the security of
property, was to deny the claimed inconsistency. It is always
in the individual's long-term or real interests if not in his short-
term or apparent interests to seek the general happiness. Difficulties still remain, however. One is that if this identity of
interests holds, and if men are rationally capable of distinguishing their real from their apparent interests, the fundamental
assumption of Bentham's theory of penal law, that there is no
such identity of interests in the absence of penal sanctions,
becomes untenable. Another objection raised by Macaulay is
that, even if such an identity exists, it would be unrealistic and
dangerous to base constitutional experiments on the supposition
that men will rationally follow their 'real' interests, particularly
if their short-term needs are overwhelming, as those of the poor
must necessarily be. The Utilitarian response was that the real
world can be made to conform to the rational world of theory,
education can bring men to the recognition of the inexorable
connection between their own and the general happiness. So, in
the last resort, the Benthamites' belief in democracy rested on
their precedent belief in the possibility of constructing a comprehensive science of man and society. So compelling were the
conclusions of such a science that men must accept them if
exposed at all to argument; and it was precisely the development of general rationality that would enable a democracy to
work as they hoped, for the principle of utility.

4. NOTE ON THE TEXTS

James Mill wrote a number of articles, including that on
Government, for the *Supplement* to the fifth edition of the
Encyclopaedia Britannica. The *Supplement* was planned in 1814
and was issued as a whole in six volumes in 1824. It had, however, been appearing in half volumes at intervals from December 1815. Volume IV, in which the article on Government

appeared, was published in two parts in December 1819 and September 1820, Mill's article on Government falling into the second half volume. The article was published in pamphlet form from the 'Traveller Office' on 5 May 1821, the publishers mentioning that the article had already been 'reprinted in parts, in different numbers of the Traveller Evening Paper'. Apart from its republication in the collected Supplement in 1824, the article was republished twice later in the 1820s, firstly in a collection of four of Mill's contributions to the *Supplement, Essays on Government, Jurisprudence, Liberty of the Press, and Law of Nations,* and secondly in a collection of seven contributions, *Essays on I. Government, II. Jurisprudence, III. Liberty of the Press, IV. Prisons and Prison Discipline, V. Colonies, VI. Law of Nations, VII. Education.* Both of these collections are undated and their dating presents a problem. The seven-essay collection, which is the one Macaulay uses in his attack on the 'Essay on Government' in the *Edinburgh Review* of March 1829, is dated 1828 in the *Review,* but recent investigation suggests dates of 1823 for the four essay collection and 1824–5 for the seven-essay collection.[57]

The 1821 edition of the 'Essay' is a straight reprint of the *Encyclopaedia* article, but a large number of revisions were made for the four essay collection. Save for one minor variation, the 'Essay on Government' in the seven-essay collection is a reprint of the four-essay edition. Since this is the last of the editions and also the one used by Macaulay, it is the one reprinted here. Most of the changes from the original *Supplement* article consist of minor corrections of typography, grammar, and punctuation, and we have not given an exhaustive list of variations. However those variations have been cited in numbered footnotes which may be thought to vary the meaning of the text.

Macaulay's articles and the *Westminster Review*'s replies are reprinted from the *Edinburgh Review* and *Westminster Review.* There was naturally a good deal of cross-quotation in these articles and these quotations have been omitted where this can be done without damage to the argument. The omissions are all indicated and a cross-reference given in square brackets to the page in this edition on which the omitted passage may be found.

[57] Robert A. Fenn: 'James Mill's Political Thought', Thesis submitted to the University of London for the degree of Doctor of Philosophy, 1971, Appendix, pp. 80–4.

II

Essay on Government

by James Mill

I. *The End of Government; viz. the Good or Benefit for the Sake of which it exists.*

THE question with respect to Government is a question about the adaptation of means to an end. Notwithstanding the portion of discourse which has been bestowed upon this subject, it is surprising to find, on a close inspection, how few of its principles are settled. The reason is, that the ends and means have not been analyzed; and it is only a general and undistinguishing conception of them, which is found in the minds of the greatest number of men. Things, in this situation, give rise to interminable disputes; more especially when the deliberation is subject, as here, to the strongest action of personal interest.

In a discourse, limited as the present, it would be obviously vain to attempt the accomplishment of such a task as that of the analysis we have mentioned. The mode, however, in which the operation should be conducted, may perhaps be described, and evidence enough exhibited to shew in what road we must travel, to approach the goal at which so many have vainly endeavoured to arrive.

The end of Government has been described in a great variety of expressions. By Locke it was said to be 'the public good'; by others it has been described as being 'the greatest happiness of the greatest number.' These, and equivalent expressions, are just; but they are defective, inasmuch as the particular ideas which they embrace are indistinctly announced; and different conceptions[1] are by means of them raised in different minds, and even in the same mind on different occasions.

It is immediately obvious, that a wide and difficult field is presented, and that the whole science of human nature must be explored, to lay a foundation for the science of Government.

To understand what is included in the happiness of the greatest number, we must understand what is included in the happiness of the individuals of whom it is composed.

That dissection of human nature which would be necessary for exhibiting, on proper evidence, the primary elements into which human happiness may be resolved, it is not compatible with the present design to undertake. We must content ourselves with assuming certain results.

We may allow, for example, in general terms, that the lot of

[1] '... different combinations ...'

every human being is determined by his pains and pleasures; and that his happiness corresponds with the degree in which his pleasures are great, and his pains are small.

Human pains and pleasures are derived from two sources:— They are produced, either by our fellow-men, or by causes independent of other men.

We may assume it as another principle, that the concern of Government is with the former of these two sources; that its business is to increase to the utmost the pleasures, and diminish to the utmost the pains, which men derive from one another.

Of the laws of nature, on which the condition of man depends, that which is attended with the greatest number of consequences, is the necessity of labour for obtaining the means of subsistence, as well as the means of the greatest part of our pleasures. This is, no doubt, the primary cause of Government; for, if nature had produced spontaneously all the objects which we desire, and in sufficient abundance for the desires of all, there would have been no source of dispute or of injury among men; nor would any man have possessed the means of ever acquiring authority over another.

The results are exceedingly different, when nature produces the objects of desire not in sufficient abundance for all. The source of dispute is then exhaustless; and every man has the means of acquiring authority over others, in proportion to the quantity of those objects which he is able to possess.

In this case, the end to be obtained, through Government as the means, is, to make that distribution of the scanty materials of happiness, which would insure the greatest sum of it in the members of the community, taken altogether, preventing every individual, or combination of individuals, from interfering with that distribution, or making any man to have less than his share.

When it is considered that most of the objects of desire, and even the means of subsistence, are the product of labour, it is evident that the means of insuring labour must be provided for as the foundation of all.

The means for the insuring of labour are of two sorts; the one made out of the matter of evil, the other made out of the matter of good.

The first sort is commonly denominated force; and, under its application, the labourers are slaves. This mode of procuring labour we need not consider; for, if the end of Government be to produce the greatest happiness of the greatest number, that end cannot be attained by making the greatest number slaves.

The other mode of obtaining labour is by allurement, or the advantage which it brings. To obtain all the objects of desire in the greatest possible quantity, we must obtain labour in the greatest possible quantity; and, to obtain labour in the greatest possible quantity, we must raise to the greatest possible height the advantage attached to labour. It is impossible to attach to labour a greater degree of advantage than the whole of the product of labour. Why so? Because, if you give more to one man than the produce of his labour, you can do so only by taking it away from the produce of some other man's labour. The greatest possible happiness of society is, therefore, attained by insuring to every man the greatest possible quantity of the produce of his labour.

How is this to be accomplished? For it is obvious that every man, who has not all the objects of his desire, has inducement to take them from any other man who is weaker than himself: and how is he to be prevented?[2]

One mode is sufficiently obvious; and it does not appear that there is any other: The union of a certain number of men, to protect one another. The object, it is plain, can best be attained when a great number of men combine, and delegate to a small number the power necessary for protecting them all. This is Government.[3]

With respect to the end of Government, or that for the sake of

[2] '... and how is this to be prevented?

[3] One Mode is sufficiently obvious; and it does not appear that there is any other. It is the union of a certain number of men, agreeing to protect one another; and the object is best accomplished when a great number of men combine together, and delegate to a small number the power necessary for protecting them all.— This is Government. And it thus appears, that it is for the sake of property that Government exists.

[Footnote added]

'It may be remarked that the conclusion to which we have thus arrived coincides exactly with the doctrine of Locke:—"The great and chief end", says he, "of men's uniting into Commonwealths, and putting themselves under Government, is the preservation of their property"—*Second Treatise concerning Government*, ch. ix. This more certainly appears, when it is considered that by far the greater part of injuries to person, committed by human beings, are, in some way or other, on account of property.'

which it exists, it is not conceived to be necessary, on the present occasion, that the analysis should be carried any further. What follows is an attempt to analyze the means.

II. *The Means of attaining the End of Government; viz. Power, and Securities against the Abuse of that Power.*

Two things are here to be considered; the power with which the small number are entrusted; and the use which they are to make of it.

With respect to the first, there is no difficulty. The elements, out of which the power of coercing others is fabricated, are obvious to all. Of these we shall, therefore, not lengthen this article by any explanation.

All the difficult questions of Government relate to the means of restraining those, in whose hands are lodged the powers necessary for the protection of all, from making bad use of it.

Whatever would be the temptations under which individuals would lie, if there was no Government, to take the objects of desire from others weaker than themselves, under the same temptations the members of Government lie, to take the objects of desire from the members of the community, if they are not prevented from doing so. Whatever, then, are the reasons for establishing Government, the very same exactly are the reasons for establishing securities, that those entrusted with the powers necessary for protecting others make use of them for that purpose solely, and not for the purpose of taking from the members of the community the objects of desire.

III. *That the requisite Securities against the Abuse of Power, are not found in any of the simple Forms of Government.*

There are three modes in which it may be supposed that the powers for the protection of the community are capable of being exercised. The community may undertake the protection of itself, and of its members. The powers of protection may be placed in the hands of a few. And, lastly, they may be placed in the hands of an individual. The Many, The Few, The One; These varieties appear to exhaust the subject. It is not possible to conceive any hands, or combination of hands, in which the powers of protection can be lodged, which will not fall under one or other of those descriptions. And these varieties correspond

to the three forms of Government, the Democratical, the Aristocratical, and the Monarchical.

It will be necessary to look somewhat closely at each of these
forms in their order.

1. THE DEMOCRATICAL.—It is obiously impossible that the
community in a body can be present to afford protection to each
of its members. It must employ individuals for that purpose.
Employing individuals, it must choose them; it must lay down
the rules under which they are to act; and it must punish them,
if they act in disconformity to those rules. In these functions are
included the three great operations of Government—Administration, Legislation, and Judicature. The community, to
perform any of these operations, must be assembled. This circumstance alone seems to form a conclusive objection against the
democratical form. To assemble the whole of a community as
often as the business of Government requires performance would
almost preclude the existence of labour; hence that of property;
and hence the existence of the community itself.

There is another objection, not less conclusive. A whole community would form a numerous assembly. But all numerous
assemblies are essentially incapable of business. It is unnecessary
to be tedious in the proof of this proposition. In an assembly,
everything must be done by speaking and assenting. But where
the assembly is numerous, so many persons desire to speak, and
feelings, by mutual inflammation, become so violent, that calm
and effectual deliberation is impossible.

It may be taken, therefore, as a position,[4] from which there
will be no dissent, that a community in mass is ill adapted for
the business of Government. There is no principle more in conformity with the sentiments and the practice of the people than
this. The management of the joint affairs of any considerable
body of the people they never undertake for themselves. What
they uniformly do is, to choose a certain number of themselves
to be the actors in their stead. Even in the case of a common
Benefit Club, the members choose a Committee of Management
and content themselves with a general control.

2. THE ARISTOCRATICAL.—This term applies to all those
cases, in which the powers of Government are held by any
number of persons intermediate between a single person and the

4 '... as a proposition ...'

majority. When the number is small, it is common to call the Government an Oligarchy; when it is considerable, to call it an Aristocracy. The cases are essentially the same; because the motives which operate in both are the same. This is a proposition which carries, we think, its own evidence along with it. We, therefore, assume it as a point which will not be disputed.

The source of evil is radically different, in the case of Aristocracy, from what it is in that of Democracy.

The Community cannot have an interest opposite to its interest. To affirm this would be a contradiction in terms. The Community within itself, and with respect to itself, can have no sinister interest. One Community may intend the evil of another; never its own. This is an indubitable proposition, and one of great importance. The Community may act wrong from mistake. To suppose that it could from design, would be to suppose that human beings can wish their own misery.[5]

The circumstances, from which the inaptitude of the community, as a body, for the business of Government, arises, namely, the inconvenience of assembling them, and the inconvenience of their numbers when assembled, do not necessarily exist in the case of Aristocracy. If the number of those who hold among them the powers of Government is so great, as to make it inconvenient to assemble them, or impossible for them to deliberate calmly when assembled, this is only an objection to so extended an Aristocracy, and has no application to an Aristocracy not too numerous, when assembled, for the best exercise of deliberation.

The question is, whether such an Aristocracy may be trusted to make that use of the powers of Government which is most conducive to the end for which Government exists?

There may be a strong presumption that any Aristocracy, monopolizing the powers of Government, would not possess intellectual powers in any very high perfection. Intellectual powers are the offspring of labour. But an hereditary Aristocracy are deprived of the strongest motives to labour. The greater part of them will, therefore, be defective in those mental powers. This is one objection, and an important one, though not the greatest.

[5] '. . . would be to suppose this absurdity, that human beings can wish their own misery.

We have already observed, that the reason for which Government exists is, that one man, if stronger than another, will take from him whatever that other possesses and he desires. But if one man will do this, so will several. And if powers are put into the hands of a comparatively small number, called an Aristocracy, powers which make them stronger than the rest of the community, they will take from the rest of the community as much as they please of the objects of desire. They will, thus, defeat the very end for which Government was instituted. The unfitness, therefore, of an Aristocracy to be entrusted with the powers of Government, rests on demonstration.

3. THE MONARCHICAL.—It will be seen, and therefore words to make it manifest are unnecessary, that, in most respects, the Monarchical form of Government agrees with the Aristocratical, and is liable to the same objections.

If Government is founded upon this, as a law of human nature, that a man, if able, will take from others anything which they have and he desires, it is sufficiently evident that when a man is called a King, it does not change his nature; so that when he has got power to enable him to take from every man what he pleases, he will take whatever he pleases. To suppose that he will not, is to affirm that Government is unnecessary; and that human beings will abstain from injuring one another of their own accord.

It is very evident that this reasoning extends to every modification of the smaller number. Whenever the powers of Government are placed in any hands other than those of the community, whether those of one man, of a few, or of several, those principles of human nature which imply that Government is at all necessary, imply that those persons will make use of them to defeat the very end for which Government exists.

IV. *An Objection stated—and answered.*

One observation, however, suggests itself. Allowing, it may be said, that this deduction is perfect, and the inference founded upon it indisputable, it is yet true, that if there were no Government, every man would be exposed to depredation from every man; but, under an Aristocracy, he is exposed to it only from a few; under a Monarchy, only from one.

This is a highly important objection, and deserves to be minutely investigated.

It is sufficiently obvious, that, if every man is liable to be deprived of what he possesses at the will of every man stronger than himself, the existence of property is impossible; and, if the existence of property is impossible, so also is that of labour, of the means of subsistence for an enlarged community, and hence of the community itself. If the members of such a community are liable to deprivation by only a few hundred men, the members of an Aristocracy, it may not be impossible to satiate that limited number with a limited portion of the objects belonging to all. Allowing this view of the subject to be correct, it follows, that the smaller the number of hands into which the powers of Government are permitted to pass, the happier it will be for the community; that an Oligarchy, therefore, is better than an Aristocracy, and a Monarchy better than either.

This view of the subject deserves to be the more carefully considered, because the conclusion to which it leads is the same with that which has been adopted and promulgated, by some of the most profound and most benevolent investigators of human affairs. That Government by one man, altogether unlimited and uncontrolled, is better than Government by any modification of Aristocracy, is the celebrated opinion of Mr. Hobbes, and of the French *Economists*, supported on reasonings which it is not easy to controvert. Government by the many, they with reason considered an impossibility. They inferred, therefore, that, of all the possible forms of Government, absolute Monarchy is the best.

Experience, if we look only at the outside of the facts, appears to be divided on this subject. Absolute Monarchy, under Neros and Caligulas, under such men as Emperors of Morocco and Sultans of Turkey, is the scourge of human nature. On the other side, the people of Denmark, tired out with the oppression of an Aristocracy, resolved that their King should be absolute; and, under their absolute Monarch, are as well governed as any people in Europe. In Greece, notwithstanding the defects of Democracy, human nature ran a more brilliant career than it has ever done in any other age or country.

As the surface of history affords, therefore, no certain principle of decision, we must go beyond the surface, and penetrate to the springs within.

When it is said that one man, or a limited number of men, will soon be satiated with the objects of desire, and, when they have taken from the community what suffices to satiate them, will protect its members in the enjoyment of the remainder, an important element of the calculation is left out. Human beings are not a passive substance. If human beings, in respect to their rulers, were the same as sheep in respect to their shepherd; and if the King, or the Aristocracy, were as totally exempt from all fear of resistance from the people, and all chance of obtaining more obedience from severity, as the shepherd in the case of the sheep, it does appear that there would be a limit to the motive for taking to one's self the objects of desire. The case will be found to be very much altered when the idea is taken into the account, first, of the resistance to his will which one human being may expect from another; and secondly, of that perfection in obedience which fear alone can produce.

That one human being will desire to render the person and property of another subservient to his pleasures, notwithstanding the pain or loss of pleasure which it may occasion to that other individual, is the foundation of Government. The desire of the object implies the desire of the power necessary to accomplish the object. The desire, therefore, of that power which is necessary to render the persons and properties of human beings subservient to our pleasures, is a grand governing law of human nature.

What is implied in that desire of power; and what is the extent to which it carries the actions of men; are the questions which it is necessary to resolve, in order to discover the limit which nature has set to the desire, on the part of a King, or an Aristocracy, to inflict evil upon the community for their own advantage.

Power is a means to an end. The end is, every thing, without exception, which the human being calls pleasure, and the removal of pain. The grand instrument for attaining what a man likes is the actions of other men. Power, in its most appropriate signification, therefore, means, security for the conformity between the will of one man and the acts of other men. This, we presume, is not a proposition which will be disputed. The master has power over his servant, because when he wills him to do so and so,—in other words, expresses a desire that he would do so and so, he possesses a kind of security that the actions of the man will correspond to his desire. The general commands his soldiers to perform certain operations, the King commands his subjects to act in a certain manner, and their power is complete or not complete, in proportion as the conformity is complete or not complete between the actions willed and the actions performed. The actions of other men, considered as means for the attainment of the objects of our desire, are perfect or imperfect, in proportion as they are or are not certainly and invariably correspondent to our will. There is no limit, therefore, to the demand of security for the perfection of that correspondence. A man is never satisfied with a smaller degree, if he can obtain a greater. And as there is no man whatsoever, whose acts, in some degree or other, in some way or other, more immediately or more remotely, may not have some influence as means to our ends, there is no man, the conformity of whose acts to our will we would not give something to secure. The demand, therefore, of power over the acts of other men is really boundless. It is boundless in two ways; boundless in the number of persons to whom we would extend it, and boundless in its degree over the actions of each.

It would be nugatory to say, with a view to explain away this important principle, that some human beings may be so remotely connected with our interests, as to make the desire of a conformity between our will and their actions evanescent. It is quite enough to assume, what nobody will deny, that our desire of that conformity is unlimited, in respect to all those men whose actions can be supposed to have any influence on our pains and pleasures. With respect to the rulers of a community, this at least is certain, that they have a desire for the conformity between their will and the actions of every man in the community. And for our present purpose, this is as wide a field as we need to embrace.

With respect to the community, then, we deem it an established truth, that the rulers, one or a few, desire an exact conformity between their will and the acts of every member of the community. It remains for us to inquire to what description of acts it is the nature of this desire to give existence.

There are two classes of means by which the conformity

between the will of one man and the acts of other men may be accomplished. The one is pleasure, the other pain.

With regard to securities of the pleasurable sort for obtaining a conformity between one man's will and the acts of other men, it is evident, from experience, that when a man possesses a command over the objects of desire, he may, by imparting those objects to other men, insure, to a great extent, conformity between his will and their actions. It follows, and is also matter of experience, that the greater the quantity of the objects of desire, which he may thus impart to other men, the greater is the number of men between whose actions and his own will he can insure a conformity. As it has been demonstrated that there is no limit to the number of men whose actions we desire to have conformable to our will, it follows, with equal evidence, that there is no limit to the command which we desire to possess over the objects which ensure this result.[6]

It is, therefore, not true, that there is, in the mind of a King, or in the minds of an Aristocracy, any point of saturation with the objects of desire. The opinion, in examination of which we have gone through the preceding analysis, that a King or an Aristocracy may be satiated with the objects of desire, and, after being satiated, leave to the members of the community the greater part of what belongs to them, is an opinion founded upon a partial and incomplete view of the laws of human nature.

We have next to consider the securities of the painful sort which may be employed for attaining conformity between the acts of one man and the will of another.

We are of opinion, that the importance of this part of the subject has not been duly considered; and that the business of Government will be ill understood, till its numerous consequences have been fully developed.

Pleasure appears to be a feeble instrument of obedience in comparison with pain. It is much more easy to despise pleasure than pain. Above all, it is important to consider, that in this class of instruments is included the power of taking away life, and with it of taking away not only all the pleasures of reality, but, what goes so far beyond them, all the pleasures of hope.

---

[6] '. . . to the command which there are motives for endeavouring to possess over the objects of desire.'

This class of securities is, therefore, incomparably the strongest. He who desires obedience, to a high degree of exactness, cannot be satisfied with the power of giving pleasure, he must have the power of inflicting pain: He who desires it, to the highest possible degree of exactness, must desire power of inflicting pain sufficient at least to insure that degree of exactness; that is, an unlimited power of inflicting pain; for, as there is no possible mark by which to distinguish what is sufficient and what is not, and as the human mind sets no bounds to its avidity for the securities of what it deems eminently good, it is sure to extend, beyond almost any limits, its desire of the power of giving pain to others.

It may, however, be said, that how inseparable a part soever of human nature it may appear to be, to desire to possess unlimited power of inflicting pain upon others, it does not follow, that those who possess it will have a desire to make use of it.[7]

This is the next part of the inquiry upon which we have to enter; and we need not add that it merits all the attention of those who would possess correct ideas upon a subject which involves the greatest interests of mankind.

The chain of inference, in this case, is close and strong, to a most unusual degree. A man desires that the actions of other men shall be instantly and accurately correspondent to his will. He desires that the actions of the greatest possible number shall be so. Terror is the grand instrument. Terror can work only through assurance that evil will follow any want of conformity between the will and the actions willed. Every failure must, therefore, be punished. As there are no bounds to the mind's desire of its pleasure, there are of course no bounds to its desire of perfection in the instruments of that pleasure. There are, therefore, no bounds to its desire of exactness in the conformity between its will and the actions willed; and, by consequence, to the strength of that terror which is its procuring cause. Every, the most minute, failure, must be visited with the heaviest infliction: and, as failure in extreme exactness must frequently happen, the occasions of cruelty must be incessant.

We have thus arrived at several conclusions of the highest

[7] '. . . pain to others.
So much with respect to the motive for having and holding powers of inflicting pain upon others. It may, however, . . .'

possible importance. We have seen, that the very principle of human nature upon which the necessity of Government is founded, the propensity of one man to possess himself of the objects of desire at the cost of another, leads on, by infallible sequence, where power over a community is attained, and nothing checks, not only to that degree of plunder which leaves the members (excepting always the recipients and instruments of the plunder) the bare means of subsistence, but to that degree of cruelty which is necessary to keep in existence the most intense terror.

The world affords some decisive experiments upon human nature, in exact conformity with these conclusions. An English Gentleman may be taken as a favourable specimen of civilization, of knowledge, of humanity, of all the qualities, in short, that make human nature estimable. The degree in which he desires to possess power over his fellow-creatures, and the degree of oppression to which he finds motives for carrying the exercise of that power, will afford a standard from which, assuredly, there can be no appeal. Wherever the same motives exist, the same conduct, as that displayed by the English Gentleman, may be expected to follow, in all men not farther advanced in human excellence than himself. In the West Indies, before that vigilant attention of the English nation, which now, for thirty years, has imposed so great a check upon the masters of slaves, there was not a perfect absence of all check upon the dreadful propensities of power. But yet it is true, that these propensities led English Gentlemen, not only to deprive their slaves of property, and to make property of their fellow-creatures, but to treat them with a degree of cruelty, the very description of which froze the blood of those of their countrymen, who were placed in less unfavourable circumstances. The motives of this deplorable conduct are exactly those which we have described above, as arising out of the universal desire to render the actions of other men exactly conformable to our will. It is of great importance to remark, that not one item in the motives which led English Gentlemen to make slaves of their fellow-creatures, and to reduce them to the very worst condition in which the negroes have been found in the West Indies, can be shown to be wanting, or to be less strong in the set of motives, which universally operate upon the men who have power over their fellow-creatures. It is proved, therefore, by the closest deduction from the acknowledged laws of human nature, and by direct and decisive experiments, that the ruling One, or the ruling Few, would, if checks did not operate in the way of prevention, reduce the great mass of the people subject to their power, at least to the condition of negroes in the West Indies.*

We have thus seen, that of the forms of Government, which have been called the three simple forms, not one is adequate to the ends which Government is appointed to secure; that the community itself, which alone is free from motives opposite to those ends, is incapacitated by its numbers from performing the business of Government; and that whether Government is intrusted to one or a few, they have not only motives opposite to those ends, but motives which will carry them, if unchecked, to inflict the greatest evils.

These conclusions are so conformable to ordinary conceptions, that it would hardly have been necessary, if the development had not been of importance for some of our subsequent investigations, to have taken any pains with the proof of them. In this country, at least, it will be remarked, in conformity with so many writers, that the imperfection of the three simple forms of Government is apparent; that the ends of Government can be attained in perfection only, as under the British Constitution, by an union of all the three.

V. *That the requisite Securities are not found in a Union of the Three simple Forms of Government;—Doctrine of the Constitutional Balance.*

The doctrine of the union of the three simple forms of Government is the next part of this important subject which we are called upon to examine.

The first thing which it is obvious to remark upon it, is, that it has been customary, in regard to this part of the inquiry, to beg the question. The good effects which have been ascribed to the union of the three simple forms of Government, have been *supposed*; and the supposition has commonly been allowed. No proof has been adduced; or if any thing have the appearance of proof, it has only been a reference to the British Constitution.

---

* An acute sense of this important truth is expressed by the President **Montes**-quieu; 'C'est une experience eternelle, que tout homme qui a du pouvoir est **porte a** en abuser; il va jusqu'a ce qu'il trouve des limites.'—*Esp. de Loix, L.* xi. *c.* 4.

The British Constitution, it has been said, is an union of the three simple forms of Government; and the British Government is excellent. To render the instance of the British Government in any degree a proof of the doctrine in question, it is evident that three points must be established; 1st, That the British Government is not in show, but in substance, an union of the three simple forms, 2dly, That it has peculiar excellence; and 3dly, That its excellence arises from the union so supposed, and not from any other cause. As these points have always been taken for granted without examination, the question with respect to the effects of an union of the three simple forms of Government may be considered as yet unsolved.

The positions which we have already established with regard to human nature, and which we assume as foundations, are these: That the actions of men are governed by their wills, and their wills by their desires: That their desires are directed to pleasure and relief from pain as *ends*, and to wealth and power as the principal means: That to the desire of these means there is no limit; and that the actions which flow from this unlimited desire are the constituents whereof bad Government is made.[8] Reasoning correctly from these acknowledged laws of human nature, we shall presently discover what opinion, with respect to the mixture of the different species of Government, it will be incumbent upon us to adopt.

The theory in question implies, that of the powers of Government, one portion is held by the King, one by the Aristocracy, and one by the people. It also implies, that there is on the part of each of them a certain unity of will, otherwise they would not act as three separate powers. This being understood, we proceed to the inquiry.

From the principles which we have already laid down, it follows, That of the objects of human desire—and, speaking more definitely, of the means to the ends of human desire, namely, wealth and power—each of the three parties will endeavour to obtain as much as possible.

After what has been said, it is not suspected that any reader will deny this proposition; but it is of importance that he keep in his mind a very clear conception of it.

If any expedient presents itself to any of the supposed parties,

[8] '... which flow from that desire are the constituents ...'

effectual to this end, and not opposed to any preferred object of pursuit, we may infer, with certainty, that it will be adopted. One effectual expedient is not more effectual than obvious. Any two of the parties, by combining, may swallow up the third. That such combination will take place, appears to be as certain as any thing which depends upon human will; because there are strong motives in favour of it, and none that can be conceived in opposition to it. Whether the portions of power, as originally distributed to the parties, be supposed to be equal or unequal, the mixture of three of the kinds of Government, it is thus evident, cannot possibly exist.

This proposition appears to be so perfectly proved, that we do not think it necessary to dwell here upon the subject. As a part, however, of this doctrine, of the mixture of the simple forms of Government, it may be proper to inquire, whether an union may not be possible of two of them.

Three varieties of this union may be conceived; the union of the Monarchy with Aristocracy, or the union of either with Democracy.

Let us first suppose that Monarchy is united with Aristocracy. Their power is equal or not equal. If it is not equal, it follows, as a necessary consequence, from the principles which we have already established, that the stronger will take from the weaker, till it engrosses the whole. The only question, therefore, is, What will happen when the power is equal.

In the first place, it seems impossible that such equality should ever exist. How is it to be established? Or by what criterion is it to be ascertained? If there is no such criterion, it must, in all cases, be the result of chance. If so, the chances against it are as infinite to one. The idea, therefore, is wholly chimerical and absurd.

Besides, a disposition to overrate one's own advantages, and underrate those of other men, is a known law of human nature.[9] Suppose, what would be little less than miraculous, that equality were established, this propensity would lead each of the parties to conceive itself the strongest. The consequence would be that they would go to war, and contend till one or other was subdued. Either those laws of human nature, upon which all reasoning with respect to Government proceeds, must be denied,

[9] 'Besides, an overweening propensity, a disposition . . .'

and then the utility of Government itself may be denied,[10] or this conclusion is demonstrated. Again, if this equality were established, is there a human being who can suppose that it would last? If any thing be known about human affairs it is this, that they are in perpetual change. If nothing else interfered, the difference of men in respect of talents, would abundantly produce the effect. Suppose your equality to be established at the time when your King is a man of talents, and suppose his successor to be the reverse; your equality no longer exists. The moment one of the parties is superior, it begins to profit by its superiority, and the inequality is daily increased. It is unnecessary to extend the investigation to the remaining cases, the union of democracy with either of the other two kinds of Government. It is very evident that the same reasoning would lead to the same results.

In this doctrine of the mixture of the simple forms of Government, is included the celebrated theory of the Balance among the component parts of a Government. By this, it is supposed, that, when a Government is composed of Monarchy, Aristocracy, and Democracy, they balance one another, and by mutual checks produce good government. A few words will suffice to show, that, if any theory deserve the epithets of 'wild, visionary, chimerical,' it is that of the Balance. If there are three powers, how is it possible to prevent two of them from combining to swallow up the third?

The analysis which we have already performed, will enable us to trace rapidly the concatenation of causes and effects in this imagined case.

We have already seen that the interest of the community, considered in the aggregate, or in the democratical point of view, is, that each individual should receive protection, and that the powers which are constituted for that purpose should be employed exclusively for that purpose. As this is a proposition wholly indisputable, it is also one to which all correct reasoning upon matters of Government must have a perpetual reference.

We have also seen that the interest of the King, and of the governing Aristocracy, is directly the reverse; it is to have unlimited power over the rest of the community, and to use it for their own advantage. In the supposed case of the Balance of the

[10] '. . . may be disputed . . .'

Monarchical, Aristocratical, and Democratical powers, it cannot
be for the interest of either the Monarchy or the Aristocracy to
combine with the Democracy; because it is the interest of the
Democracy, or community at large, that neither the King nor
the Aristocracy should have one particle of power, or one particle of the wealth of the community, for their own advantage.

The Democracy or Community have all possible motives to
endeavour to prevent the Monarchy and Aristocracy from
exercising power, or obtaining the wealth of the community,
for their own advantage: The Monarchy and Aristocracy have
all possible motives for endeavouring to obtain unlimited power
over the persons and property of the community: The consequence is inevitable; they have all possible motives for combining to obtain that power, and unless the people have power
enough to be a match for both, they have no protection. The
balance, therefore, is a thing, the existence of which, upon
the best possible evidence, is to be regarded as impossible. The
appearances which have given colour to the supposition are
altogether delusive.

VI. *In the Representative System alone the Securities for good Government are to be found.*

What then is to be done? For, according to this reasoning,
we may be told that good Government appears to be impossible.
The people, as a body, cannot perform the business of Government for themselves. If the powers of Government are entrusted
to one man, or a few men, and a Monarchy, or governing
Aristocracy, is formed, the results are fatal: And it appears that
a combination of the simple forms is impossible.

Notwithstanding the truth of these propositions, it is not yet
proved that good Government is unattainable.[11] For though the
people, who cannot exercise the powers of Government themselves, must entrust them to some one individual or set of
individuals, and such individuals will infallibly have the
strongest motives to make a bad use of them, it is possible that
checks may be found sufficient to prevent them. The next subject of inquiry, then, is the doctrine of checks. It is sufficiently
conformable to the established and fashionable opinions to say,

---

[11] 'Notwithstanding the certainty of these propositions, it is not yet proved that
good Government is impossible.'

that, upon the right constitution of checks, all goodness of Government depends. To this proposition we fully subscribe. Nothing, therefore, can exceed the importance of correct conclusions upon this subject. After the developments already made, it is hoped that the inquiry will be neither intricate nor unsatisfactory.

In the grand discovery of modern times, the system of representation, the solution of all the difficulties, both speculative and practical, will perhaps be found. If it cannot, we seem to be forced upon the extraordinary conclusion, that good Government is impossible. For as there is no individual, or combination of individuals, except the community itself, who would not have an interest in bad Government, if entrusted with its powers; and as the community itself is incapable of exercising those powers, and must entrust them to some individual or combination of individuals, the conclusion is obious: The Community itself must check those individuals, else they will follow their interest, and produce bad Government.

But how is it the Community can check? The community can act only when assembled: And then it is incapable of acting.

The community, however, can chuse Representatives: And the question is, whether the Representatives of the Community can operate as a check?

VII. *What is required in a Representative Body to make it a Security for good Government?*

We may begin by laying down two propositions, which appear to involve a great portion of the inquiry; and about which it is unlikely that there will be any dispute.

I. The checking body must have a degree of power sufficient for the business of checking.

II. It must have an identity of interest with the community; otherwise it will make a mischievous use of its power.[12]

I. To measure the degree of power which is requisite upon any occasion, we must consider the degree of power which is necessary to be overcome. Just as much as suffices for that

---

[12] '. . . use of its power.

The first question relates to the degree of power which is necessary to perform the business of checking. We need hardly excite the reader's attention to the importance of this inquiry: for upon this, it is evident, every thing depends.

To measure the degree of power . . .'

purpose is requisite, and no more. We have then to inquire what power it is which the Representatives of the community, acting as a check, need power to overcome. The answer here is easily given. It is all that power, wheresoever lodged, which they, in whose hands it is lodged, have an interest in misusing. We have already seen, that to whomsoever the community entrusts the powers of Government, whether one, or a few, they have an interest in misusing them. All the power, therefore, which the one or the few, or which the one and the few combined, can apply to insure the accomplishment of their sinister ends, the checking body must have power to overcome, otherwise its check will be unavailing. In other words, there will be no check.

This is so exceedingly evident, that we hardly think it necessary to say another word in illustration of it. If a King is prompted by the inherent principles of human nature to seek the gratification of his will; and if he finds an obstacle in that pursuit, he removes it, of course, if he can. If any man, or any set of men, oppose him, he overcomes them, if he is able; and to prevent him, they must, at the least, have equal power with himself.

The same is the case with an Aristocracy. To oppose them with success in pursuing their interest at the expense of the community, the checking body must have power successfully to resist whatever power they possess. If there is both a King and an Aristocracy, and if they would combine to put down the checking force, and to pursue their mutual interest at the expense of the community, the checking body must have sufficient power successfully to resist the united power of both King and Aristocracy.

These conclusions are not only indisputable, but the very theory of the British Constitution is erected upon them. The House of Commons, according to that theory, is the checking body. It is also an admitted doctrine, that if the King had the power of bearing down any opposition to his will that could be made by the House of Commons; or if the King and the House of Lords combined had the power of bearing down its opposition to their joint will, it would cease to have the power of checking them; it must, therefore, have a power sufficient to overcome the united power of both.

II. All the questions which relate to the degree of power

necessary to be given to that checking body, on the perfection of whose operations all the goodness of Government depends, are thus pretty easily solved. The grand difficulty consists in finding the means of constituting a checking body, the powers of which shall not be turned against the community for whose protection it is created.

There can be no doubt, that, if power is granted to a body of men, called Representatives, they, like any other men, will use their power, not for the advantage of the community, but for their own advantage, if they can. The only question is, therefore, how they can be prevented? In other words, how are the interests of the Representatives to be identified with those of the community?

Each Representative may be considered in two capacities; in his capacity of Representative, in which he has the exercise of power over others, and in his capacity of Member of the Community, in which others have the exercise of power over him.

If things were so arranged, that, in his capacity of Representative, it would be impossible for him to do himself so much good by mis-government, as he would do himself harm in his capacity of member of the community, the object would be accomplished. We have already seen, that the amount of power assigned to the checking body cannot be diminished beyond a certain amount. It must be sufficient to overcome all resistance on the part of all those in whose hands the powers of Government are lodged. But if the power assigned to the Representative cannot be diminished in amount, there is only one other way in which it can be diminished, and that is, in duration.

This, then, is the instrument; lessening duration is the instrument, by which, if by any thing, the object is to be attained. The smaller the period of time during which any man retains his capacity of Representative, as compared with the time in which he is simply a member of the community, the more difficult it will be to compensate the sacrifice of the interests of the longer period, by the profits of mis-government during the shorter.

This is an old and approved method of identifying, as nearly as possible, the interests of those who rule, with the interests of those who are ruled. It is in pursuance of this advantage, that the Members of the British House of Commons have always been chosen for a limited period. If the Members were hereditary, or even if they were chosen for life, every inquirer would immediately pronounce that they would employ, for their own advantage, the powers entrusted to them; and that they would go just as far in abusing the persons and properties of the people, as their estimate of the powers and spirit of the people to resist them would allow them to contemplate as safe.

As it thus appears, by the consent of all men, from the time when the Romans made their Consuls annual, down to the present day, that the end is to be attained by limiting the duration, either of the acting, or (which is better) of the checking power, the next question is, to what degree should the limitation proceed?[13]

The general answer is plain. It should proceed, till met by over-balancing inconveniences on the other side. What then are the inconveniences which are likely to flow from a too limited duration?

They are of two sorts; those which affect the performance of the service, for which the individuals are chosen, and those which arise from the trouble of election. It is sufficiently obvious, that the business of Government requires time to perform it. The matter must be proposed, and deliberated upon, a resolution must be taken, and executed. If the powers of Government were to be shifted from one set of hands to another every day, the business of Government could not proceed. Two conclusions, then, we may adopt with perfect certainty; that whatsoever time is necessary to perform the periodical round of the stated operations of Government, should be allotted to those who are invested with the checking powers; and secondly, that no time, which is not necessary for that purpose, should by any means be allotted to them. With respect to the inconvenience arising from frequency of election, though it is evident that the trouble of election, which is always something, should not be repeated oftener than is necessary, no great allowance will need to be made for it, because it may easily be reduced to an inconsiderable amount.

As it thus appears, that limiting the duration of their power is a security against the sinister interest of the people's Representatives, so it appears that it is the only security of which the nature of the case admits. The only other means which could be

---

[13] '... the duration, either of the principal, or (what is better) of the checking power ...,'

employed to that end, would be punishment on account of abuse. It is easy, however, to see, that punishment could not be effectually applied. Previous to punishment, definition is required of the punishable acts; and proof must be established of the commission. But abuses of power may be carried to a great extent, without allowing the means of proving a determinate offence. No part of political experience is more perfect than this.

If the limiting of duration be the only security, it is unnecessary to speak of the importance which ought to be attached to it.

In the principle of limiting the duration of the power delegated to the Representaties of the people, is not included the idea of changing them. The same individual may be chosen any number of times. The check of the short period, for which he is chosen, and during which he can promote his sinister interest, is the same upon the man who has been chosen and re-chosen twenty times, as upon the man who has been chosen for the first time. And there is good reason for always re-electing the man who has done his duty, because the longer he serves, the better acquainted he becomes with the business of the service. Upon this principle of re-choosing, or of the permanency of the individual, united with the power of change, has been recommended the plan of permanent service with perpetual power of removal. This, it has been said, reduces the period within which the Representative can promote his sinister interest to the narrowest possible limits; because the moment when his Constituents begin to suspect him, that moment they may turn him out: on the other hand, if he continues faithful, the trouble of election is performed once for all, and the man serves as long as he lives. Some disadvantages, on the other hand, would accompany this plan. The present, however, is not the occasion on which the balance of different plans is capable of being adjusted.

VIII. *What is required in the Elective Body to secure the requisite Properties in the Representative Body.*

Having considered the means which are capable of being employed for identifying the interest of the Representatives, when chosen, with that of the persons who choose them, it remains that we endeavour to bring to view the principles which ought to guide in determining who the persons are by whom the act of choosing ought to be performed.

It is most evident, that upon this question, every thing depends. It can be of no consequence to insure, by shortness of duration, a conformity between the conduct of the Representatives and the will of those who appoint them, if those who appoint them have an interest opposite to that of the community; because those who choose will, according to the principles of human nature, make choice of such persons as will act according to their wishes. As this is a direct inference from the very principle on which Government itself is founded, we assume it as indisputable.

We have seen already, that if one man has power over others placed in his hands, he will make use of it for an evil purpose; for the purpose of rendering those other men the abject instruments of his will. If we, then, suppose, that one man has the power of choosing the Representatives of the people, it follows, that he will choose men, who will use their power as Representatives for the promotion of this his sinister interest.

We have likewise seen, that when a few men have power given them over others, they will make use of it exactly for the same ends, and to the same extent, as the one man. It equally follows, that, if a small number of men have the choice of the Representatives, such Representatives will be chosen as will promote the interests of that small number, by reducing, if possible, the rest of the community to be the abject and helpless slaves of their will.

In all these cases, it is obvious and indisputable, that all the benefits of the Representative system are lost. The Representative system is, in that case, only an operose and clumsy machinery for doing that which might as well be done without it; reducing the community to subjection, under the One, or the Few.

When we say the Few, it is seen that, in this case, it is of no importance whether we mean a few hundreds, or a few thousands, or even many thousands. The operation of the sinister interest is the same; and the fate is the same, of all that part of the community over whom the power is exercised. A numerous Aristocracy has never been found to be less oppressive than an Aristocracy confined to a few.

The general conclusion, therefore, which is evidently established is this; that the benefits of the Representative system are lost, in all cases in which the interests of the choosing body are not the same with those of the community.

It is very evident, that if the community itself were the choosing body, the interest of the community and that of the choosing body would be the same. The question is, whether that of any portion of the community, if erected into the choosing body, would remain the same?

One thing is pretty clear, that all those individuals whose interests are indisputably included in those of other individuals, may be struck off without inconvenience. In this light may be viewed all children, up to a certain age, whose interests are involved in those of their parents. In this light, also, women may be regarded, the interest of almost all of whom is involved either in that of their fathers or in that of their husbands.

Having ascertained that an interest, identical with that of the whole community, is to be found in the aggregate males, of an age to be regarded as *sui juris*, who may be regarded as the natural Representatives of the whole population, we have to go on, and inquire, whether this requisite quality may not be found in some less number, some aliquot part of that body.

As degrees of mental qualities are not easily ascertained, outward and visible signs must be taken to distinguish, for this purpose, one part of these males from another. Applicable signs of this description appear to be three; Years, Property, Profession or Mode of Life.

According to the first of these means of distinction, a portion of the males, to any degree limited, may be taken, by prescribing an advanced period of life at which the power of voting for a Representative should commence. According to the second, the elective body may be limited, by allowing a vote to those only who possess a certain amount of property or of income. According to the third, it may be limited, by allowing a vote only to such persons as belong to certain professions, or certain connexions and interests. What we have to inquire is, if the interest of the number, limited and set apart, upon any of those principles, as the organ of choice for a body of Representatives, will be the same with the interest of the community?

With respect to the first principle of selection, that of age, it would appear that a considerable latitude may be taken without inconvenience. Suppose the age of forty were prescribed, as that at which the right of Suffrage should commence; scarcely any laws could be made for the benefit of all the men of forty which would not be laws for the benefit of all the rest of the community.

The great principle of security here is, that the men of forty have a deep interest in the welfare of the younger men; for otherwise it might be objected, with perfect truth, that, if decisive power were placed in the hands of men of forty years of age, they would have an interest, just as any other detached portion of the community, in pursuing that career which we have already described, for reducing the rest of the community to the state of abject slaves. But the great majority of old men have sons, whose interest they regard as an essential part of their own.[14] This is a law of human nature. There is, therefore, no great danger that, in such an arrangement as this, the interests of the young would be greatly sacrificed to those of the old.

We come next to the inquiry, whether the interest of a body of electors, constituted by the possession of a certain amount of property or income, would be the same with the interest of the community?

It will not be disputed, that, if the qualification were raised so high that only a few hundreds possessed it, the case would be exactly the same with that of the consignment of the Electoral Suffrage to an Aristocracy. This we have already considered, and have seen that it differs in form rather than substance from a simple Aristocracy. We have likewise seen, that it alters not the case in regard to the community, whether the Aristocracy be some hundreds or many thousands. One thing is, therefore, completely ascertained, that a pecuniary qualification, unless it were very low, would only create an Aristocratical Government, and produce all the evils which we have shown to belong to that organ of misrule.[15]

This question, however, deserves to be a little more minutely considered. Let us next take the opposite extreme. Let us suppose that the qualification is very low, so low as to include the great majority of the people. It would not be easy for the people

[14] 'But it so happens (and it is a fully established law of human nature), that the great majority of old men . . .'

[15] '. . . ascertained that, unless the qualification be very low, it would only create an Aristocratical Government on a broad basis, and be accompanied with all the evils which we have shown to belong to an Aristocratical Government.'

who have very little property, to separate their interests from those of the people who have none. It is not the interest of those who have little property to give undue advantages to the posses-sion of property, which those who have the great portions of it would turn against themselves.

It may, therefore, be said, that there would be no evil in a low qualification. It can hardly be said, however, on the other hand, that there would be any good; for if the whole mass of the people who have some property would make a good choice, it will hardly be pretended that, added to them, the compara-tively small number of those who have none, and whose minds are naturally and almost necessarily governed by the minds of those who have, would be able to make the choice a bad one.

We have ascertained, therefore, two points. We have ascer-tained that a very low qualification is of no use, as affording no security for a good choice beyond that which would exist if no pecuniary qualification was required. We have likewise ascer-tained, that a qualification so high as to constitute an Aristo-cracy of wealth, though it were a very numerous one, would leave the community without protection, and exposed to all the evils of unbridled power. The only question, therefore, is, whether, between these extremes, there is any qualification which would remove the right of Suffrage from the people of small, or of no property, and yet constitute an elective body, the interest of which would be identical with that of the community?

It is not easy to find any satisfactory principle to guide us in our researches, and to tell us where we should fix. The qualifica-tion must either be such as to embrace the majority of the population, or some thing less than the majority. Suppose, in the first place, that it embraces the majority, the question is, whether the majority would have an interest in oppressing those who, upon this supposition, would be deprived of political power? If we reduce the calculation to its elements, we shall see that the interest which they would have, of this deplorable kind, though it would be something, would not be very great. Each man of the majority, if the majority were constituted the governing body, would have something less than the benefit of oppressing a single man. If the majority were twice as great as the minority, each man of the majority would only have one-half the benefit of oppressing a single man. In that case, the benefits of good Government, accruing to all, might be expected to overbalance to the several members of such an elective body the benefits of misrule peculiar to themselves. Good Government, would, therefore, have a tolerable security. Suppose, in the second place, that the qualification did not admit a body of electors so large as the majority, in that case, taking again the calculation in its elements, we shall see that each man would have a benefit equal to that derived from the oppression of more than one man; and that, in proportion as the elective body constituted a smaller and smaller minority, the benefit of misrule to the elective body would be increased, and bad Government would be insured.

It seems hardly necessary to carry the analysis of the pecuniary qualification, as the principle for choosing an elective body, any farther.

We have only remaining the third plan for constituting an elective body. According to the scheme in question, the best elective body is that which consists of certain classes, professions, or fraternities. The notion is, that when these fraternities or bodies are represented, the community itself is represented. The way in which, according to the patrons of this theory, the effect is brought about, is this. Though it is perfectly true, that each of these fraternities would profit by misrule, and have the strongest interest in promoting it; yet, if three or four such fraternities are appointed to act in conjunction, they will not profit by misrule, and will have an interest in nothing but good Government.

This theory of Representation we shall not attempt to trace farther back than the year 1793. In the debate on the motion of Mr. (now Earl) Grey, for a Reform in the System of Representation, on the 6th of May, of that year, Mr. Jenkinson, the present Earl of Liverpool, brought forward this theory of Representation, and urged it in opposition to all idea of Reform in the British House of Commons, in terms as clear and distinct as those in which it has recently been clothed by leading men on both sides of that House. We shall transcribe the passage from the speech of Mr. Jenkinson, omitting, for the sake of abbreviation, all those expressions which are unnecessary for conveying a knowledge of the plan, and of the reasons upon which it was founded.

'Supposing it agreed,' he said, 'that the House of Commons is meant to be a legislative body, representing all descriptions of men in the country, he supposed every person would agree, that the landed interest ought to have the preponderant weight. The landed interest was, in fact, the *stamina* of the country. In the second place, in a commercial country like this, the manufacturing and commercial interest ought to have a considerable weight, secondary to the landed interest, but secondary to the landed interest only. But was this all that was necessary? There were other descriptions of people, which, to distinguish them from those already mentioned, he should style professional people, and whom he considered as absolutely necessary to the composition of a House of Commons. By professional people, he meant those Members of the House of Commons who wished to raise themselves to the great offices of the State; those that were in the army, those that were in the navy, those that were in the law.' He then, as a reason for desiring to have those whom he calls 'professional people' in the composition of the House of Commons, gives it as a fact, that country Gentlemen and Merchants seldom desire, and seldom have motives for desiring, to be Ministers and the other great Officers of State. These Ministers and Officers, however, ought to be made out of the House of Commons. Therefore, you ought to have 'professional people' of whom to make them. Nor was this all. 'There was another reason why these persons were absolutely necessary. We were constantly in the habit of discussing in that House all the important concerns of the State. It was necessary, therefore, that there should be persons in the practice of debating such questions.' 'There was a third reason, which, to his mind, was stronger than all the rest. Suppose that in that House there were only country Gentlemen, they would not then be the Representatives of the nation, but of the landholders. Suppose there were in that House only commercial persons, they would not be the Representatives of the nation, but of the commercial interest of the nation. Suppose the landed and commercial interest could both find their way into the House. The landed interest would be able, if it had nothing but the commercial interest to combat with, to prevent that interest from having its due weight in the

Constitution. All descriptions of persons in the country would thus, in fact, be at the mercy of the landholders.' He adds, 'the professional persons are, then, what makes this House the Representatives of the people. They have collectively no *esprit de corps*, and prevent any *esprit de corps* from affecting the proceedings of the House. Neither the landed nor commercial interest can materially affect each other, and the interests of the different professions of the country are fairly considered. The Honourable Gentleman (Mr. Grey), and the petition on this table, rather proposed uniformity of election. His ideas were the reverse—that the modes of election ought to be as varied as possible, because, if there was but one mode of election, there would, generally speaking, be but one description of persons in that House, and by a varied mode of election only could that variety be secured.'

There is great vagueness undoubtedly in the language here employed; and abundant wavering and uncertainty in the ideas. But the ideas regarding this theory appear in the same half-formed state, in every speech and writing, in which we have seen it adduced. The mist, indeed, by which it has been kept surrounded, alone creates the difficulty; because it cannot be known precisely how any thing is good or bad, till it is precisely known what it is.

According to the ideas of Lord Liverpool, the landholders ought to be represented; the merchants and manufacturers ought to be represented; the officers of the army and navy ought to be represented; and the practitioners of the law ought to be represented. Other patrons of the scheme have added, that literary men ought to be represented. And these, we believe, are almost all the fraternities, which have been named for this purpose, by any of the advocates of representation by clubs. To insure the choice of Representatives of the landholders, landholders must be the choosers; to insure the choice of Representatives of the merchants and manufacturers, merchants and manufacturers must be the choosers; and so with respect to the other fraternities, whether few or many. Thus it must be at least in *substance;* whatever the form, under which the visible acts may be performed. According to the scheme in question, these several fraternities are represented *directly*, the rest of the community is *not* represented directly; but it will be said by the patrons of the scheme, that it is represented *virtually*, which, in this case, answers the same purpose.

From what has already been ascertained, it will appear certain, that each of these fraternities has its sinister interest, and will be led to seek the benefit of misrule, if it is able to obtain it. This is frankly and distinctly avowed by Lord Liverpool. And by those by whom it is not avowed, it seems impossible to suppose that it should be disputed.

Let us now, then, observe the very principle upon which this theory must be supported. Three, or four, or five, or more clubs of men, have unlimited power over the whole community put into their hands. These clubs have, each, and all of them, an interest, an interest the same with that which governs all other rulers, in misgovernment, in converting the persons and properties of the rest of the community wholly to their own benefit. Having this interest, says the theory, they will not make use of it, but will use all their powers for the benefit of the community. Unless this proposition can be supported, the theory is one of the shallowest by which the pretenders to political wisdom have ever exposed themselves.

Let us resume the proposition. Three, or four, or five fraternities of men, composing a small part of the community, have all the powers of government placed in their hands. If they oppose and contend with one another, they will be unable to convert these powers to their own benefit. If they agree, they will be able to convert them wholly to their own benefit, and to do with the rest of the community just what they please. The patrons of this system of Representation assume, that these fraternities will be sure to take that course which is *contrary* to their interest. The course which is *according* to their interest, appears as if it had never presented itself to their imaginations!

There being two courses which the clubs may pursue, one contrary to their interest, the other agreeable to it, the patrons of the club system must prove, they must place it beyond all doubt, that the clubs will follow the first course, and not follow the second: if not, the world will laugh at a theory which is founded upon a direct contradiction of one of the fundamental principles of human nature.

In supposing that clubs or societies of men are governed, like men individually, by their interests, we are surely following a pretty complete experience. In the idea that a certain number of those clubs can unite to pursue a common interest, there is surely nothing more extraordinary, than that as many individuals should unite to pursue a common interest. Lord Liverpool talks of an *esprit de corps* belonging to a class of landholders, made up of the different bodies of landholders in every county in the kingdom. He talks of an *esprit de corps* in a class of merchants and manufacturers, made up of the different bodies of merchants and manufacturers in the several great towns and manufacturing districts in the kingdom. What, then, is meant by an *esprit de corps?* Nothing else but a union for the pursuit of a common interest. To the several clubs supposed in the present theory, a common interest is created by the very circumstance of their composing the representing and represented bodies. Unless the patrons of this theory can prove to us, contrary to all experience, that a common interest cannot create an *esprit de corps* in men in combinations, as well as in men individually, we are under the necessity of believing, that an *esprit de corps* would be formed in the classes separated from the rest of the community for the purposes of Representation; that they would pursue their common interest; and inflict all the evils upon the rest of the community to which the pursuit of that interest would lead.

It is not included in the idea of this union for the pursuit of a common interest, that the clubs or sets of persons appropriated to the business of Representation should totally harmonize. There would, no doubt, be a great mixture of agreement and disagreement among them. But there would, if experience is any guide, or if the general laws of human nature have any power, be sufficient agreement to prevent their losing sight of the common interest; in other words, for insuring all that abuse of power which is useful to the parties by whom it is exercised.

The real effect of this motley Representation, therefore, would only be to create a motley Aristocracy; and, of course, to insure that kind of misgovernment which it is the nature of Aristocracy to produce, and to produce equally, whether it is a uniform, or a variegated Aristocracy; whether an Aristocracy all of landowners; or an Aristocracy in part landowners, in part merchants and manufacturers, in part officers of the army and navy, and in part lawyers.

We have now, therefore, examined the principles of the Representative system, and have found in it all that is necessary to constitute a security for good government. We have seen in what manner it is possible to prevent in the Representatives the rise of an interest different from that of the parties who choose them, namely by giving them little time, not dependent upon the will of those parties: We have likewise seen in what manner identity of interest may be insured between the electoral body and the rest of the community: We have, therefore, discovered the means by which identity of interest may be insured between the Representatives and the community at large. We have, by consequence, obtained an organ of Government which possesses that quality, without which there can be no good Government.

IX. (i) *Objection: That a perfect Representative System, if established, would destroy the Monarchy, and the House of Lords.*

The question remains, Whether this organ is competent to the performance of the whole of the business of Government? And it may be certainly answered, that it is not. It may be competent to the making of laws, and it may watch over their execution: but to the executive functions themselves, operations in detail, to be performed by individuals, it is manifestly not competent. The executive functions of Government consist of two parts, the administrative and the judicial. The administrative, in this country, belong to the King; and it will appear indubitable, that, if the best mode of disposing of the administrative powers of Government be to place them in the hands of one great functionary, not elective, but hereditary; a King such as ours, instead of being inconsistent with the Representative system, in its highest state of perfection, would be an indispensable branch of a good Government; and, even if it did not previously exist, would be established by a Representative body whose interests were identified, as above, with those of the nation.

The same reasoning will apply exactly to our House of Lords. Suppose it true, that, for the perfect performance of the business of Legislation, and of watching over the execution of the laws, a second deliberative Assembly is necessary; and that an Assembly, such as the British House of Lords, composed of the proprietors of the greatest landed estates, with dignities and privileges, is the best adapted to the end: it follows, that a body of Representatives, whose interests were identified with those of the nation, would establish such an Assembly, if it did not previously exist: for the best of all possible reasons; that they would have motives for, and none at all against it.

Those parties, therefore, who reason against any measures necessary for identifying the interests of the Representative body with those of the nation, under the plea that such a Representative body would abolish the King and the House of Lords, are wholly inconsistent with themselves. They maintain that a King and a House of Lords, such as ours, are important and necessary branches of a good Government. It is demonstratively certain that a Representative body, the interests of which were identified with those of the nation, would have no motive to abolish them, if they were not causes of bad government. Those persons, therefore, who affirm that it would certainly abolish them, affirm implicitly that they are causes of bad, and not necessary to good government. This oversight of theirs is truly surprising.

The whole of this chain of reasoning is dependent, as we stated at the beginning, upon the principle that the acts of men will be conformable to their interests. Upon this principle, we conceive that the chain is complete and irrefragable. The principle, also, appears to stand upon a strong foundation. It is indisputable that the acts of men follow their will; that their will follows their desires; and that their desires are generated by their apprehensions of good or evil; in other words, by their interests.

X. (ii) *Objection: That the People are not capable of acting agreeably to their Interests.*

The apprehensions of the people, respecting good and evil, may be just, or they may be erroneous. If just, their actions will be agreeable to their real interests. If erroneous, they will not be agreeable to their real interests, but to a false supposition of interest.[16]

---

[16] 'These apprehensions, however, may be just, or they may be erroneous. If just, the man's actions will be agreeable to his real interests. If erroneous, they will not be agreeable to his real interests, but to a false supposition of interest. This it is which creates the difficulty.'

We have seen, that, unless the Representative Body are chosen by a portion of the community the interest of which cannot be made to differ from that of the community, the interest of the community will infallibly be sacrificed to the interest of the rulers.

The whole of that party of reasoners who support Aristocratical power affirm, that a portion of the community, the interest of whom cannot be made to differ from that of the community, will not act according to their interest, but contrary to their interest. All their pleas are grounded upon this assumption. Because, if a portion of the community whose interest is the same with that of the community, would act agreeably to their own interest, they would act agreeably to the interest of the community, and the end of Government would be obtained.

If this assumption of theirs is true, the prospect of mankind is deplorable. To the evils of misgovernment they are subject by inexorable destiny. If the powers of Government are placed in the hands of persons whose interests are not identified with those of the community, the interests of the community are wholly sacrificed to those of the rulers. If so much as a checking power is held by the community, or by any part of the community, where the interests are the same as those of the community, the holders of that checking power will not, according to the assumption in question, make use of it in a way agreeable, but in a way contrary to their own interest. According to this theory, the choice is placed between the evils which will be produced by design, the design of those who have the power of oppressing the rest of the community, and an interest in doing it; and the evils which may be produced by mistake, the mistake of those who, if they acted agreeably to their own interest, would act well.

Supposing that this theory were true, it would still be a question, between these two sets of evils, whether the evils arising from the design of those who have motives to employ the powers of Government for the purpose of reducing the community to the state of abject slaves of their will, or the evils arising from the misconduct of those who never produce evil but when they mistake their own interest, are the greatest evils.

Upon the most general and summary view of this question, it

appears that the proper answer cannot be doubtful. They who have a fixed, invariable interest in acting ill, will act ill invariably. They who act ill from mistake, will often act well, sometimes even by accident, and in every case in which they are enabled to understand their interest, by design.

There is another, and a still more important ground of preference. The evils which are the produce of interest and power united, the evils on the one side, are altogether incurable: the effects are certain, while that conjunction which is the cause of them remains. The evils which arise from mistake are not incurable; for, if the parties who act contrary to their interest had a proper knowledge of that interest, they would act well. What is necessary, then, is knowledge. Knowledge, on the part of those whose interests are the same as those of the community, would be an adequate remedy. But knowledge is a thing which is capable of being increased; and the more it is increased the more the evils on this side of the case would be reduced.

Supposing, then, the theory of will opposed to interest to be correct, the practical conclusion would be, as there is something of a remedy to the evils arising from this source, none whatever to the evils arising from the conjunction of power and sinister interest, to adopt the side which has the remedy, and to do whatever is necessary for obtaining the remedy in its greatest possible strength, and for applying it with the greatest possible efficacy.

It is no longer deniable that a high degree of knowledge is capable of being conveyed to such a portion of the community, as would have interests the same with those of the community. This being the only resource for good government, those who say that it is not yet attained stand in this dilemma; either they do not desire good government, which is the case with all those who derive advantage from bad; or they will be seen employing their utmost exertions to increase the quantity of knowledge in the body of the community.

The practical conclusion, then, is actually the same, whether we embrace or reject the assumption that the community are little capable of acting according to their own interest.

That assumption, however, deserves to be considered. And it would need a more minute consideration than the space to which we are confined will enable us to bestow upon it.

One caution, first of all, we should take along with us; and it is this, That all those persons who hold the powers of Government, without having an identity of interests with the community; all those persons who share in the profits which are made by the abuse of those powers; and all those persons whom the example and representations of the two first classes influence; will be sure to represent the community, or a part having an identity of interest with the community, as incapable, in the highest degree, of acting according to their own interest; it being clear that they who have not an identity of interest with the community ought to hold the powers of Government no longer, if those who have that identity of interest could be expected to act in any tolerable conformity with their interest.[17] All representations from that quarter, therefore, of their incapability so to act, are to be received with suspicion. They come from interested parties; they come from parties who have the strongest possible interest to deceive themselves, and to endeavour to deceive others.

It is impossible that the interested endeavours of all those parties should not propagate, and for a long time successfully uphold, such an opinion, to whatever degree it might be found, upon accurate inquiry, to be without foundation.

A parallel case may be given. It was the interest of the priesthood, when the people of Europe were all of one religion, that the laity should take their opinions exclusively from them; because, in that case, the laity might be rendered subservient to the will of the Clergy, to any possible extent; and as all opinions were to be derived professedly from the Bible, they withdrew from the laity the privilege of reading it. When the opinions which produced the Reformation, and all the blessings which may be traced to it, began to ferment, the privilege of the Bible was demanded. The demand was resisted by the Clergy, upon the very same assumption which we have now under

[17] '... are made by the abuse of those powers, and all those persons whom the examples and representations of the two first classes, who, from the very supposition of their having the powers of Government, must have the power of setting the fashion, and of influencing to a large extent, the public mind,—all those persons will be sure to represent the community, or a part having an identity of interest with the community, as incapable, in the highest degree, of acting according to their own interest; because this is the only resource of those who hold the powers of Government without having that identity of interest; it being clear that they ought to hold them no longer, if those who have that identity of interest could be expected to act in any tolerable conformity with their interest.'

contemplation. 'The people did not understand their own interest. They would be sure to make a bad use of the Bible. They would derive from it not right opinions, but all sorts of wrong opinions.'*

There can be no doubt that the assumption, in the religious case, was borne out by still stronger appearance of evidence, than it is in the political. The majority of the people may be supposed less capable of deriving correct opinions from the Bible, than of judging who is the best man to act as a Representative.

Experience has fully displayed the nature of the assumption in regard to religion. The power bestowed upon the people, of judging for themselves, has been productive of good effects, to a degree which has totally altered the condition of human nature, and exalted man to what may be called a different stage of existence.

For what reason then, is it, we are called upon to believe, that, if a portion of the community, having an identity of interests with the whole community, have the power of choosing Representatives, they will act wholly contrary to their interests, and make a bad choice?

Experience, it will be said, establishes this conclusion. We see that the people do not act according to their interests, but very often in opposition to them.

The question is between a portion of the community, which, if entrusted with power, would have an interest in making a bad use of it, and a portion which, though entrusted with power, would not have an interest in making a bad use of it. The former are any small number whatsoever; who, by the circumstance of being entrusted with power, are constituted an Aristocracy.

From the frequency, however great, with which those who compose the mass of the community act in opposition to their interests, no conclusion can, in this case, be drawn, without a comparison of the frequency with which those, who are placed in contrast with them, act in opposition to theirs. Now, it may with great confidence, be affirmed, that as great a proportion of those who compose the Aristocratical body of any country, as of those who compose the rest of the community, are distinguished

---

* A most instructive display of these and similar artifices for the preservation of mischievous power, after the spirit of the times is felt to be hostile to it, may be seen in Father Paul's *History of the Council of Trent.*

for a conduct unfavourable to their interests. Prudence is a more general characteristic of the people who are without the advantages of fortune, than of the people who have been thoroughly subject to their corruptive operation. It may surely be said, that if the powers of Government must be entrusted to persons incapable of good conduct, they were better entrusted to incapables who have an interest in good government, than to incapables who have an interest in bad.

It will be said, that a conclusion ought not to be drawn from the unthinking conduct of the great majority of an Aristocratical body, against the capability of such a body for acting wisely in the management of public affairs; because the body will always contain a certain proportion of wise men, and the rest will be governed by them. Nothing but this can be said with pertinency. And, under certain modifications, this may be said with truth. The wise and good in any class of men do, to all general purposes, govern the rest. The comparison, however, must go on. Of that body, whose interests are identified with those of the community, it may also be said, that if one portion of them are unthinking, there is another portion wise; and that, in matters of state, the less wise would be governed by the more wise, not less certainly than in that body, whose interests, if they were entrusted with power, could not be identified with those of the community.

If we compare in each of these two contrasted bodies the two descriptions of persons, we shall not find that the foolish part of the Democratical body are more foolish than that of the Aristocratical, nor the wise part less wise.

Though, according to the opinions which fashion has propagated, it may appear a little paradoxical, we shall probably find the very reverse.

That there is not only as great a proportion of wise men in that part of the community which is not the Aristocracy, as in that which is; but that, under the present state of education, and the diffusion of knowledge, there is a much greater, we presume, there are few persons who will be disposed to dispute. It is to be observed, that the class which is universally described as both the most wise and the most virtuous part of the community, the middle rank, are wholly included in that part of the community which is not the Aristocratical. It is also not disputed, that in

Great Britain the middle rank are numerous, and form a large proportion of the whole body of the people. Another proposition may be stated, with a perfect confidence of the concurrence of all those men who have attentively considered the formation of opinions in the great body of society, or, indeed, the principles of human nature in general. It is, that the opinions of that class of the people, who are below the middle rank, are formed, and their minds are directed by that intelligent, that virtuous rank, who come the most immediately in contact with them, who are in the constant habit of intimate communication with them, to whom they fly for advice and assistance in all their numerous difficulties, upon whom they feel an immediate and daily dependence, in health and in sickness, in infancy and in old age, to whom their children look up as models for their imitation, whose opinions they hear daily repeated, and account it their honour to adopt. There can be no doubt that the middle rank, which gives to science, to art, and to legislation itself, their most distinguished ornaments, and is the chief source of all that has exalted and refined human nature, is that portion of the community of which, if the basis of Representation were ever so far extended, the opinion would ultimately decide. Of the people beneath them, a vast majority would be sure to be guided by their advice and example.

The incidents which have been urged as exceptions to this general rule, and even as reasons for rejecting it, may be considered as contributing to its proof. What signify the irregularities of a mob, more than half composed, in the greater number of instances, of boys and women, and disturbing, for a few hours or days, a particular town? What signifies the occasional turbulence of a manufacturing district, peculiarly unhappy from a very great deficiency of a middle rank, as there the population almost wholly consists of rich manufacturers and poor workmen; with whose minds no pains are taken by anybody; with whose afflictions there is no virtuous family of the middle rank to sympathize; whose children have no good example of such a family to see and to admire; and who are placed in the highly unfavourable situation of fluctuating between very high wages in one year, and very low wages in another? It is altogether futile with regard to the foundation of good government to say that this or the other portion of the people may, at this, or the other time, depart from the wisdom of the middle rank. It is enough that the great majority of the people never cease to be guided by that rank; and we may, with some confidence, challenge the adversaries of the people to produce a single instance to the contrary in the history of the world.

III

Mill's Essay on Government: Utilitarian Logic and Politics

Edinburgh Review, no. xcvii (March 1829), Article vii.

OF those philosophers who call themselves Utilitarians, and whom others generally call Benthamites, Mr Mill is, with the exception of the illustrious founder of the sect, by far the most distinguished. The little work now before us contains a summary of the opinions held by this gentleman and his brethren, on several subjects most important to society. All the seven Essays, of which it consists, abound in curious matter. But at present we intend to confine our remarks to the Treatise on Government, which stands first in the volume. On some future occasion, we may perhaps attempt to do justice to the rest.

It must be owned, that, to do justice to any composition of Mr Mill is not, in the opinion of his admirers, a very easy task. They do not, indeed, place him in the same rank with Mr Bentham; but the terms in which they extol the disciple, though feeble when compared with the hyperboles of adoration employed by them in speaking of the master, are as strong as any sober man would allow himself to use concerning Locke or Bacon. The Essay before us is perhaps the most remarkable of the works to which Mr Mill owes his fame. By the members of his sect, it is considered as perfect and unanswerable. Every part of it is an article of their faith; and the damnatory clauses, in which their creed abounds far beyond any theological symbol with which we are acquainted, are strong and full against all who reject any portion of what is so irrefragably established. No man, they maintain, who has understanding sufficient to carry him through the first proposition of Euclid, can read this masterpiece of demonstration, and honestly declare that he remains unconvinced.

We have formed a very different opinion of this work. We think that the theory of Mr Mill rests altogether on false principles, and that even on those false principles he does not reason logically. Nevertheless, we do not think it strange that his speculations should have filled the Utilitarians with admiration. We have been for some time past inclined to suspect that these people, whom some regard as the lights of the world, and others as incarnate demons, are in general ordinary men, with narrow understandings, and little information. The contempt which they express for elegant literature, is evidently the contempt of ignorance. We apprehend that many of them are persons who, having read little or nothing, are delighted to be rescued from the sense of their own inferiority by some teacher, who assures them that the studies which they have neglected are of no value, puts five or six phrases into their mouths, lends them an odd number of the Westminster Review, and in a month transforms them into philosophers. Mingled with these smatterers, whose attainments just suffice to elevate them from the insignificance of dunces to the dignity of bores, and to spread dismay among their pious aunts and grandmothers, there are, we well know, many well-meaning men, who have really read and thought much; but whose reading and meditation have been almost exclusively confined to one class of subjects; and who, consequently, though they possess much valuable knowledge respecting those subjects, are by no means so well qualified to judge of a great system as if they had taken a more enlarged view of literature and society.

Nothing is more amusing or instructive than to observe the manner in which people, who think themselves wiser than all the rest of the world, fall into snares which the simple good sense of their neighbours detects and avoids. It is one of the principal tenets of the Utilitarians, that sentiment and eloquence serve only to impede the pursuit of truth. They therefore affect a quakerly plainness, or rather a cynical negligence and impurity of style. The strongest arguments, when clothed in brilliant language, seem to them so much wordy nonsense. In the mean time they surrender their understandings, with a facility found in no other party, to the meanest and most abject sophisms, provided those sophisms come before them disguised with the externals of demonstration. They do not seem to know that logic has its illusions as well as rhetoric,—that a fallacy may lurk in a syllogism as well as in a metaphor.

Mr Mill is exactly the writer to please people of this description. His arguments are stated with the utmost affectation of precision; his divisions are awfully formal; and his style is generally as dry as that of Euclid's Elements. Whether this be a merit, we must be permitted to doubt. Thus much is certain, that the ages in which the true principles of philosophy were least understood, were those in which the ceremonial of logic was most strictly observed, and that the time from which we date the rapid progress of the experimental sciences was also the time at which a less exact and formal way of writing came into use.

The style which the Utilitarians admire, suits only those subjects on which it is possible to reason *a priori*. It grew up with
the verbal sophistry which flourished during the dark ages.
With that sophistry it fell before the Baconian philosophy, in
the day of the great deliverance of the human mind. The inductive method not only endured, but required, greater freedom
of diction. It was impossible to reason from phenomena up to
principles, to mark slight shades of difference in quality, or to
estimate the comparative effect of two opposite considerations
between which there was no common measure, by means of the
naked and meagre jargon of the schoolmen. Of those schoolmen,
Mr Mill has inherited both the spirit and the style. He is an
Aristotelian of the fifteenth century, born out of due season. We
have here an elaborate treatise on Government, from which, but
for two or three passing allusions, it would not appear that the
author was aware that any governments actually existed
among men. Certain propensities of Human Nature are
assumed; and from these premises the whole science of Politics
is synthetically deduced! We can scarcely persuade ourselves
that we are not reading a book written before the time of Bacon
and Galileo,—a book written in those days in which physicians
reasoned from the nature of heat to the treatment of fever, and
astronomers proved syllogistically that the planets could have
no independent motion,—because the heavens were incorruptible, and nature abhorred a vacuum!

The reason, too, which Mr Mill has assigned for taking this
course strikes us as most extraordinary.

'Experience,' says he, 'if we look only at the outside of the
facts, appears to be *divided* on this subject. Absolute monarchy,
under Neros and Caligulas, under such men as the Emperors of
Morocco and Sultans of Turkey, is the scourge of human nature.
On the other side, the people of Denmark, tired out with the
oppression of an aristocracy, resolved that their king should be
absolute; and, under their absolute monarch, are as well governed
as any people in Europe.'

This Mr Mill actually gives as a reason for pursuing the *a
priori* method. But, in our judgment, the very circumstances
which he mentions, irresistibly prove that the *a priori* method
is altogether unfit for investigations of this kind, and that the
only way to arrive at the truth is by induction. *Experience* can

never be divided, or even appear to be divided, except with reference to some hypothesis. When we say that one fact is inconsistent with another fact, we mean only that it is inconsistent with *the theory* which we have founded on that other fact. But, if the fact be certain, the unavoidable conclusion is, that our theory is false; and in order to correct it, we must reason back from an enlarged collection of facts to principles.

Now here we have two governments which, by Mr Mill's own account, come under the same head in his *theoretical* classification. It is evident, therefore, that, by reasoning on that theoretical classification, we shall be brought to the conclusion that these two forms of government must produce the same effects. But Mr Mill himself tells us, that they do not produce the same effects. Hence he infers, that the only way to get at truth is to place implicit confidence in that chain of proof *a priori*, from which it appears that they must produce the same effects! To believe at once in a theory, and in a fact which contradicts it, is an exercise of faith sufficiently hard: But, to believe in a theory *because* a fact contradicts it, is what neither philosopher nor pope ever before required. This, however, is what Mr Mill demands of us. He seems to think that if all despots, without exception, governed ill, it would be unnecessary to prove, by a synthetical argument, what would then be sufficiently clear from experience. But as some despots will be so perverse as to govern well, he finds himself compelled to prove the impossibility of their governing well, by that synthetical argument, which would have been superfluous had not the facts contradicted it. He reasons *a priori*, because the phenomena are not what, by reasoning *a priori*, he will prove them to be. In other words, he reasons *a priori* because, by so reasoning, he is certain to arrive at a false conclusion!

In the course of the examination to which we propose to subject the speculations of Mr Mill, we shall have to notice many other curious instances of that turn of mind which the passage above quoted indicates.

The first chapter of his Essay relates to the ends of government. The conception on this subject, he tells us, which exists in the minds of most men, is vague and undistinguishing. He first assumes, justly enough, that the end of government is 'to increase to the utmost the pleasures, and diminish to the utmost the pains, which men derive from each other.' He then proceeds to show, with great form, that 'the greatest possible happiness of society is attained by insuring to every man the greatest possible quantity of the produce of his labour.' To effect this is, in his opinion, the end of government. It is remarkable that Mr Mill, with all his affected display of precision, has here given a description of the ends of government far less precise than that which is in the mouths of the vulgar. The first man with whom Mr Mill may travel in a stage-coach, will tell him that government exists for the protection of the *persons* and property of men. But Mr Mill seems to think that the preservation of property is the first and only object. It is true, doubtless, that many of the injuries which are offered to the persons of men, proceed from a desire to possess their property. But the practice of vindictive assassination, as it has existed in some parts of Europe—the practice of fighting wanton and sanguinary duels, like those of the sixteenth and seventeenth centuries, in which bands of seconds risked their lives as well as the principals;—these practices, and many others which might be named, are evidently injurious to society; and we do not see how a government which tolerated them could be said 'to diminish to the utmost the pains which men derive from each other.' Therefore, according to Mr Mill's very correct assumption, such a government would not perfectly accomplish the end of its institution. Yet such a government might, as far as we can perceive, 'insure to every man the greatest possible quantity of the produce of his labour.' Therefore such a government might, according to Mr Mill's subsequent doctrine, perfectly accomplish the end of its institution. The matter is not of much consequence, except as an instance of that slovenliness of thinking which is often concealed beneath a peculiar ostentation of logical neatness.

Having determined the ends, Mr Mill proceeds to consider the means. For the preservation of property, some portion of the community must be intrusted with power. This is Government; and the question is, how are those to whom the necessary power is intrusted to be prevented from abusing it?

Mr Mill first passes in review the simple forms of government. He allows that it would be inconvenient, if not physically impossible, that the whole community should meet in a mass; it follows, therefore, that the powers of government cannot be directly exercised by the people. But he sees no objection to pure and direct Democracy, except the difficulty which we have mentioned ... ['The community ... great importance.' p. 60]

Mr Mill then proceeds to demonstrate, that a purely Aristocratical form of government is necessarily bad ... ['The reason ... rests on demonstration.' p. 61].

In exactly the same manner Mr Mill proves absolute Monarchy to be a bad form of government ... ['If government ... for which government exists.' p. 61]

But is it not possible that a king or an aristocracy may soon be saturated with the objects of their desires, and may then protect the community in the enjoyment of the rest? Mr Mill answers in the negative. He proves, with great pomp, that every man desires to have the actions of every other correspondent to his will. Others can be induced to conform to our will only by motives derived from pleasure or from pain. The infliction of pain is of course direct injury; and even if it take the milder course, in order to produce obedience by motives derived from pleasure, the government must confer favours. But, as there is no limit to its desire of obedience, there will be no limit to its disposition to confer favours; and, as it can confer favours only by plundering the people, there will be no limit to its disposition to plunder the people. 'It is therefore not true, that there is in the mind of a king, or in the minds of an aristocracy, any point of saturation with the objects of desire.'

Mr Mill then proceeds to show, that as monarchical and oligarchical governments can influence men by motives drawn from pain, as well as by motives drawn from pleasure, they will carry their cruelty, as well as their rapacity, to a frightful extent. ... ['The chain of inference ... most intense terror.' pp. 66–7]

During the last two centuries, some hundreds of absolute princes have reigned in Europe. Is it true, that their cruelty has kept in existence the most intense degree of terror, that their rapacity has left no more than the bare means of subsistence to any of their subjects, their ministers and soldiers excepted? Is this true of all of them? Of one half of them? Of one tenth part of them? Of a single one? Is it true, in the full extent, even of Philip the Second, of Lewis the Fifteenth, or of the Emperor Paul? But it is scarcely necessary to quote history. No man of common sense, however ignorant he may be of books, can be imposed on by Mr Mill's argument; because no man of common sense can live among his fellow-creatures for a day without seeing innumerable facts which contradict it. It is our business, however, to point out its fallacy; and happily the fallacy is not very recondite.

We grant that rulers will take as much as they can of the objects of their desires; and that when the agency of other men is necessary to that end, they will attempt by all means in their power to enforce the prompt obedience of such men. But what are the objects of human desire? Physical pleasure, no doubt, in part. But the mere appetites which we have in common with the animals, would be gratified almost as cheaply and easily as those of the animals are gratified, if nothing were given to taste, to ostentation, or to the affections. How small a portion of the income of a gentleman in easy circumstances is laid out merely in giving pleasurable sensations to the body of the possessor! The greater part even of what is spent on his kitchen and his cellar, goes not to titillate his palate, but to keep up his character for hospitality, to save him from the reproach of meanness in housekeeping, and to cement the ties of good neighbourhood. It is clear, that a king or an aristocracy may be supplied to satiety with mere corporal pleasures, at an expense which the rudest and poorest community would scarcely feel.

Those tastes and propensities which belong to us as reasoning and imaginative beings, are not indeed so easily gratified. There is, we admit, no point of saturation with objects of desire which come under this head. And therefore the argument of Mr Mill will be just, unless there be something in the nature of the objects of desire themselves which is inconsistent with it. Now, of these objects there is none which men in general seem to desire more than the good opinion of others. The hatred and contempt of the public are generally felt to be intolerable. It is probable, that our regard for the sentiments of our fellow-creatures springs by association from a sense of their ability to hurt or to serve us. But be this as it may, it is notorious, that when the habit of mind of which we speak has once been formed, men feel extremely solicitous about the opinions of those by whom it is most improbable, nay, absolutely impossible, that they should ever be in the slightest degree injured or benefited. The desire of posthumous fame, and the dread of posthumous reproach and execration, are feelings, from the influence of which scarcely any man is perfectly free, and which in many men are powerful and constant motives of action. As we are afraid that, if we handle this part of the argument after our own manner, we shall incur the reproach of sentimentality, a word which, in the sacred language of the Benthamites, is synonymous with idiocy, we will quote what Mr Mill himself says on the subject, in his Treatise on Jurisprudence.

Pains from the moral source are the pains derived from the unfavourable sentiments of mankind. . . . These pains are capable of rising to a height with which hardly any other pains incident to our nature can be compared. There is a certain degree of unfavourableness in the sentiments of his fellow-creatures, under which hardly any man, not below the standard of humanity, can endure to live.

The importance of this powerful agency, for the prevention of injurious acts, is too obvious to need to be illustrated. If sufficiently at command, it would almost supersede the use of other means . . .

To know how to direct the unfavourable sentiments of mankind, it is necessary to know in as complete, that is, in as comprehensive, a way as possible, what it is which gives them birth. Without entering into the metaphysics of the question, it is a sufficient practical answer, for the present purpose, to say that the unfavourable sentiments of man are excited by every thing which hurts them.

It is strange that a writer who considers the pain derived from the unfavourable sentiments of others as so acute, that, if sufficiently at command, it would supersede the use of the gallows and the tread-mill, should take no notice of this most important restraint, when discussing the question of Government. We will attempt to deduce a theory of politics in the mathematical form, in which Mr Mill delights, from the premises with which he has himself furnished us.

PROPOSITION I. THEOREM.

No rulers will do any thing which may hurt the people.

This is the thesis to be maintained; and the following we humbly offer to Mr Mill, as its syllogistic demonstration.

No rulers will do that which produces pain to themselves.

But the unfavourable sentiments of the people will give pain to them.

Therefore no rulers will do any thing which may excite the unfavourable sentiments of the people.

But the unfavourable sentiments of the people are excited by every thing which hurts them.

Therefore no rulers will do any thing which may hurt the people, which was the thing to be proved.

Having thus, as we think, not unsuccessfully imitated Mr Mill's logic, we do not see why we should not imitate what is at least equally perfect in its kind, his self-complacency, and proclaim our *Εὔρηκα* in his own words: 'The chain of inference, in this case, is close and strong to a most unusual degree.'

The fact is, that when men, in treating of things which cannot be circumscribed by precise definitions, adopt this mode of reasoning, when once they begin to talk of power, happiness, misery, pain, pleasure, motives, objects of desire, as they talk of lines and numbers, there is no end to the contradictions and absurdities into which they fall. There is no proposition so monstrously untrue in morals or politics that we will not undertake to prove it, by something which shall sound like a logical demonstration, from admitted principles.

Mr Mill argues, that if men are not inclined to plunder each other, government is unnecessary; and that, if they are so inclined, the powers of government, when intrusted to a small number of them, will necessarily be abused. Surely it is not by propounding dilemmas of this sort, that we are likely to arrive at sound conclusions in any moral science. The whole question is a question of degree. If all men preferred the moderate approbation of their neighbours, to any degree of wealth, or grandeur, or sensual pleasure, government would be unnecessary. If all men desired wealth so intensely as to be willing to brave the hatred of their fellow creatures for sixpence, Mr Mill's argument against monarchies and aristocracies would be true to the full extent. But the fact is, that all men have some desires which impel them to injure their neighbours, and some desires which impel them to benefit their neighbours. Now, if there were a community consisting of two classes of men, one of which should be principally influenced by the one set of motives, and the other by the other, government would clearly be necessary to restrain the class which was eager for plunder, and careless of reputation: and yet the powers of government might be safely

intrusted to the class which was chiefly actuated by the love of
approbation. Now, it might, with no small plausibility, be
maintained, that, in many countries, *there are* two classes which,
in some degree, answer to this description; that the poor compose the class which government is established to restrain; and
the people of some property the class to which the powers of
government may without danger be confided. It might be said,
that a man who can barely earn a livelihood by severe labour, is
under stronger temptations to pillage others than a man who
enjoys many luxuries. It might be said, that a man who is lost
in the crowd is less likely to have the fear of public opinion before his eyes, than a man whose station and mode of living render him conspicuous. We do not assert all this. We only say,
that it was Mr Mill's business to prove the contrary; and that,
not having proved the contrary, he is not entitled to say, 'that
those principles which imply that government is at all necessary,
imply that an aristocracy will make use of its power to defeat
the end for which governments exist.' This is not true, unless it
be true that a rich man is as likely to covet the goods of
his neighbours as a poor man; and that a poor man is as likely
to be solicitous about the opinions of his neighbours as a rich
man.

But we do not see that, by reasoning *a priori* on such subjects
as these, it is possible to advance one single step. We know that
every man has some desires which he can gratify only by hurting
his neighbours, and some which he can gratify only by pleasing
them. Mr Mill has chosen to look only at one-half of human
nature, and to reason on the motives which impel men to
oppress and despoil others, as if they were the only motives by
which men could possibly be influenced. We have already
shown that, by taking the other half of the human character,
and reasoning on it as if it were the whole, we can bring out a
result diametrically opposite to that at which Mr Mill has
arrived. We can, by such a process, easily prove that any form
of government is good, or that all government is superfluous.

We must now accompany Mr Mill on the next stage of his
argument. Does any combination of the three simple forms of
government afford the requisite securities against the abuse of
power? Mr Mill complains, that those who maintain the affirmative generally beg the question, and proceeds to settle

the point by proving, after his fashion, that no combination of the three simple forms, or of any two of them, can possibly exist . . . ['From the principles . . . to obtain that power.' pp. 69–72]

If any part of this passage be more eminently absurd than another, it is, we think, the argument by which Mr Mill proves that there cannot be an union of monarchy and aristocracy. Their power, he says, must be equal or not equal. But of equality there is no criterion. Therefore the chances against its existence are as infinity to one. If the power be not equal, then it follows, from the principles of human nature, that the stronger will take from the weaker, till it has engrossed the whole.

Now, if there be no criterion of equality between two portions of power, there can be no common measure of portions of power. Therefore it is utterly impossible to compare them together. But where two portions of power are of the same kind, there is no difficulty in ascertaining, sufficiently for all practical purposes, whether they are equal or unequal. It is easy to judge whether two men run equally fast, or can lift equal weights. Two arbitrators, whose joint decision is to be final, and neither of whom can do any thing without the assent of the other, possess equal power. Two electors, each of whom has a vote for a borough, possess, in that respect, equal power. If not, all Mr Mill's political theories fall to the ground at once. For if it be impossible to ascertain whether two portions of power are equal, he never can show that, even under a system of universal suffrage, a minority might not carry every thing their own way, against the wishes and interests of the majority.

Where there are two portions of power differing in kind, there is, we admit, no criterion of equality. But then, in such a case, it is absurd to talk, as Mr Mill does, about the stronger and the weaker. Popularly, indeed, and with reference to some particular objects, these words may very fairly be used. But to use them mathematically, is altogether improper. If we are speaking of a boxing-match, we may say that some famous bruiser has greater bodily power than any man in England. If we are speaking of a pantomime, we may say the same of some very agile Harlequin. But it would be talking nonsense to say, in general, that the power of Harlequin either exceeded that of the pugilist, or fell short of it.

If Mr Mill's argument be good as between different branches of a legislature, it is equally good as between sovereign powers. Every government, it may be said, will, if it can, take the objects of its desires from every other. If the French government can subdue England, it will do so. If the English government can subdue France, it will do so. But the power of England and France is either equal or not equal. The chance that it is not exactly equal is as infinity to one, and may safely be left out of the account; and then the stronger will infallibly take from the weaker, till the weaker is altogether enslaved.

Surely the answer to all this hubbub of unmeaning words is the plainest possible. For some purposes, France is stronger than England. For some purposes, England is stronger than France. For some, neither has any power at all. France has the greater population, England the greater capital; France has the greater army, England the greater fleet. For an expedition to Rio Janeiro or the Philippines, England has the greater power. For a war on the Po or the Danube, France has the greater power. But neither has power sufficient to keep the other in quiet subjection for a month. Invasion would be very perilous; the idea of complete conquest on either side utterly ridiculous. This is the manly and sensible way of discussing such questions. The *ergo*, or rather the *argal*, of Mr Mill, cannot impose on a child. Yet we ought scarcely to say this; for we remember to have heard *a child* ask whether Bonaparte was stronger than an elephant!

Mr Mill reminds us of those philosophers of the sixteenth century, who, having satisfied themselves *a priori* that the rapidity with which bodies descended to the earth varied exactly as their weights, refused to believe the contrary on the evidence of their own eyes and ears. The British constitution, according to Mr Mill's classification, is a mixture of monarchy and aristocracy; one House of Parliament being composed of hereditary nobles, and the other almost entirely chosen by a privileged class, who possess the elective franchise on account of their property, or their connexion with certain corporations. Mr Mill's argument proves that, from the time that these two powers were mingled in our government, that is, from the very first dawn of our history, one or the other must have been constantly encroaching. According to him, moreover, all the encroachments must have

been on one side. For the first encroachment could only have
been made by the stronger, and that first encroachment would
have made the stronger stronger still. It is, therefore, matter of
absolute demonstration, that either the Parliament was stronger
than the Crown in the reign of Henry VIII., or that the Crown
was stronger than the Parliament in 1641. 'Hippocrate dira ce
que lui plaira,' says the girl in Moliere; 'mais le cocher est
mort.' Mr Mill may say what he pleases; but the English constitution is still alive. That, since the Revolution, the Parliament has possessed great power in the state, is what nobody
will dispute. The King, on the other hand, can create new
peers, and can dissolve Parliaments. William sustained severe
mortifications from the House of Commons, and was, indeed,
unjustifiably oppressed. Anne was desirous to change a ministry
which had a majority in both Houses. She watched her moment
for a dissolution, created twelve Tory peers, and succeeded.
Thirty years later, the House of Commons drove Walpole from
his seat. In 1784, George III. was able to keep Mr Pitt in office,
in the face of a majority of the House of Commons. In 1804, the
apprehension of a defeat in Parliament compelled the same
King to part from his most favoured minister. But in 1807, he
was able to do exactly what Anne had done nearly a hundred
years before. Now, had the power of the King increased during
the intervening century, or had it remained stationary? Is it
possible that the one lot among the infinite number should have
fallen to us? If not, Mr Mill has proved that one of the two
parties must have been constantly taking from the other. Many
of the ablest men in England think that the influence of the
Crown has, on the whole, increased since the reign of Anne.
Others think that the Parliament has been growing in strength.
But of this there is no doubt, that both sides possessed great
power then, and possess great power now. Surely, if there were
the least truth in the argument of Mr Mill, it could not possibly
be a matter of doubt, at the end of a hundred and twenty years,
whether the one side or the other had been the gainer.

But we ask pardon. We forgot that a fact, irreconcilable with
Mr Mill's theory, furnishes, in his opinion, the strongest reason
for adhering to the theory. To take up the question in another
manner, is it not plain that there may be two bodies, each possessing a perfect and entire power, which cannot be taken from

it without its own concurrence? What is the meaning of the words stronger and weaker, when applied to such bodies as these? The one may, indeed, by physical force altogether destroy the other. But this is not the question. A third party, a general of their own, for example, may, by physical force, subjugate them both: Nor is there any form of government, Mr Mill's Utopian democracy not excepted, secure from such an occurrence. We are speaking of the powers with which the constitution invests the two branches of the legislature; and we ask Mr Mill how, on his own principles, he can maintain that one of them will be able to encroach on the other, if the consent of the other be necessary to such encroachment?

Mr Mill tells us, that if a government be composed of the three simple forms, which he will not admit the British constitution to be, two of the component parts will inevitably join against the third. Now, if two of them combine and act as one, this case evidently resolves itself into the last; and all the observations which we have just made will fully apply to it. Mr Mill says, that 'any two of the parties, by combining, may swallow up the third;' and afterwards asks, 'How it is possible to prevent two of them from combining to swallow up the third?' Surely Mr Mill must be aware, that in politics two is not always the double of one. If the concurrence of all the three branches of the legislature be neccessary to every law, each branch will possess constitutional power sufficient to protect it against any thing but that physical force, from which no form of government is secure. Mr Mill reminds us of the Irishman, who could not be brought to understand how one juryman could possibly starve out eleven others.

But is it certain that two of the branches of the legislature will combine against the third? 'It appears to be as certain,' says Mr Mill, 'as any thing which depends upon human will; because there are strong motives in favour of it, and none that can be conceived in opposition to it.' He subsequently sets forth what these motives are. The interest of the democracy is, that each individual should receive protection. The interest of the King and the aristocracy is, to have all the power that they can obtain, and to use it for their own ends. Therefore the King and the aristocracy have all possible motives for combining against the people. If our readers will look back to the passage quoted

above, they will see that we represent Mr Mill's argument quite
fairly.

Now we should have thought that, without the help of either
history or experience, Mr Mill would have discovered, by the
light of his own logic, the fallacy which lurks, and indeed
scarcely lurks, under this pretended demonstration. The interest of the King may be opposed to that of the people. But is it
identical with that of the aristocracy? In the very page which
contains this argument, intended to prove that the King and the
aristocracy will coalesce against the people, Mr Mill attempts to
show that there is so strong an opposition of interest between
the King and the aristocracy, that if the powers of government
are divided between them, the one will inevitably usurp the
power of the other. If so, he is not entitled to conclude that
they will combine to destroy the power of the people, merely because their interests may be at variance with those of the people.
He is bound to show, not merely that in all communities the
interest of a king must be opposed to that of the people, but also
that, in all communities, it must be more directly opposed to the
interest of the people than to the interest of the aristocracy. But
he has not shown this. Therefore he has not proved his proposition on his own principles. To quote history would be a mere
waste of time. Every schoolboy, whose studies have gone so far
as the Abridgements of Goldsmith, can mention instances in
which sovereigns have allied themselves with the people against
the aristocracy, and in which the nobles have allied themselves
with the people against the sovereign. In general, when there
are three parties, every one of which has much to fear from the
others, it is not found that two of them combine to plunder the
third. If such a combination be formed, it scarcely ever effects
its purpose. It soon becomes evident which member of the co-
alition is likely to be the greater gainer by the transaction. He
becomes an object of jealousy to his ally, who, in all probability,
changes sides, and compels him to restore what he has taken.
Every body knows how Henry VIII. trimmed between Francis
and the Emperor Charles. But it is idle to cite examples of the
operation of a principle which is illustrated in almost every page
of history, ancient or modern, and to which almost every state
in Europe has, at one time or another, been indebted for its in-
dependence.

Mr Mill has now, as he conceives, demonstrated that the simple forms of government are bad, and that the mixed forms cannot possibly exist. There is still, however, it seems, a hope for mankind.

In the grand discovery of modern times, the system of representation, the solution of all the difficulties, both speculative and practical, will perhaps be found. If it cannot, we seem to be forced upon the extraordinary conclusion, that good government is impossible. For as there is no individual or combination of individuals, except the community itself, who would not have an interest in bad government, if intrusted with its powers, and as the community itself is incapable of exercising those powers, and must intrust them to certain individuals, the conclusion is obvious: the community itself must check those individuals, else they will follow their interest, and produce bad government. But how is it the community can check? The community can act only when assembled; and when assembled, it is incapable of acting. The community, however, can choose representatives.

The next question is—How must the representative body be constituted? Mr Mill lays down two principles, about which, he says, 'it is unlikely that there will be any dispute.'

'First, The checking body must have a degree of power sufficient for the business of checking.

Secondly, It must have an identity of interest with the community. Otherwise, it will make a mischievous use of its power.'

The first of these propositions certainly admits of no dispute. As to the second, we shall hereafter take occasion to make some remarks on the sense in which Mr Mill understands the words, 'interest of the community.'

It does not appear very easy, on Mr Mill's principles, to find out any mode of making the interest of the representative body identical with that of the constituent body. The plan proposed by Mr Mill is simply that of very frequent election. 'As it appears,' says he, 'that limiting the duration of their power is a security against the sinister interest of the people's representatives, so it appears that it is the only security of which the nature of the case admits.' But all the arguments by which Mr Mill has proved monarchy and aristocracy to be pernicious, will, as it appears to us, equally prove this security to be no security at all. Is it not clear that the representatives, as soon as they are elected, are an aristocracy, with an interest opposed to the interest of the community? Why should they not pass a law for extending the term of their power from one year to ten years, or declare themselves senators for life? If the whole legislative power is given to them, they will be constitutionally competent to do this. If part of the legislative power is withheld from them, to whom is that part given? Is the people to retain it, and to express its assent or dissent in primary assemblies? Mr Mill himself tells us that the community can only act when assembled, and that, when assembled, it is incapable of acting. Or is it to be provided, as in some of the American republics, that no change in the fundamental laws shall be made without the consent of a convention, specially elected for the purpose? Still the difficulty recurs: Why may not the members of the convention betray their trust, as well as the members of the ordinary legislature? When private men, they may have been zealous for the interests of the community. When candidates, they may have pledged themselves to the cause of the constitution. But as soon as they are a convention, as soon as they are separated from the people, as soon as the supreme power is put into their hands, commences that interest, opposite to the interest of the community, which must, according to Mr Mill, produce measures opposite to the interests of the community. We must find some other means, therefore, of checking this check upon a check; some other prop to carry the tortoise, that carries the elephant, that carries the world.

We know well that there is no real danger in such a case. But there is no danger, only because there is no truth in Mr Mill's principles. If men were what he represents them to be, the letter of the very constitution which he recommends would afford no safeguard against bad government. The real security is this, that legislators will be deterred by the fear of resistance and of infamy, from acting in the manner which we have described. But restraints, exactly the same in kind, and differing only in degree, exist in all forms of government. That broad line of distinction which Mr Mill tries to point out between monarchies and aristocracies on the one side, and democracies on the other, has in fact no existence. In no form of government is there an absolute identity of interest between the people and their rulers. In every form of government, the rulers stand in some awe of the people. The fear of resistance and the sense of shame operate, in a certain degree, on the most absolute kings and the most illiberal oligarchies. And nothing but the fear of resistance and the sense of shame preserves the freedom of the most democratic communities from the encroachments of their annual and biennial delegates.

We have seen how Mr Mill proposes to render the interest of the representative body identical with that of the constituent body. The next question is, in what manner the interest of the constituent body is to be rendered identical with that of the community. Mr Mill shows that a minority of the community, consisting even of many thousands, would be a bad constituent body, and, indeed, merely a numerous aristocracy . . . ['The benefits . . . would be the same. pp. 78–9]

On these grounds Mr Mill recommends that all males of mature age, rich and poor, educated and ignorant, shall have votes. But why not the women too? This question has often been asked in parliamentary debate, and has never, to our knowledge, received a plausible answer. Mr Mill escapes from it as fast as he can. But we shall take the liberty to dwell a little on the words of the oracle. 'One thing,' says he, 'is pretty clear, that all those individuals whose interests are involved in those of other individuals, may be struck off without inconvenience . . .
'. . . . In this light Women may be regarded, the interest of almost all of whom is involved either in that of their fathers, or in that of their husbands.'

If we were to content ourselves with saying, in answer to all the arguments in Mr Mill's Essay, that the interest of a king is involved in that of the community, we should be accused, and justly, of talking nonsense. Yet such an assertion would not, as far as we can perceive, be more unreasonable than that which Mr Mill has here ventured to make. Without adducing one fact, without taking the trouble to perplex the question by one sophism, he placidly dogmatizes away the interests of one half of the human race. If there be a word of truth in history, women have always been, and still are, over the greater part of the globe, humble companions, playthings, captives, menials, beasts of burden. Except in a few happy and highly civilized communities, they are strictly in a state of personal slavery. Even in those countries where they are best treated, the laws are generally unfavourable to them, with respect to almost all the points in which they are most deeply interested.

Mr Mill is not legislating for England or the United States; but for mankind. Is then the interest of a Turk the same with that of the girls who compose his harem? Is the interest of a Chinese the same with that of the woman whom he harnesses to his plough? Is the interest of an Italian the same with that of the daughter whom he devotes to God? The interest of a respectable Englishman may be said, without any impropriety, to be identical with that of his wife. But why is it so? Because human nature is *not* what Mr Mill conceives it to be; because civilized men, pursuing their own happiness in a social state, are not Yahoos fighting for carrion; because there is a pleasure in being loved and esteemed, as well as in being feared and servilely obeyed. Why does not a gentleman restrict his wife to the bare maintenance which the law would compel him to allow her, that he may have more to spend on his personal pleasures? Because, if he loves her, he has pleasure in seeing her pleased; and because, even if he dislikes her, he is unwilling that the whole neighbourhood should cry shame on his meanness and ill-nature. Why does not the legislature, altogether composed of males, pass a law to deprive women of all civil privileges whatever, and reduce them to the state of slaves? By passing such a law, they would gratify what Mr Mill tells us is an inseparable part of human nature, the desire to possess unlimited power of inflicting pain upon others. That they do not pass such a law, though they have the power to pass it, and that no man in England wishes to see such a law passed, proves that the desire to possess unlimited power of inflicting pain is not inseparable from human nature.

If there be in this country an identity of interest between the two sexes, it cannot possibly arise from any thing but the pleasure of being loved, and of communicating happiness. For that it does not spring from the mere instinct of sex, the treatment which women experience over the greater part of the world abundantly proves. And if it be said that our laws of marriage have produced it, this only removes the argument a step further; for those laws have been made by males. Now, if the kind feelings of one half of the species be a sufficient security for the happiness of the other, why may not the kind feelings of a monarch or an aristocracy be sufficient at least to prevent them from grinding the people to the very utmost of their power?

If Mr Mill will examine why it is that women are better treated in England than in Persia, he may perhaps find out, in the course of his inquiries, why it is that the Danes are better governed than the subjects of Caligula.

We now come to the most important practical question in the whole Essay. Is it desirable that all males arrived at years of discretion should vote for representatives, or should a pecuniary qualification be required? Mr Mill's opinion is, that the lower the qualification the better; and that the best system is that in which there is none at all . . . ['The qualification . . . would be insured.' pp. 81–2]

The first remark which we have to make on this argument is, that, by Mr Mill's own account, even a government in which every human being should vote would still be defective. For, under a system of universal suffrage, the majority of the electors return the representative, and the majority of the representatives make the law. The whole people may vote, therefore, but only the majority govern. So that, by Mr Mill's own confession, the most perfect system of government conceivable, is one in which the interest of the ruling body to oppress, though not great, is something.

But is Mr Mill in the right, when he says that such an interest could not be very great? We think not. If, indeed, every man in the community possessed an equal share of what Mr Mill calls the objects of desire, the majority would probably abstain from plundering the minority. A large minority would offer a vigorous resistance; and the property of a small minority would not repay the other members of the community for the trouble of dividing it. But it happens that in all civilized communities there is a small minority of rich men, and a great majority of poor men. If there were a thousand men with ten pounds a-piece, it would not be worthwhile for nine hundred and ninety of them to rob ten, and it would be a bold attempt for six hundred of them to rob four hundred. But if ten of them had a hundred thousand pounds a-piece, the case would be very different. There would then be much to be got, and nothing to be feared.

'That one human being will desire to render the person and property of another subservient to his pleasures, notwithstanding the pain or loss of pleasure which it may occasion to that other individual, is,' according to Mr Mill, 'the foundation of government.' That the property of the rich minority can be made subservient to the pleasures of the poor majority, will scarcely be denied. But Mr Mill proposes to give the poor majority power over the rich minority. Is it possible to doubt to what, on his own principles, such an arrangement must lead?

It may perhaps be said that, in the long run, it is for the interest of the people that property should be secure, and that therefore they will respect it. We answer thus:—It cannot be pretended that it is not for the immediate interest of the people to plunder the rich. Therefore, even if it were quite certain that, in the long run, the people would, as a body, lose by doing so, it would not necessarily follow that the fear of remote ill consequences would overcome the desire of immediate acquisitions. Every individual might flatter himself that the punishment would not fall on him. Mr Mill himself tells us, in his Essay on Jurisprudence, that no quantity of evil which is remote and uncertain will suffice to prevent crime.

But we are rather inclined to think that it would, on the whole, be for the interest of the majority to plunder the rich. If so, the Utilitarians will say, that the rich *ought* to be plundered. We deny the inference. For, in the first place, if the object of government be the greatest happiness of the greatest number, the intensity of the suffering which a measure inflicts must be taken into consideration, as well as the number of the sufferers. In the next place, we have to notice one most important distinction which Mr Mill has altogether overlooked. Throughout his Essay, he confounds the community with the species. He talks of the greatest happiness of the greatest number: but when we examine his reasonings, we find that he thinks only of the greatest number of a single generation.

Therefore, even if we were to concede, that all those arguments of which we have exposed the fallacy, are unanswerable, we might still deny the conclusion at which the essayist arrives. Even if we were to grant that he had found out the form of government which is best for the majority of the people now

living on the face of the earth, we might still without inconsistency maintain that form of government to be pernicious to
mankind. It would still be incumbent on Mr Mill to prove
that the interest of every generation is identical with the interest
of all succeeding generations. And how on his own principles he
could do this we are at a loss to conceive.

The case, indeed, is strictly analogous to that of an aristocratical government. In an aristocracy, says Mr Mill, the few,
being invested with the powers of government, can take the
objects of their desires from the people. In the same manner,
every generation in turn can gratify itself at the expense of posterity,—priority of time, in the latter case, giving an advantage
exactly corresponding to that which superiority of station gives
in the former. That an aristocracy will abuse its advantage, is,
according to Mr Mill, matter of demonstration. Is it not
equally certain, that the whole people will do the same; that, if
they have the power, they will commit waste of every sort on the
estate of mankind, and transmit it to posterity impoverished and
desolated?

How is it possible for any person who holds the doctrines of
Mr Mill to doubt, that the rich, in a democracy such as that
which he recommends, would be pillaged as unmercifully as under a Turkish Pacha? It is no doubt for the interest of the
next generation, and it may be for the remote interest of the
present generation, that property should be held sacred. And
so no doubt it will be for the interest of the next Pacha, and
even for that of the present Pacha, if he should hold office long,
that the inhabitants of his Pachalik should be encouraged to
accumulate wealth. Scarcely any despotic sovereign has plundered his subjects to a large extent, without having reason before the end of his reign to regret it. Every body knows how
bitterly Louis the Fourteenth, towards the close of his life,
lamented his former extravagance. If that magnificent prince
had not expended millions on Marli and Versailles, and tens of
millions on the aggrandizement of his grandson, he would not
have been compelled at last to pay servile court to low-born
money-lenders, to humble himself before men, on whom, in the
days of his pride, he would not have vouchsafed to look, for
the means of supporting even his own household. Examples to
the same effect might easily be multiplied. But despots, we see,

do plunder their subjects, though history and experience tell them, that by prematurely exacting the means of profusion, they are in fact devouring the seed-corn, from which the future harvest of revenue is to spring. Why then should we suppose that the people will be deterred from procuring immediate relief and enjoyment by the fear of distant calamities, of calamities which perhaps may not be fully felt till the times of their grandchildren?

These conclusions are strictly drawn from Mr Mill's own principles: and, unlike most of the conclusions which he has himself drawn from those principles, they are not, as far as we know, contradicted by facts. The case of the United States is not in point. In a country where the necessaries of life are cheap and the wages of labour high, where a man who has no capital but his legs and arms may expect to become rich by industry and frugality, it is not very decidedly even for the immediate advantage of the poor to plunder the rich; and the punishment of doing so would very speedily follow the offence. But in countries in which the great majority live from hand to mouth, and in which vast masses of wealth have been accumulated by a comparatively small number, the case is widely different. The immediate want is, at particular seasons, craving, imperious, irresistible. In our own time, it has steeled men to the fear of the gallows, and urged them on the point of the bayonet. And if these men had at their command that gallows, and those bayonets, which now scarcely restrain them, what is to be expected? Nor is this state of things one which can exist only under a bad government. If there be the least truth in the doctrines of the school to which Mr Mill belongs, the increase of population will necessarily produce it every where. The increase of population is accelerated by good and cheap government. Therefore, the better the government, the greater is the inequality of conditions: and the greater the inequality of conditions, the stronger are the motives which impel the populace to spoliation. As for America, we appeal to the twentieth century.

It is scarcely necessary to discuss the effects which a general spoliation of the rich would produce. It may indeed happen, that where a legal and political system full of abuses is inseparably bound up with the institution of property, a nation may gain by a single convulsion, in which both perish together. The price is fearful: But if, when the shock is over, a new order of things should arise, under which property may enjoy security, the industry of individuals will soon repair the devastation. Thus we entertain no doubt that the revolution was, on the whole, a most salutary event for France. But would France have gained, if, ever since the year 1793, she had been governed by a democratic convention? If Mr Mill's principles be sound, we say that almost her whole capital would by this time have been annihilated. As soon as the first explosion was beginning to be forgotten, as soon as wealth again began to germinate, as soon as the poor again began to compare their cottages and salads with the hotels and banquets of the rich, there would have been another scramble for property, another maximum, another general confiscation, another reign of terror. Four or five such convulsions following each other, at intervals of ten or twelve years, would reduce the most flourishing countries of Europe to the state of Barbary or the Morea.

The civilized part of the world has now nothing to fear from the hostility of savage nations. Once the deluge of barbarism has passed over it, to destroy and to fertilize; and in the present state of mankind we enjoy a full security against that calamity. That flood will no more return to cover the earth. But is it possible that, in the bosom of civilization itself, may be engendered the malady which shall destroy it? Is it possible that institutions may be established which, without the help of earthquake, of famine, of pestilence, or of the foreign sword, may undo the work of so many ages of wisdom and glory, and gradually sweep away taste, literature, science, commerce, manufactures, every thing but the rude arts necessary to the support of animal life? Is it possible, that in two or three hundred years, a few lean and half-naked fishermen may divide with owls and foxes the ruins of the greatest of European cities— may wash their nets amidst the relics of her gigantic docks, and build their huts out of the capitals of her stately cathedrals? If the principles of Mr Mill be sound, we say without hesitation, that the form of government which he recommends will assuredly produce all this. But if these principles be unsound, if the reasonings by which we have opposed them be just, the higher and middling orders are the natural representatives of the human race. Their interest may be opposed, in some things, to that of their poorer contemporaries, but it is identical with that of the innumerable generations which are to follow.

Mr Mill concludes his Essay, by answering an objection often made to the project of universal suffrage—that the people do not understand their own interests. We shall not go through his arguments on this subject, because, till he has proved, that it is for the interest of the people to respect property, he only makes matters worse, by proving that they understand their interests. But we cannot refrain from treating our readers with a delicious *bonne bouche* of wisdom, which he has kept for the last moment.

The opinions of that class of the people who are below the middle rank are formed, and their minds are directed, by that intelligent, that virtuous rank, who come the most immediately in contact with them, who are in the constant habit of intimate communication with them, to whom they fly for advice and assistance in all their numerous difficulties, upon whom they feel an immediate and daily dependence in health and in sickness, in infancy and in old age, to whom their children look up as models for their imitation, whose opinions they hear daily repeated, and account it their honour to adopt. There can be no doubt that the middle rank, which gives to science, to art, and to legislation itself, their most distinguished ornaments, and is the chief source of all that has exalted and refined human nature, is that portion of the community, of which, if the basis of representation were ever so far extended, the opinion would ultimately decide. Of the people beneath them, a vast majority would be sure to be guided by their advice and example.

This single paragraph is sufficient to upset Mr Mill's theory. Will the people act against their own interest? Or will the middle rank act against its own interest? Or is the interest of the middle rank identical with the interest of the people? If the people act according to the directions of the middle rank, as Mr Mill says that they assuredly will, one of these three questions must be answered in the affirmative. But if any one of the three be answered in the affirmative, his whole system falls to the ground. If the interest of the middle rank be identical with that of the people, why should not the powers of government be intrusted to that rank? If the powers of government were intrusted to that rank, there would evidently be an aristocracy of wealth; and 'to constitute an aristocracy of wealth, though it were a very numerous one, would,' according to Mr Mill, 'leave the community without protection, and exposed to all the evils of unbridled power.' Will not the same motives which induce the middle classes to abuse one kind of power, induce them to abuse another? If their interest be the same with that of the people, they will govern the people well. If it be opposite to that of the people, they will advise the people ill. The system of universal suffrage, therefore, according to Mr Mill's own account, is only a device for doing circuitously, what a representative system, with a pretty high qualification, would do directly.

So ends this celebrated Essay. And such is this philosophy, for which the experience of three thousand years is to be discarded; this philosophy, the professors of which speak as if it had guided the world to the knowledge of navigation and alphabetical writing; as if, before its dawn, the inhabitants of Europe had lived in caverns and eaten each other! We are sick, it seems, like the children of Israel, of the objects of our old and legitimate worship. We pine for a new idolatry. All that is costly and all that is ornamental in our intellectual treasures must be delivered up, and cast into the furnace—and there comes out this Calf!

Our readers can scarcely mistake our object in writing this article. They will not suspect us of any dispositon to advocate the cause of absolute monarchy, or of any narrow form of oligarchy, or to exaggerate the evils of popular government. Our object at present is, not so much to attack or defend any particular system of polity, as to expose the vices of a kind of reasoning utterly unfit for moral and political discussions; of a kind of reasoning which may so readily be turned to purposes of falsehood, that it ought to receive no quarter, even when by accident it may be employed on the side of truth.

Our objection to the Essay of Mr Mill is fundamental. We believe that it is utterly impossible to deduce the science of government from the principles of human nature.

What proposition is there respecting human nature which is absolutely and universally true? We know of only one: and that is not only true, but identical; that men always act from self-interest. This truism the Utilitarians proclaim with as much

pride as if it were new, and as much zeal as if it were important.
But in fact, when explained, it means only that men, if they can,
will do as they choose. When we see the actions of a man, we
know with certainty what he thinks his interest to be. But it is
impossible to reason with certainty from what *we* take to be his
interest to his actions. One man goes without a dinner, that he
may add a shilling to a hundred thousand pounds: another runs
in debt to give balls and masquerades. One man cuts his father's
throat to get possession of his old clothes: another hazards his
own life to save that of an enemy. One man volunteers on a for-
lorn hope: another is drummed out of a regiment for cowardice.
Each of these men has, no doubt, acted from self-interest. But
we gain nothing by knowing this, except the pleasure, if it be
one, of multiplying useless words. In fact, this principle is just as
recondite, and just as important, as the great truth, that whatever is, is. If a philosopher were always to state facts in the
following form—'There is a shower: but whatever is, is; therefore, there is a shower,' his reasoning would be perfectly sound;
but we do not apprehend that it would materially enlarge the
circle of human knowledge. And it is equally idle to attribute
any importance to a proposition, which, when interpreted, means
only that a man had rather do what he had rather do.

If the doctrine that men always act from self-interest, be laid
down in any other sense than this—if the meaning of the word
self-interest be narrowed so as to exclude any one of the motives
which may by possibility act on any human being,—the proposition ceases to be identical; but at the same time it ceases to be
true.

What we have said of the word 'self-interest' applies to all the
synonymes and circumlocutions which are employed to convey
the same meaning; pain and pleasure, happiness and misery,
objects of desire, and so forth.

The whole art of Mr Mill's Essay consists in one simple trick
of legerdemain. It consists in using words of the sort which we
have been describing, first in one sense and then in another.
Men will take the objects of their desire if they can. Unques-
tionably:—but this is an identical proposition: For an object of
desire means merely a thing which a man will procure if he can.
Nothing can possibly be inferred from a maxim of this kind.
When we see a man take something, we shall know that it was

an object of his desire. But till then, we have no means of judging with certainty what he desires, or what he will take. The general proposition, however, having been admitted, Mr Mill proceeds to reason as if men had no desires but those which can be gratified only by spoliation and oppression. It then becomes easy to deduce doctrines of vast importance from the original axiom. The only misfortune is, that by thus narrowing the meaning of the word desire, the axiom becomes false, and all the doctrines consequent upon it are false likewise.

When we pass beyond those maxims which it is impossible to deny without a contradiction in terms, and which, therefore, do not enable us to advance a single step in practical knowledge, we do not believe that it is possible to lay down a single general rule respecting the motives which influence human actions. There is nothing which may not, by association or by comparison, become an object either of desire or of aversion. The fear of death is generally considered as one of the strongest of our feelings. It is the most formidable sanction which legislators have been able to devise. Yet it is notorious that, as Lord Bacon has observed, there is no passion by which that fear has not been often overcome. Physical pain is indisputably an evil; yet it has been often endured, and even welcomed. Innumerable martyrs have exulted in torments which made the spectators shudder; and, to use a more homely illustration, there are few wives who do not long to be mothers.

Is the love of approbation a stronger motive than the love of wealth? It is impossible to answer this question generally, even in the case of an individual with whom we are very intimate. We often say, indeed, that a man loves fame more than money, or money more than fame. But this is said in a loose and popular sense; for there is scarcely a man who would not endure a few sneers for a great sum of money, if he were in pecuniary distress; and scarcely a man, on the other hand, who, if he were in flourishing circumstances, would expose himself to the hatred and contempt of the public for a trifle. In order, therefore, to return a precise answer, even about a single human being, we must know what is the amount of the sacrifice of reputation demanded, and of the pecuniary advantage offered, and in what situation the person to whom the temptation is proposed stands at the time. But when the question is propounded generally about the whole species, the impossibility of answering is still more evident. Man differs from man; generation from generation; nation from nation. Education, station, sex, age, accidental associations, produce infinite shades of variety.

Now, the only mode in which we can conceive it possible to deduce a theory of government from the principles of human nature, is this. We must find out what are the motives which, in a particular form of government, impel rulers to bad measures, and what are those which impel them to good measures. We must then compare the effect of the two classes of motives; and according as we find the one or the other to prevail, we must pronounce the form of government in question good or bad.

Now let it be supposed that, in aristocratical and monarchical states, the desire of wealth, and other desires of the same class, always tend to produce misgovernment, and that the love of approbation, and other kindred feelings, always tend to produce good government. Then, if it be impossible, as we have shown that it is, to pronounce generally which of the two classes of motives is the more influential, it is impossible to find out, *a priori*, whether a monarchical or aristocratical form of government be good or bad.

Mr Mill has avoided the difficulty of making the comparison, by very coolly putting all the weights into one of the scales,— by reasoning as if no human being had ever sympathized with the feelings, been gratified by the thanks, or been galled by the execrations, of another.

The case, as we have put it, is decisive against Mr Mill; and yet we have put it in a manner far too favourable to him. For in fact, it is impossible to lay it down as a general rule, that the love of wealth in a sovereign always produces misgovernment, or the love of approbation good government. A patient and far-sighted ruler, for example, who is less desirous of raising a great sum immediately, than of securing an unencumbered and progressive revenue, will, by taking off restraints from trade, and giving perfect security to property, encourage accumulation, and entice capital from foreign countries. The commercial policy of Prussia, which is perhaps superior to that of any government in the world, and which puts to shame the absurdities of our republican brethren on the other side of the Atlantic, has probably sprung from the desire of an absolute ruler to enrich himself. On the other hand, when the popular estimate of virtues and vices is erroneous, which is too often the case, the love of approbation leads sovereigns to spend the wealth of the nation on useless shows, or to engage in wanton and destructive wars. If then we can neither compare the strength of two motives, nor determine with certainty to what description of actions either motive will lead, how can we possibly deduce a theory of government from the nature of man?

How then are we to arrive at just conclusions on a subject so important to the happiness of mankind? Surely by that method, which, in every experimental science to which it has been applied, has signally increased the power and knowledge of our species,—by that method for which our new philosophers would substitute quibbles scarcely worthy of the barbarous respondents and opponents of the middle ages,—by the method of Induction;—by observing the present state of the world,—by assiduously studying the history of past ages,—by sifting the evidence of facts,—by carefully combining and contrasting those which are authentic,—by generalizing with judgment and diffidence,—by perpetually bringing the theory which we have constructed to the test of new facts,—by correcting, or altogether abandoning it, according as those new facts prove it to be partially or fundamentally unsound. Proceeding thus,—patiently,—diligently,—candidly,—we may hope to form a system as far inferior in pretension to that which we have been examining, and as far superior to it in real utility, as the prescriptions of a great physician, varying with every stage of every malady, and with the constitution of every patient, to the pill of the advertising quack, which is to cure all human beings, in all climates, of all diseases.

This is that noble Science of Politics, which is equally removed from the barren theories of the Utilitarian sophists, and from the petty craft, so often mistaken for statesmanship by minds grown narrow in habits of intrigue, jobbing, and official etiquette;—which, of all sciences, is the most important to the welfare of nations,—which, of all sciences, must tends to expand and invigorate the mind,—which draws nutriment and ornament from every part of philosophy and literature, and dispenses, in return, nutriment and ornament to all. We are sorry and surprised when we see men of good intentions and good natural abilities abandon this healthful and generous study, to pore over speculations like those which we have been examining. And we should heartily rejoice to find that our remarks had induced any person of this description to employ, in researches of real utility, the talents and industry which are now wasted on verbal sophisms, wretched of their wretched kind.

As to the greater part of the sect, it is, we apprehend, of little consequence, what they study, or under whom. It would be more amusing, to be sure, and more reputable, if they would take up the old republican cant, and declaim about Brutus and Timoleon, the duty of killing tyrants, and the blessedness of dying for liberty. But, on the whole, they might have chosen worse. They may as well be Utilitarians as jockeys or dandies. And though quibbling about self-interest and motives, and objects of desire, and the greatest happiness of the greatest number, is but a poor employment for a grown man, it certainly hurts the health less than hard drinking, and the fortune less than high play: it is not much more laughable than phrenology, and is immeasurably more humane than cock-fighting.

IV

'Greatest Happiness' Principle

Westminster Review, vol. xxi (July 1829), Article xvi.

IV

Greatest Happiness Principle

A good enemy is sometimes worth a host of friends. In such a position the Edinburgh Review is placed, by the assault of arms made nominally against the author of the Essays, but announced at the top of the alternate pages as directed against what are there denominated Utilitarian logic and politics. If the author in question has been attacked where he was right and let alone where he was wrong, and an opening made for advancing the opinions intended to be opposed,—it may be said in courtly language (which means the language of law courts), that the learned brother has taken little by his motion.

The pith of the charge against the author of the Essays is, that he has written 'an elaborate treatise on government,' and 'deduced the whole science from the assumption of certain propensities of human nature.' Now in the name of Sir Richard Birnie and all saints, from what else *should* it be deduced? What did ever any body imagine to be the end, object, and design of government *as it ought to be*, but the same operation on an extended scale, which that meritorious chief magistrate conducts on a limited one at Bow-street; to wit, the preventing one man from injuring another? Imagine then, that the whiggery of Bow-street were to rise up against the proposition that their science was to be deduced from 'certain propensities of human nature,' and thereon were to ratiocinate as follows.

How then are we to arrive at just conclusions on a subject so important to the happiness of mankind? Surely by that method, which, in every experimental science to which it has been applied, has signally increased the power and knowledge of our species,—by that method for which our new philosophers would substitute quibbles scarcely worthy of the barbarous respondents and opponents of the middle ages,—by the method of Induction;—by observing the present state of the world,—by assiduously studying the history of past ages,—by sifting the evidence of facts,—by carefully combining and contrasting those which are authentic,—by generalizing with judgment and diffidence,—by perpetually bring the theory which we have constructed to the test of new facts,—by correcting, or altogether abandoning it, according as those new facts prove it to be partially or fundamentally unsound. Proceeding thus,—patiently,—diligently,—candidly,—we may hope to form a system as far inferior in pretension to that which we have been examining, and as far superior to it in real utility, as the prescriptions of a great physician, varying with every stage of every malady, and with the constitution of every patient, to the pill of the advertising quack, which is to cure all human beings, in all climates, of all diseases.

Fancy now,—only fancy,—the delivery of these wise words at Bow-street; and think how speedily the practical catch-poles would reply, that all this might be very fine, but as far as they had studied history, the naked story was after all, that numbers of men had a propensity to thieving, and their business was to catch them; that they too had been sifters of facts, and, to say the truth, their simple opinion was, that their brethren of the red waistcoat (though they should be sorry to think ill of any man), had some how contracted a leaning to the other side, and were more bent on puzzling the case for the benefit of the defendants, than on doing the duty of good officers and true. Such would beyond all doubt be the sentence passed on such trimmers in the microcosm of Bow-Street. It might not absolutely follow that they were in a plot to rob the goldsmiths shops, or to set fire to the House of Commons; but it would be quite clear that they had got *a feeling*,—that they were in process of siding with the thieves,—and that it was not to them that any man must look, who was anxious that pantries should be safe.

If indeed it could be proved, that Bow-street at large had been mistaken in its men;—that the flash gentlemen to whom it had been in the habit of much directing its surveillance, were in reality meritorious persons filled with zeal for the public good, and in short the best and only representatives and guardians of the public interests;—then indeed, the opinion of the ancient and venerable thief-takers would fall down before the new discovery. And this it is, the Whigs essay to prove.

And first, 'that it is not true that all despots govern ill;'— whereon the world is in a mistake, and the Whigs have the true light. And for proof, principally,—that the king of Denmark is not Caligula. To which the answer is, that the king of Denmark is not a despot. He was put in his present situation, by the people turning the scale in his favour in a balanced contest between himself and the nobility. And it is quite clear that the same power would turn the scale the other way, the moment a king of Denmark should take into his head to be Caligula. It is of little consequence by what congeries of letters the majesty of Denmark is typified in the royal press of Copenhagen, while the real fact is that the sword of the people is suspended over his head in case of ill behaviour, as effectually as in other countries where more noise is made upon the subject. Every body believes the sovereign of Denmark to be a good and virtuous gentleman; but there is no more superhuman merit in his being so, than in the case of a rural squire who does not shoot his land-steward, or quarter his wife with his yeomanry sabre.

It is true that there are partial exceptions to the rule, that all men use power as badly as they dare. There may have been such things as amiable negro-drivers and sentimental masters of press-gangs; and here and there, among the odd freaks of human nature, there may have been specimens of men who were 'No tyrants, though bred up to tyranny.' But it would be as wise to recommend wolves for nurses at the Foundling, on the credit of Romulus and Remus, as to substitute the exception for the general fact, and advise mankind to take to trusting to arbitrary power on the credit of these specimens.

Secondly, that a government not under the control of the community (for there is no question upon any other) '*may soon be saturated.*' Tell it not in Bow-street, whisper it not in Hatton-garden,—that there is a plan for preventing injustice by 'saturation.' With what peals of unearthly merriment, would Minos, Æacus, and Rhadamanthus be aroused upon their benches, if the 'light wings of saffron and of blue' should bear this theory into their grim domains. Why do not the owners of pocket-handkerchiefs try to 'saturate?' Why does not the cheated publican beg leave to check the gulosity of his defrauder with a *repetatur haustus*, and the pummelled plaintiff neutralize the malice of his adversary by requesting to have the rest of the beating in presence of the court,—if it is not that such conduct would run counter to all the conclusions of experience, and be the procreation of the mischief it affected to destroy. Woeful is the man, whose wealth depends on his having more than somebody else can be persuaded to take from him; and woeful also is the people that is in such a case.

Thirdly, that 'though there may be some tastes and propensities that have no point of saturation, there exists a sufficient check in the desire of the good opinion of others.' The misfortune of this argument is, that no man cares for the good opinion of those he has been accustomed to wrong. If oysters have opinions, it is probable they think very ill of those who eat them in August; but small is the effect upon the autumnal glutton that engulphs their gentle substances within his own. The planter and the slave-driver care just as much about negro opinion, as the epicure about the sentiments of oysters. M. Ude throwing live eels into the fire as a kindly method of divesting them of the unsavoury oil that lodges beneath their skins, is not more convinced of the immense aggregate of good which arises to the lordlier parts of the creation, than is the gentle peer who strips his fellow man of country and of family for a wild-fowl slain. The goodly land-owner, who lives by morsels squeezed indiscriminately from the waxy hands of the cobbler and the polluted ones of the nightman, is in no small degree the object of both hatred and contempt; but it is to be feared that he is a long way from feeling them to be intolerable. The principle of '*At mihi plaudo, Ipse domi, simul ac nummos contemplor in arcâ,*' is sufficient to make a wide interval between the opinions of the plaintiff and defendant in such cases. In short, to banish law and leave all plaintiffs to trust to the desire of reputation on the opposite side, would only be transporting the theory of the Whigs, from the House of Commons to Westminster Hall.

Fourthly, the Edinburgh Reviewers are of opinion, that

'it might, with no small plausibility, be maintained, that, in many countries, there are two classes which, in some degree, answer to this description;' [viz.] 'that the poor compose the class which government is established to restrain; and the people of some property the class to which the powers of government may without danger be confided.'

They take great pains, it is true, to say this and not to say it. They shuffle and creep about, to secure a hole to escape at, if 'what they do not assert' should be found in any degree inconvenient. A man might waste his life in trying to find out whether the Misses of the Edinburgh mean to say Yes or No in their political coquetry. But whichever way the lovely spinsters may decide, it is diametrically opposed to history and the evidence of facts, that the poor *are* the class whom there is any difficulty in restraining. It is not the poor but the rich, that have a propensity to take the property of other people. There is no instance upon earth, of the poor having combined to take away the property of the rich; and all the instances habitually brought forward as examples of it, are gross misrepresentations, founded upon the most necessary acts of self-defence on the part of the most numerous classes. Such a misrepresentation is the common one of the Agrarian law; which was nothing but an attempt on the part of the Roman people to get back some part of what had been taken from them by undisguised robbery. Such another is the stock example of the French Revolution, appealed to by the Edinburgh Review in the actual case. It is utterly untrue that the French Revolution took place because 'the poor began to compare their cottages and salads with the hotels and banquets of the rich;' it took place because they were robbed of their cottages and salads to support the hotels and banquets of their oppressors. It is utterly untrue that there was either a scramble for property or a general confiscation; the classes who took part with the foreign invader lost their property, as they would have done here, and ought to do everywhere. All these are the vulgar errors of the man on the lion's back,—which the lion will set to rights when he can tell his own story. History is nothing but the relation of the sufferings of the poor from the rich; except precisely so far as the numerous classes of the community have contrived to keep the virtual power in their hands, or in other words, to establish free governments. If a poor man injures the rich, the law is instantly at his heels; the injuries of the rich towards the poor are always inflicted *by* the law. And to enable the rich to do this to any extent that may be practicable or prudent, there is clearly only one postulate required, which is, that the rich shall make the law.

This appears to be sufficient, for the Edinburgh Review, in this place. A more useful and agreeable office remains, in endeavouring to give the history of the common-sense principle of morals and politics, and to promote its diffusion.

The first time the phrase of 'the principle of utility' was brought decidedly into notice, was in the 'Essays, by David Hume,' published about the year 1742. In that work it is mentioned as the name of a principle which might be made the foundation of a system of morals, in opposition to a system then in vogue, which was founded on what was called the 'moral sense.' The ideas, however, there attached to it, are vague, and defective in practical application.

Nearly at the same time appeared in French the celebrated work of Helvetius '*Sur L'Esprit.*' In this a commencement was made, of the application of the principle to practical use. A connection was established between the ideas attached to the word 'happiness,' and those attached to the words 'pleasure' and 'pain;' by which a great advance was made in the developement of the meaning of the terms 'utility' and 'principle of utility.'

In 1749 appeared the work of David Hartley known by the title of 'Hartley on Man.' It at first consisted of two volumes octavo; which by the abridgements of Dr. Priestley were afterwards reduced to one. In this a greater number of species were ranked under the two heads of pleasure and pain, than in the work of Helvetius; but the collection was still exceedingly defective.

In the year 1768 appeared a pamphlet of Dr. Priestley's, written, as was his custom, in a hasty manner, and with little precise method; but containing in one of its pages the express phrase 'the greatest happiness of the greatest number.' And this was represented as a principle containing the only rational foundation of rules for human conduct.

In the same year this pamphlet fell into the hands of Mr. Bentham at Oxford; he being at that time not quite twenty-one years of age. Like Archimedes on the discovery of the principle of hydrostatics, he exclaimed Σϋρηκα, and from that page of that pamphlet, was drawn the phrase, the import of which it has been the object of his subsequent writings to diffuse.

In 1776 came out Mr. Bentham's first publication, entitled 'A Fragment on Government.' In this he employed the phrase of Priestley's which had made so strong an impression on his mind; and endeavoured to enforce its reception as the radical principle of government, in preference to the fiction of Locke denominated 'the original contract.' In 1781 was begun the printing of his 'Introduction to the Principles of Morals and Legislation;' but it was not till 1789 that it was brought into the state in which it now appears. In this was seen the first inventory that had been attempted, of the different forms of stimulus to human action called 'motives;' each motive being accompanied by a reference to the corresponding pleasure or pain, in the prospect of which it has its origin.

In 1817 appeared his tract entitled 'Springs of Action;' which is composed of a pretty extensive Table, elucidated by notes. In this was added for the first time a list of 'interests;' each interest being referred to its corresponding motive, as the motives were to pleasures or to pains.

In the course of the construction of this Table, occasion was given for observing the expression of approbation or the contrary, which in the case of almost every species of motive, is introduced into its designation, according to the colouring desired to be given to it by the speaker. Hence in most cases there were found to be three sorts of designations; one in which the expression of approbation was superadded; another, in which there was the expression of disapprobation; and a third, which presented the original idea without either. The extent to which these kinds of adjuncts were employed as instruments of deception, induced the author of the Table to mark the difference between the classes by appropriate denominations. The terms chosen by him for the two classes which depart in opposite directions from the unadulterated idea, were *eulogistic*, or if preferred, approbative,—and its Greek opposite *dyslogistic*, or if preferred, disapprobative. All new terms have a portion of stiffness; but the proof of their goodness, is the degree in which they finally wind themselves into the practice of mankind. On this ground, there are appearances, that the Greek terms here mentioned, possess a force and spirit, at least to Grecian ears, that will confer on them the durability the Roman emperor complained of being unable to bestow.

On his entrance upon the *moral* (including the *political*) branch of science as it then existed, it appeared to him to be in nearly the same condition as that in which Lord Bacon found the *physical*. The matter of what was called the science, was composed of a more or less copious assemblage of words; and the instruction attempted, consisted principally in conveying information of the relation borne by the import of one of these words to the import of another,—but with an almost total absence of any endeavour to trace the relations of the things typified to each other in the way of cause and effect. Hence, as '*Fiat experimentum*' was the aphorism of Bacon, so '*Fiat observatio*' seemed to be the aphorism demanded in the present case. An Imperial dilettante, or a Colonial Secretary, may be able to pursue his studies by making original experiments upon mankind. But unofficial philosophers must be content to classify appearances as they arise; without attempting to direct the course of their succession.

In proceeding to make trial of the application of the new principle, it was in the first instance very open to observation, that by far the greatest part of what is done in the way of legislation, is done by making a choice of evils. No government can be without coercion; and the degree in which its ends can be obtained by reward, is so comparatively small, that it may almost be left out of consideration altogether. But if the object of government is to effect an end by means of pains, there appeared strong *primâ facie* reason for believing, that the object of a *good* government must be to prevent a greater evil at the expense of a less; and this led rapidly to a vague surmise,—a wandering suspicion mixed with hope, like 'love's youngest dream,'—that the object of good government might possibly be the carrying the diminution of evil, or the increase of happiness, to its *maximum*. This was the vision of which the prophet caught a glance from his Pisgah, and straightway girded himself to enter on the promised land.

And here was to be encountered in the outset the perplexing question, of *why* the production of the maximum of happiness ought to be the object of government. One possible response was, that it is the production of good. But why ought a government to follow after the production of good?—for to say that it cannot be a good government without it, is at best only an identical proposition. Cicero would have answered that it was because it was virtuous, becoming, or perhaps god-like; and philosopher Square would have said, it was because it was according to the fitness of things. But these are all reasons *à l'antique;* and would not in this day content a Mechanics Institute. Something might perhaps be done towards an answer, by Euclid's mode improperly included under the title of *reductio ad absurdum*, or defying any body to prove that the object of government should be any thing else. For if it is any thing else, the object must be the production of a smaller quantity of good instead of a greater; or in other words, the production of relative evil—which is an unmaintainable proposition *s'il y en avait jamais*. But the real answer appeared to be, that men at large *ought* not to allow a government to afflict them with more evil or less good, than they can help. What a *government* ought to do, is a mysterious and searching question, which those may answer who know what it means; but what other men ought to do, is a question of no mystery at all. The word *ought*, if it means any thing, must have reference to some kind of interest or motives; and what interest a government has in doing right, when it happens to be interested in doing wrong, is a question for the school-men. The fact appears to be, that *ought* is not predicable of governments. The question is not why governments are bound not to do this or that, but why other men should let them if they can help it. The point is not to determine why the lion should not eat sheep, but why men should eat their own mutton if they can.

It might, perhaps, be objected in this place, that the obligation may be solved into the fact, that men would not consent to obey a government that acted on the principle of diminishing the possible quantity of happiness, and therefore the members of the government are interested in preventing their own overthrow. But the misfortune is, that this solution does not extend to the most needful case; which is that of the successful establishment of an open and avowed diminution of human happiness by the exercise of government. The system of Colonial Slavery, is an overt instance of this kind; but still it is not overthrown. The danger of overthrow, therefore, is not a competent answer to the question 'Why the aggregate of human happiness should not be diminished by law in the West Indies.'

The only rivals of any note to the new principle which were brought forward, were those known by the names of the 'moral sense,' and the 'original contract.' The new principle superseded the first of these, by presenting it with a guide for its decisions; and the other, by making it unnecessary to resort to a remote and imaginary contract, for what was clearly the business of every man and every hour. Throughout the whole horizon of morals and of politics, the consequences were glorious and vast. It might be said without danger of exaggeration, that they who sat in darkness had seen a great light. The mists in which mankind had jousted against each other were swept away, as when the sun of astronomical science arose in the full developement of the principle of Gravitation. If the object of legislation was the greatest happiness, *Morality* was the promotion of the same end by the conduct of the individual; and by analogy, the happiness of the world was the Morality of Nations. The awful names of Justice and Liberty,—which men had long felt after, if haply they might comprehend them,—ceased to designate unknown powers; and *Justice* stood forth as the rule of appropriation which produced the greatest happiness, while *Liberty* was the being subject to no restraints except what were necessary for the promotion of the same end. *Rights*, were what by the same rule men *ought* to have; not the miserable technicality, of what laws and lawyers might have left them. Or if preferred, they were the securities which individuals could not be unprovided with, without a diminution of the aggregate of happiness. Rights, therefore, in this sense, were no more abrogated by the absence of enjoyment, than Moral rules are abrogated by the absence of obedience; and in this sense it was, that men had murmured of their *Natural* and *Imprescriptible* rights. What men *ought* to have—that is, what it is for the advancement of the aggregate happiness that they should have—depends neither on lawyers nor on kings, but on the constitution of things imprinted by the Maker; and is consequently immutable like that. *Equality*, meant equality in the safety of such rights as the rule of the greatest happiness assigned; and it was an easy inference from practical observation, that in the case of all the most important rights, the assignment was uniform to all mankind. The *Sovereignty of the people*, meant the acknowledgment of the essential right of the community to obtain its own happiness in its own way; and a *Constitution*, meant a reserved rule or rules, which in the exercise of this sovereignty it was not committed to the delegated rulers to infringe. A *Legitimate* government, was such a government as was established or assented to by the community, in the uncontrolled exercise of its last-mentioned right; and the *Illegitimate*, were all besides. A *Free* government, was one which not only was legitimate, but in which the members of the community actually exercised an effective portion of the direction of their own concerns, either by the means of representatives or otherwise; and in proportion to the degree in which this exercise was extended and secured, was the degree in which freedom could be predicated of the result. A *Constitutional* government, was one in which there was an acknowledgment of the reserved rule or rules denominated a Constitution; a necessary ingredient of a free government, but not identical in terms. Lastly, a glimpse had been received from beyond the Atlantic, of the possibility of such an institution as a *Constitutional Majority*, or committing the charge of alterations in the Constitution itself, to, for instance, a threefold majority of the ordinary delegates, as a provision in the last resort, for what of change may be demanded by the imperfection of human foresight and the flow of time. All the sublime obscurities, which had haunted the mind of man from the first formation of society,—the phantoms whose steps had been on earth, and their heads among the clouds,— marshalled themselves at the sound of this new principle of connection and of union, and stood a regulated band, where all was order, symmetry, and force. What men had struggled for and bled, while they saw it but as through a glass darkly,—was made the object of substantial knowledge and lively apprehension. The bones of sages and of patriots stirred within their tombs, that what they dimly saw and followed, had become the world's common heritage. And the great result was wrought by no supernatural means, nor produced by any unparallelable concatenation of events. It was foretold by no oracles, and ushered by no portents; but was brought about by the quiet and reiterated exercise of God's first gift of common sense. Even religions bowed before the discovered rule; and the reason why the divine origin of the Koran and the Vedas was to be disallowed, was because they could not endure the test, which heaven in the exercise of its simpler Providence had revealed to human apprehension. Fanatics and bigots might frown; but good men of all creeds hailed the appearance of peace on earth and good-will towards men, in the establishment of the principle which made human happiness the end of all studies, and the land-mark of all toils.

Subordinate to the greater results of the discovery, were many other inferences both in morals and in politics. The innumerable questions which had been agitated concerning the merit or demerit of certain actions, were now found to be decided by a rule perfectly within the reach of human application, and which exhibited itself as a rigid touchstone of other systems. The paradox of the Stoics was dissolved by simple transposition; and instead of virtue making happiness, what makes the general happiness was virtue. But it was in the relations which pass under the name of the political, that its agency was most decisive. If the happiness of men was the object of government, it was plain that this object was to be obtained by their being governed with a view to their own interest, and not to the interest of somebody else. And the way to effect this, was that they should govern *themselves*, or which amounts to the same thing in the view proposed, should hold an effectual check over those to whom the reins of government are committed. That a community of any great extent should govern by the constant act and deed of all its members, was as palpably inconvenient, amounting to the impracticable, as that the owner of a large fortune should be his own steward, butler, groom, huntsman, coachman, all in one. But it no more followed in one case than in the other, that the impracticability of exercising these offices except by delegate, derogates from the complete and perfect right to superintend their exercise by others. The sovereignty of the community, like that of the rich proprietor over his corks and his curry-combs, is an essential, not an active sovereignty. It is a sovereignty which can only be well exercised by delegating its execution to others under rules; but it is not on that account less real or less solid.

But if the community is to hold an effectual check over those who are to govern for it, the government, or at all events some integral and indispensable branch of it, must be committed to individuals chosen by the community at large or by its subdivisions. The Whigs say not,—and that it should be committed to somebody else, meaning themselves; and on this they and the community are at issue. And here rises to view the greatest political invention of the moderns; which is the system of Representation. And the plain and simple *rationale* of the right of Representation, unembarrassed with the consideration of what it may be one dishonest man's interest to defend or another's to acquire, is that all should be admitted equally, and that when all are so admitted and not before, each man possesses the full enjoyment of all the influence his wealth, talents, or reputation, can confer on him without infringing on the happiness of others. The principle of this is as clear, as that of the right of equal admission to the market. The equality of admission, does not make men possess an equality of influence when they are there. On the contrary it is precisely then, that the rich man has the just advantage of the influence, which there is no intention to deny him. The fallacy is in stating, that the rich cannot have their proper influence in the market, unless the poor are kept out besides. Property should be represented; but then it should be every body's property; the fallacy is, that it should be only the property of those who happen to have a great deal. And as in the common market, so in the greater market of election. In such a contest of interests, every man's influence would fetch exactly what it was worth; and the theory which claims for the rich not only the influence of their riches, but the exclusion of the poor besides, is as visibly and demonstrably unjust, as in the market case produced as parallel. This furnishes the foundation of the right of *Universal Suffrage;* a right which no reasonable man that understands it will ever consent to disavow, however remote the actual condition of society may be from its practical enjoyment. To think common sense at home, is a luxury that might have been indulged in in Egypt; even though all the surrounding world worshipped a crocodile or a monkey. Closely connected with the *universality* of suffrage, is the opportunity of its frequent exercise. For the only practical way of preserving a check over those appointed to the directorship of the great Company, is to send them back to their constituents frequently; and the more frequent the reference, the more perfect the check. And the period which would occur to every man who had no sinister interests to promote, would be that it should be *annual.* The organ of the Whigs once undertook to ask, why the period should be precisely a year, and what virtue there was in a planet's periodic time, that should connect it with a seat in parliament. To which the answer is by asking, why men do other things yearly, and not, for instance, every eighteen months. Why do men make up their accounts once a year, hold Long Vacations once a year, keep their birth-days once a year, visit their friends once a year, physic and purge, eat mince-pies, issue Army-lists and the Red Book, and take the sacrament by Act of Parliament,—if it is not that the necessary connection of the seasons with many of the acts of man, makes it highly convenient for him to bind up his other actions in the same routine, and hence in all things that require regularity of performance, his option is in reality to do them once a year, or once in two. But between these, there is a gulph, which passed, leads easily to once in seven, or once in ten. The tradesman who should defer making up his accounts to a second year, would soon bring them to a conclusion in the Fleet; and if all the members of the community had as lively a sense of their interests as the tenant of a chandler's shop, they would be equally jealous of the laxity of delay. Sensible men make their stand upon the right side of the gulph; and fools upon the other.

On these two important points of Universal Suffrage and its Annual exercise, the objections oftenest urged relate to some impracticability or difficulty to arise in the execution. On which it may be answered, that if an intelligent committee was appointed, with instructions to devise the mode in which the greatest obstacles should be thrown in the way of the quiet exercise of the operation of appointing representatives, it would clearly devise the actual one. In the first place, it is plain, that it would advise the compression of the power of choice into the hands of a few; that there might be a physical possibility of the few being bribed. Secondly, it would recommend the extension of the period of service; in order that it might be better worth while for the candidates to bribe, and that the electors might be enabled to indulge in riot on an occasion that occurs but seldom, in a way they could not do if it occurred more frequently. Thirdly and lastly, it would suggest that each man's way of voting should be published, in order that the greatest possible scope might be given to the operation of party feelings, and no man be able to escape by holding his peace. This is what a sensible committee would recommend; and, by consequence, it is what sensible men on the other side would recommend to be undone. It is evident at sight, that the difficulties suggested are not only factitious and artificial, but require great pains to secure and keep them in existence. It would be as much easier to take men's votes annually than septennially, as for a boy to comb his hair daily than once a week,—if the management was in the hands of those who had an interest in its success. And the votes of an entire population might be taken with as much facility as a census, if the way that leads to such a result was followed, instead of the way that does not. When the lion builds its own cage, interests hostile to the good of the community will pare their own claws. But whether their claws are pared or not, it is satisfactory to know what arrangements are directed to the good of the community, and what are curiously and scientifically adjusted to its opposite.

These are the principles against which the Whigs have directed the small battery of their wit; which was more than it was politic to do, upon the strength of 'past renown and antiquated power.' Among other specimens of their ingenuity, they think they embarrass the subject, by asking why, on the principles in question, women should not have votes as well as men. *And why not?*—

'Gentle shepherd, tell me why.'—

If the mode of election was what it ought to be, there would be no more difficulty in women voting for a representative in parliament, than for a director at the India House. The world will find out at some time, that the readiest way to secure justice on some points, is to be just on all;—that the whole is easier to accomplish than the part;—and that whenever the camel is driven through the eye of the needle, it would be simple folly and debility that would leave a hoof behind.

Another of their perverted ingenuities is, that 'they are rather inclined to think,' that it would, on the whole, be for the interest of the majority to plunder the rich; and if so, the Utilitarians will say, that the rich *ought* to be plundered. On which it is sufficient to reply, that for the majority to plunder the rich, would amount to a declaration that nobody should be rich; which, as all men wish to be rich, would involve a suicide of hope. And as nobody has shown a fragment of reason why such a proceeding should be for the general happiness, it does not follow that the 'Utilitarians' would recommend it. The Edinburgh Reviewers have a waiting gentlewoman's ideas of 'Utilitarianism.' It is unsupported by any thing but the pitiable 'We are rather inclined to think'—and is utterly contradicted by the whole course of history and human experience besides,— that there is either danger or possibility of such a consummation as the majority agreeing on the plunder of the rich. There have been instances in human memory, of their agreeing to plunder rich oppressors, rich traitors, rich enemies,—but the rich *simpliciter*, never. It is as true now as in the days of Harrington, that 'a people never will, nor ever can, never did, nor ever shall, take up arms for levelling.' All the commotions in the world have been for something else; and 'levelling' is brought forward as the blind, to conceal what the other was.

The real errors of the author of the 'Essays,' may be concluded under the lawyer-like mistake, of pouncing on the technical and secondary meaning of terms, to the exclusion of the primary. As lawyers and law-makers became anxious to secure the adherence of mankind to their decisions, they found a strong interest in representing that *their law* was right, and right was *their law*. They were not only to be the servants of Astrea, but they were to be Astrea herself. Hence they applied themselves to suppress all reference to the awful though obscure ideas which men possessed, of a power to which both law and lawyers were meant to be subservient; the object being to transfer to themselves the reverence intended for the other. The only wonder is, that when they went to the secondary sense, they did not go to the ternary, and declare that the word justice meant nothing but a justice of the peace. With deference, however, to their authority, the original sense of words exists as ever; and 'seeking justice and doing right,' *does not* mean seeking Coke and doing Blackstone.

But as all knowledge is only the accumulation of improvements, the very title of the principle in question was found susceptible of progressive melioration. Its first name, 'the Principle of Utility,' was defective in as much as it did not express the nature and extent of the utility intended; and the same objection extended to the terms 'Utilitarian' and 'Utilitarianism.' It may be useful to a thief to steal; but it is useful to the community at large, that men should not steal; and it was this last utility, and not the first, which was intended, but not expressed. Its next denomination was, the principle of 'the Greatest Happiness of the Greatest Number.' This was erroneous by superfluity; and was in fact attempting to say the same thing twice instead of once. Though nothing in the writings of any of the proposers supported such a construction, it was liable to be represented as maintaining, that if, for example, a nation was composed of a million of black men and a million and one of white, the white were justified in sacrificing as much as they pleased of the happiness of the million, for the sake of any increase that might be made to the happiness of the million and one. The latest improvement, therefore, of the philosopher whose long life has been dedicated to the diffusion of the principle,—and of which the present Article has to boast of being the announcement and the organ,—is to dismiss the superfluous 'greatest number,' and declare that the just object of politics and morals, is simply 'THE GREATEST HAPPINESS.' In this manner the magnificent proposition emerges clearly, and disentangled from its accessary. And the accessary proposition is, that the greatest aggregate of happiness must always include the happiness of the greatest number. For the greatest number must always be composed of those who individually possess a comparatively small portion of the good things of life; and if any thing is taken from one of these to give to the others, it is plain that what he loses in happiness, is greater than what the others gain. It is the mathematical assertion, that a quantity x is greater in comparison of a small quantity it is taken from, than of a large one it is added to. It is the avowal that half-a-crown is of more consequence to the porter that loses it, than to the Duke of Bedford who should chance to find it;—that a chief portion of the baseness of the rich man who seized the poor's ewe lamb, consisted in taking what caused so much greater pain to the sufferer, than happiness to the receiver.

It would clearly be very desirable to compress the expression of 'The Principle of the Greatest Aggregate of Happiness,' or its conjugates, into a single term. Those who object indiscriminately to inventions in nomenclature, are either ignorant of their power, or jealous of their effect. It is, however, very difficult to combine the three ideas of 'greatest, aggregate, and happiness,' in a single word. What friendly efforts have failed to effect, the scorner has perhaps supplied. That name is best, which most strongly excites in the minds of friends and enemies, the impressions designed to be conveyed. It has always been permitted, to learn from an opponent. The Utilitarians shall abandon foreign titles, and 'the sacred language of the *Benthamites*' be all that shall be heard of by posterity.

V

Bentham's Defence of Mill: Utilitarian System of Philosophy

Edinburgh Review, no. xcviii (June 1829), Article i.

WE have had great reason, we think, to be gratified by the success of our late attack on the Utilitarians. We could publish a long list of the cures which it has wrought, in cases previously considered as hopeless. Delicacy forbids us to divulge names; but we cannot refrain from alluding to two remarkable instances. —A respectable lady writes to inform us, that her son, who was plucked at Cambridge last January, has not been heard to call Sir James Mackintosh a poor ignorant fool more than twice since the appearance of our article. A distinguished political writer in the Westminster and Parliamentary Reviews has borrowed Hume's History, and has actually got as far as the battle of Agincourt. He assures us that he takes great pleasure in his new study, and that he is very impatient to learn how Scotland and England became one kingdom. But the greatest compliment that we have received is, that Mr Bentham himself should have condescended to take the field in defence of Mr Mill. We have not been in the habit of reviewing Reviews; but as Mr Bentham is a truly great man, and as his party have thought fit to announce in puffs and placards that this article is written by him, and contains not only an answer to our attacks, but a developement of the 'greatest happiness principle,' with the latest improvements of the author, we shall for once depart from our general rule. However the conflict may terminate, we shall at least not have been vanquished by an ignoble hand.

Of Mr Bentham himself, we shall endeavour, even while defending ourselves against his reproaches, to speak with the respect to which his venerable age, his genius, and his public services entitle him. If any harsh expression should escape us, we trust that he will attribute it to inadvertence, to the momentary warmth of controversy,—to any thing, in short, rather than to a design of affronting him. Though we have nothing in common with the crew of Hurds and Boswells, who, either from interested motives, or from the habit of intellectual servility and dependence, pamper and vitiate his appetite with the noxious sweetness of their undiscerning praise, we are not perhaps less competent than they to appreciate his merit, or less sincerely disposed to acknowledge it. Though we may sometimes think his reasonings on moral and political questions feeble and sophistical—though we may sometimes smile at his extraordinary language—we can never be weary of admiring the amplitude of his comprehension, the keenness of his penetration, the exuberant fertility with which his mind pours forth arguments and illustrations. However sharply he may speak of us, we can never cease to revere in him the father of the philosophy of Jurisprudence. He has a full right to all the privileges of a great inventor; and, in our court of criticism, those privileges will never be pleaded in vain. But they are limited in the same manner in which, fortunately for the ends of justice, the privileges of the peerage are now limited. The advantage is personal and incommunicable. A nobleman can now no longer cover with his protection every lackey who follows his heels, or every bully who draws in his quarrel; and, highly as we respect the exalted rank which Mr Bentham holds among the writers of our time, yet when, for the due maintenance of literary police, we shall think it necessary to confute sophists, or to bring pretenders to shame, we shall not depart from the ordinary course of our proceedings because the offenders call themselves Benthamites.

Whether Mr Mill has much reason to thank Mr Bentham for undertaking his defence, our readers, when they have finished this article, will perhaps be inclined to doubt. Great as Mr Bentham's talents are, he has, we think, shown an undue confidence in them. He should have considered how dangerous it is for any man, however eloquent and ingenious he may be, to attack or to defend a book without reading it: And we feel quite convinced that Mr Bentham would never have written the article before us, if he had, before he began, perused our review with attention, and compared it with Mr Mill's Essay.

He has utterly mistaken our object and meaning. He seems to think that we have undertaken to set up some theory of government in opposition to that of Mr Mill. But we distinctly disclaimed any such design. From the beginning to the end of our article, there is not, as far as we remember, a single sentence which, when fairly construed, can be considered as indicating any such design. If such an expression can be found, it has been dropped by inadvertence. Our object was to prove, not that monarchy and aristocracy are good, but that Mr Mill had not proved them to be bad; not that democracy is bad, but that Mr Mill had not proved it to be good. The points in issue are these, Whether the famous Essay on Government be, as it has been called, a perfect solution of the great political problem, or a series of sophisms and blunders; and whether the sect which, while it glories in the precision of its logic, extols this Essay as a masterpiece of demonstration, be a sect deserving of the respect or of the derision of mankind. These, we say, are the issues; and on these we with full confidence put ourselves on the country.

It is not necessary, for the purposes of this investigation, that we should state what our political creed is, or whether we have any political creed at all. A man who cannot act the most trivial part in a farce has a right to hiss Romeo Coates—a man who does not know a vein from an artery may caution a simple neighbour against the advertisements of Doctor Eady. A complete theory of government would indeed be a noble present to mankind; but it is a present which we do not hope, and do not pretend, that we can offer. If, however, we cannot lay the foundation, it is something to clear away the rubbish—if we cannot set up truth, it is something to pull down error. Even if the subjects of which the Utilitarians treat were subjects of less fearful importance, we should think it no small service to the cause of good sense and good taste, to point out the contrast between their magnificent pretensions and their miserable performances. Some of them have, however, thought fit to display their ingenuity on questions of the most momentous kind, and on questions concerning which men cannot reason ill with impunity. We think it, under these circumstances, an absolute duty to expose the fallacy of their arguments. It is no matter of pride or of pleasure. To read their works, is the most soporific employment that we know; and a man ought no more to be proud of refuting them, than of having two legs. We must now come to close quarters with Mr Bentham, whom, we need not say, we do not mean to include in this observation. He charges us with maintaining,—

First, 'that it is not true that all despots govern ill;'—whereon the world is in a mistake, and the Whigs have the true light. And for proof, principally,—that the King of Denmark is not Caligula. . . . ['To which the answer is . . . credit of these specimens.' pp. 134–5]

Now, in the first place, we never cited the case of Denmark to prove that all despots do not govern ill. We cited it to prove that Mr Mill did not know how to reason. Mr Mill gave it as a reason for deducing the theory of government from the general laws of human nature, that the King of Denmark was not Caligula. This we said, and we still say, was absurd.

In the second place, it was not we, but Mr Mill, who said that the King of Denmark was a despot. His words are these:—'The people of Denmark, tired out with the oppression of an aristocracy, resolved that their king should be absolute; and under their absolute monarch are as well governed as any people in Europe.' We leave Mr Bentham to settle with Mr Mill the distinction between a despot and an absolute king.

In the third place, Mr Bentham says, that there was in Denmark a balanced contest between the king and the nobility. We find some difficulty in believing that Mr Bentham seriously means to say this, when we consider that Mr Mill has demonstrated the chance to be as infinity to one against the existence of such a balanced contest.

Fourthly, Mr Bentham says, that in this balanced contest the people turned the scale in favour of the king against the aristocracy. But Mr Mill has demonstrated, that it cannot possibly be for the interest of the monarchy and democracy to join against the aristocracy; and that wherever the three parties exist, the king and the aristocracy will combine against the people. This, Mr Mill assures us, is as certain as any thing which depends upon human will.

Fifthly, Mr Bentham says, that if the King of Denmark were to oppress his people, the people and nobles would combine against the king. But Mr Mill has proved that it can never be for the interest of the aristocracy to combine with the democracy against the king. It is evidently Mr Bentham's opinion, that 'monarchy, aristocracy, and democracy, may balance each other, and by mutual checks produce good government.' But this is the very theory which Mr Mill pronounces to be the wildest, the most visionary, the most chimerical, ever broached on the subject of government.

We have no dispute on these heads with Mr Bentham. On the contrary, we think his explanation true—or, at least, true in part; and we heartily thank him for lending us his assistance to demolish the Essay of his follower. His wit and his sarcasm are sport to us; but they are death to his unhappy disciple.

Mr Bentham seems to imagine that we have said something implying an opinion favourable to despotism. We can scarcely suppose that, as he has not condescended to read that portion of our work which he undertook to answer, he can have bestowed much attention on its general character. Had he done so, he would, we think, scarcely have entertained such a suspicion. Mr Mill asserts, and pretends to prove, that under no despotic government does any human being, except the tools of the sovereign, possess more than the necessaries of life, and that the most intense degree of terror is kept up by constant cruelty. This, we say, is untrue. It is not merely a rule to which there are exceptions: but it is not the rule. Despotism is bad; but it is scarcely anywhere so bad as Mr Mill says that it is everywhere. This, we are sure, Mr Bentham will allow. If a man were to say that five hundred thousand people die every year in London of dram-drinking, he would not assert a proposition more monstrously false than Mr Mill's. Would it be just to charge us with defending intoxication because we might say that such a man was grossly in the wrong?

We say with Mr Bentham that despotism is a bad thing. We say with Mr Bentham that the exceptions do not destroy the authority of the rule. But this we say—that a single exception overthrows an argument, which either does not prove the rule at all, or else proves the rule to be *true without exceptions;* and such an argument is Mr Mill's argument against despotism. In this respect, there is a great difference between rules drawn from experience, and rules deduced *à priori*. We might believe that there had been a fall of snow last August, and yet not think it likely that there would be snow next August. A single occurrence opposed to our general experience would tell for very little in our calculation of the chances. But if we could once satisfy ourselves that, in *any* single right-angled triangle, the square of the hypothenuse might be less than the squares of the sides, we must reject the forty-seventh proposition of Euclid altogether. We willingly adopt Mr Bentham's lively illustration about the wolf; and we will say, in passing, that it gives us real pleasure to see how little old age has diminished the gaiety of this eminent man. We can assure him that his merriment gives us far more pleasure on his account, than pain on our own. We say with him, Keep the wolf out of the nursery, in spite of the story of Romulus and Remus. But if the shepherd who saw the wolf licking and suckling those famous twins, were, after telling this story to his companions, to assert that it was an infallible rule that no wolf ever had spared, or ever would spare, any living thing which might fall in its way—that its nature was carnivorous—and that it could not possibly disobey its nature, we think that the hearers might have been excused for staring. It may be strange, but is not inconsistent, that a wolf which has eaten ninety-nine children should spare the hundredth. But the fact, that a wolf has once spared a child is sufficient to show that there must be some flaw in a chain of reasoning, purporting to prove that wolves cannot possibly spare children.

Mr Bentham proceeds to attack another position which he conceives us to maintain:—

Secondly, That a government not under the control of the community (for there is no question upon any other) '*may soon be saturated.*' ... ['Tell it not in Bow Street ... in such a case.' p. 135]

[T]here is no great difficulty in answering the argument. The real reason which makes it absurd to think of preventing theft by pensioning off thieves is this, that there is no limit to the number of thieves. If there were only a hundred thieves in a place, and we were quite sure that no person not already addicted to theft would take to it, it might become a question, whether to keep the thieves from dishonesty by raising them above distress, would not be a better course than to employ officers against them. But the actual cases are not parallel. Every man who chooses can become a thief; but a man cannot become a king or a member of the aristocracy whenever he chooses. The number of the depredators is limited; and therefore the amount of depredation, so far as physical pleasures are concerned, must be limited also. Now, we made the remark which Mr Bentham censures with reference to physical pleasures only. The pleasures of ostentation, of taste, of revenge, and other pleasures of the same description, have, we distinctly allowed, no limit. Our words are these:—'A king or an aristocracy may be supplied to satiety with *corporal pleasures*, at an expense which the rudest and poorest community would scarcely feel.' Does Mr Bentham deny this? If he does, we leave him to Mr Mill. 'What,' says that philosopher, in his Essay on Education, 'what are the ordinary pursuits of wealth and power, which kindle to such a height the ardour of mankind? Not the mere love of eating and of drinking, or all the physical objects together which wealth can purchase or power command. With these every man is in the long run speedily satisfied.' What the difference is between being speedily satisfied and being soon saturated, we leave Mr Bentham and Mr Mill to settle together.

The word 'saturation,' however, seems to provoke Mr Bentham's mirth. It certainly did not strike us as very pure English; but, as Mr Mill used it, we supposed it to be good Benthamese. With the latter language we are not critically acquainted, though, as it has many roots in common with our mother tongue, we can contrive, by the help of a converted Utilitarian, who attends us in the capacity of Moonshee, to make out a little. But Mr Bentham's authority is of course decisive, and we bow to it.

Mr Bentham next represents us as maintaining,—

Thirdly, That 'though there may be some tastes and propensities that have no point of saturation, there exists a sufficient check in the desire of the good opinion of others.' ... ['The misfortune ... Westminster Hall.' pp. 135–6]

Now, in the first place, we never maintained the proposition which Mr Bentham puts into our mouths. We said, and say, that there is a *certain* check to the rapacity and cruelty of men, in their desire of the good opinion of others. We never said that it was sufficient. Let Mr Mill show it to be insufficient. It is enough for us to prove, that there is a set-off against the principle from which Mr Mill deduces the whole theory of government. The balance may be, and, we believe, will be, against despotism and the narrower forms of aristocracy. But what is this to the correctness or incorrectness of Mr Mill's accounts? The question is not, whether the motives which lead rulers to behave ill, are stronger than those which lead them to behave well;—but, whether we ought to form a theory of government by looking *only* at the motives which lead rulers to behave ill, and never noticing those which lead them to behave well.

Absolute rulers, says Mr Bentham, do not care for the good opinion of their subjects; for no man cares for the good opinion of those whom he has been accustomed to wrong. By Mr Bentham's leave, this is a plain begging of the question. The point at issue is this:—Will kings and nobles wrong the people? The argument in favour of kings and nobles is this:—they will not wrong the people, because they care for the good opinion of the people. But this argument Mr Bentham meets thus:—they will not care for the good opinion of the people, because they are accustomed to wrong the people.

Here Mr Mill differs, as usual, from Mr Bentham. 'The greatest princes,' says he, in his Essay on Education, 'the most despotical masters of human destiny, when asked what they aim at by their wars and conquests, would answer, if sincere, as Frederick of Prussia answered, *pous faire parler de soi;*—to occupy a large space in the admiration of mankind.' Putting Mr Mill's and Mr Bentham's principles together, we might make out very easily that 'the greatest princes, the most despotical masters of human destiny,' would never abuse their power.

A man who has been long accustomed to injure people, must also have been long accustomed to do without their love, and to endure their aversion. Such a man may not miss the pleasure of popularity; for men seldom miss a pleasure which they have long denied themselves. An old tyrant does without popularity, just as an old water-drinker does without wine. But though it is perfectly true that men who, for the good of their health, have long abstained from wine, feel the want of it very little, it would be absurd to infer that men will always abstain from wine, when their health requires that they should do so. And it would be equally absurd to say, because men who have been accustomed to oppress care little for popularity, that men will therefore necessarily prefer the pleasures of oppression to those of popularity.

Then, again, a man may be accustomed to wrong people in one point, and not in another. He may care for their good opinion with regard to one point, and not with regard to another. The Regent Orleans laughed at charges of impiety, libertinism, extravagance, idleness, disgraceful promotions. But the slightest allusion to the charge of poisoning threw him into convulsions. Louis the Fifteenth braved the hatred and contempt of his subjects during many years of the most odious and imbecile misgovernment. But when a report was spread that he used human blood for his baths, he was almost driven mad by it. Surely Mr Bentham's position, 'that no man cares for the good opinion of those whom he has been accustomed to wrong,' would be objectionable, as far too sweeping and indiscriminate, even if it did not involve, as in the present case we have shown that it does, a direct begging of the question at issue.

Mr Bentham proceeds:—

Fourthly, The Edinburgh Reviewers are of opinion, that 'it might, with no small plausibility, be maintained, that, in many countries, there are two classes which, in some degree, answer to this description;' [viz.] 'that the poor compose the class which government is established to restrain; and the people of some property, the class to which the powers of government may without danger be confided. . . . ['They take great pains . . . make the law.' pp. 136-7]

This passage is alone sufficient to prove that Mr Bentham has not taken the trouble to read our article from beginning to end. We are quite sure that he would not stoop to misrepresent it. And if he had read it with any attention, he would have perceived that all this coquetry, this hesitation, this Yes and No, this saying and not saying, is simply an exercise of the undeniable right which in controversy belongs to the defensive side— to the side which proposes to establish nothing. The affirmative of the issue and the burden of the proof are with Mr Mill, not with us. We are not bound, perhaps we are not able, to show that the form of government which he recommends is bad. It is quite enough if we can show that he does not prove it to be good. In his proof, among many other flaws, is this—He says, that if men are not inclined to plunder each other, government is unnecessary, and that, if men are so inclined, kings and aristocracies will plunder the people. Now this, we say, is a fallacy. That *some* men will plunder their neighbours if they can, is a sufficient reason for the existence of governments. But it is not demonstrated that kings and aristocracies will plunder the people, unless it be true that *all* men will plunder their neighbours if they can. Men are placed in very different situations. Some have all the bodily pleasures that they desire, and many other pleasures besides, without plundering any body. Others can scarcely obtain their daily bread without plundering. It may be true, but surely it is not self-evident, that the former class is under as strong temptations to plunder as the latter. Mr Mill was therefore bound to prove it. That he has not proved it, is one of thirty or forty fatal errors in his argument. It is not necessary that we should express an opinion, or even have an opinion on the subject. Perhaps we are in a state of perfect scepticism; but what then? Are we the theory-makers? When we bring before the world a theory of government, it will be time to call upon us to offer proof at every step. At present we stand on our undoubted logical right. We concede nothing, and we deny nothing. We say to the Utilitarian theorists,—When you prove your doctrine, we will believe it, and till you prove it, we will not believe it.

Mr Bentham has quite misunderstood what we said about the French Revolution. We never alluded to that event for the purpose of proving that the poor were inclined to rob the rich. Mr Mill's principles of human nature furnished us with that part of our argument ready-made. We alluded to the French Revolution for the purpose of illustrating the effects which general spoliation produces on society, not for the purpose of showing that general spoliation will take place under a democracy. We allowed distinctly, that in the peculiar circumstances of the French monarchy, the Revolution, though accompanied by a great shock to the institution of property, was a blessing. Surely Mr Bentham will not maintain that the injury produced by the deluge of assignats and by the maximum, fell only on the emigrants,—or that there were not many emigrants who would have staid and lived peaceably under any government, if their persons and property had been secure.

We never said that the French Revolution took place, because the poor began to compare their cottages and salads with the hotels and banquets of the rich. We were not speaking about *the causes* of the Revolution, or thinking about them. This we said, and say, that if a democratic government had been established in France, the poor, when they began to compare their cottages and salads with the hotels and banquets of the rich, would, on the supposition that Mr Mill's principles are sound have plundered the rich, and repeated without provocation all

the severities and confiscations, which, at the time of the Revolution, were committed with provocation. We say that Mr
Mill's favourite form of government would, if his own views of
human nature be just, make those violent convulsions and trans-
fers of property which now rarely happen, except, as in the case
of the French Revolution, when the people are maddened by oppression, events of annual or biennial occurrence. We gave no
opinion of our own. We give none now. We say that this proposition may be proved from Mr Mill's own premises, by steps
strictly analogous to those by which he proves monarchy and
aristocracy to be bad forms of government. To say this, is not
to say that the proposition is true. For we hold both Mr Mill's
premises and his deduction to be unsound throughout.

Mr Bentham challenges us to prove from history, that the
people will plunder the rich. What does history say to Mr
Mill's doctrine, that absolute kings will always plunder their
subjects so unmercifully as to leave nothing but a bare subsistence to any except their own creatures? If experience is to be
the test, Mr Mill's theory is unsound. If Mr Mill's reasoning
à priori be sound, the people in a democracy will plunder the
rich. Let us use one weight and one measure. Let us not
throw history aside when we are proving a theory, and take it
up again when we have to refute an objection founded on the
principles of that theory.

We have not done, however, with Mr Bentham's charges
against us. ... ['Among other specimens ... a hoof behind.'
p. 147]

Why, says or sings Mr Bentham, should not women vote?
It may seem uncivil in us to turn a deaf ear to his Arcadian
warblings. But we submit, with great deference, that it is not
our business to tell him why. We fully agree with him, that
the principle of female suffrage is not so palpably absurd, that a
chain of reasoning ought to be pronounced unsound, merely because it leads to female suffrage. We say that every argument
which tells in favour of the universal suffrage of the males, tells
equally in favour of female suffrage. Mr Mill, however, wishes
to see all men vote, but says that it is unnecessary that women
should vote; and for making this distinction, *he* gives as a reason
an assertion which, in the first place, is not true, and which, in
the next place, would, if true, overset his whole theory of human

nature; namely, that the interest of the women is identical with that of the men. We side with Mr Bentham, so far at least as this, that when we join to drive the camel through the needle, he shall go through hoof and all. We at present desire to be excused from driving the camel. It is Mr Mill who leaves the hoof behind. But we should think it uncourteous to reproach him in the language which Mr Bentham, in the exercise of his paternal authority over the sect, thinks himself entitled to employ.

Another of their perverted ingenuities is, that 'they are rather inclined to think,' that it would, on the whole, be for the interest of the majority to plunder the rich; and if so, the Utilitarians will say, that the rich *ought* to be plundered. . . . ['On which it is sufficient . . . what the other was.' pp. 147–8]

We say again and again, that we are on the defensive. We do not think it necessary to prove that a quack medicine is poison. Let the vendor prove it to be sanative. We do not pretend to show that universal suffrage is an evil. Let its advocates show it to be a good. Mr Mill tells us, that if power be given for short terms to representatives elected by all the males of mature age, it will then be for the interest of those representatives to promote the greatest happiness of the greatest number. To prove this, it is necessary that he should prove three propositions; first, that the interest of such a representative body will be identical with the interest of the constituent body; secondly, that the interest of the constituent body will be identical with that of the community; thirdly, that the interest of one generation of a community is identical with that of all succeeding generations. The two first propositions Mr Mill attempts to prove, and fails. The last he does not even attempt to prove. We therefore refuse our assent to his conclusions. Is this unreasonable?

We never even dreamed, what Mr Bentham conceives us to have maintained, that it could be for the greatest happiness of *mankind*, to plunder the rich. But we are 'rather inclined to think,' though doubtingly, and with a disposition to yield to conviction, that it may be for the pecuniary interest of the majority of a single generation in a thickly-peopled country to plunder the rich. Why we are inclined to think so we will explain, whenever we send a theory of government to an

Encyclopaedia. At present we are bound to say only that we think so, and shall think so, till somebody shows us a reason for thinking otherwise.

Mr Bentham's answer to us is simple assertion. He must not think that we mean any discourtesy by meeting it with a simple denial. The fact is, that almost all the governments that have ever existed in the civilized world, have been, in part at least, monarchical and aristocratical. The first government constituted on principles approaching to those which the Utilitarians hold, was, we think, that of the United States. That the poor have never combined to plunder the rich in the governments of the old world, no more proves that they might not combine to plunder the rich under a system of universal suffrage, than the fact, that the English Kings of the House of Brunswick have not been Neros and Domitians, proves that sovereigns may safely be intrusted with absolute power. Of what the people would do in a state of perfect sovereignty, we can judge only by indications, which, though rarely of much moment in themselves, and though always suppressed with little difficulty, are yet of great significance, and resemble those by which our domestic animals sometimes remind us that they are of kin with the fiercest monsters of the forest. It would not be wise to reason from the behaviour of a dog crouching under the lash, which is the case of the Italian people, or from the behaviour of a dog pampered with the best morsels of a plentiful kitchen, which is the case of the people of America, to the behaviour of a wolf, which is nothing but a dog run wild, after a week's fast among the snows of the Pyrenees. No commotion, says Mr Bentham, was ever really produced by the wish of levelling: the wish has been put forward as a blind; but something else has been the real object. Grant all this. But why has levelling been put forward as a blind in times of commotion, to conceal the real objects of the agitators? Is it with declarations which involve 'a suicide of hope,' that men attempt to allure others? Was famine, pestilence, slavery, ever held out to attract the people? If levelling has been made a pretence for disturbances, the argument against Mr Bentham's doctrine is as strong as if it had been the real object of disturbances.

But the great objection which Mr Bentham makes to our review, still remains to be noticed.

The pith of the charge against the author of the Essays is, that he has written 'an elaborate Treatise on Government,' and 'deduced the whole science from the assumption of certain propensities of human nature.' Now, in the name of Sir Richard Birnie, and all saints, from what else *should* it be deduced? What did ever any body imagine to be the end, object, and design of government *as it ought to be*, but the same operation, on an extended scale, which that meritorious chief magistrate conducts on a limited one at Bow Street; to wit, the preventing one man from injuring another? . . . ['Imagine, then, that the Whiggery . . . pantries should be safe.' pp. 133–4]

It would, to be sure, be very absurd in a magistrate, discussing the arrangements of a police-office, to spout in the style either of our article or Mr Bentham's; but, in substance, he would proceed, if he were a man of sense, exactly as *we* recommend. He would, on being appointed to provide for the security of property in a town, study attentively the state of the town. He would learn at what places, at what times, and under what circumstances, theft and outrage were most frequent. Are the streets, he would ask, most infested with thieves at sunset, or at midnight? Are there any public places of resort which give peculiar facilities to pickpockets? Are there any districts completely inhabited by a lawless population? Which are the flash-houses, and which the shops of receivers? Having made himself master of the facts, he would act accordingly. A strong detachment of officers might be necessary for Petticoat-Lane; another for the pit entrance of Covent-Garden Theatre. Grosvenor Square and Hamilton Place would require little or no protection. Exactly thus should we reason about government. Lombardy is oppressed by tyrants; and constitutional checks, such as may produce security to the people, are required. It is, so to speak, one of the resorts of thieves, and there is great need of police-officers. Denmark resembles one of those respectable streets, in which it is scarcely necessary to station a catchpoll, because the inhabitants would at once join to seize a thief. Yet even in such a street, we should wish to see an officer appear now and then, as his occasional superintendence would render the security more complete. And even Denmark, we think, would be better off under a constitutional form of government.

Mr Mill proceeds like a director of police, who, without asking a single question about the state of his district, should give his orders thus:—'My maxim is, that every man will take what he can. Every man in London would be a thief, but for the thief-takers. This is an undeniable principle of human nature. Some of my predecessors have wasted their time in enquiring about particular pawnbrokers, and particular alehouses. Experience is altogether divided. Of people placed in exactly the same situation, I see that one steals, and that another would sooner burn his hand off. *Therefore* I trust to the laws of human nature alone, and pronounce all men thieves alike. Let every body, high and low, be watched. Let Townsend take particular care that the Duke of Wellington does not steal the silk hand-kerchief of the lord in waiting at the levee. A person has lost a watch. Go to Lord Fitzwilliam and search him for it: He is as great a receiver of stolen goods as Ikey Solomons himself. Don't tell me about his rank, and character, and fortune. He is a man; and a man does not change his nature when he is called a lord. Either men will steal or they will not steal. If they will not, why do I sit here? If they will, his Lordship must be a thief.' The Whiggery of Bow Street would perhaps rise up against this wisdom. Would Mr Bentham think that the Whiggery of Bow Street was in the wrong?

We blamed Mr Mill for deducing his theory of government from the principles of human nature. 'In the name of Sir Richard Birnie, and all saints,' cries Mr Bentham, 'from what else should it be deduced?' In spite of this solemn adjuration, we shall venture to answer Mr Bentham's question by another. How does he arrive at those principles of human nature from which he proposes to deduce the science of government? We think that we may venture to put an answer into his mouth; for in truth there is but one possible answer. He will say—By experience. But what is the extent of this experience? Is it an experience which includes experience of the conduct of men intrusted with the powers of government; or is it exclusive of that experience? If it includes experience of the manner in which men act when intrusted with the powers of government, then those principles of human nature from which the science of government is to be deduced, can only be known after going through that inductive process by which we propose to arrive at the science of government. Our knowledge of human nature, instead of being prior in order to our knowledge of the science of government, will be posterior to it. And it would be correct to say, that by means of the science of government, and of other kindred sciences—the science of education, for example, which falls under exactly the same principle—we arrive at the science of human nature.

If, on the other hand, we are to deduce the theory of government from principles of human nature, in arriving at which principles we have not taken into the account the manner in which men act when invested with the powers of government, then those principles must be defective. They have not been formed by a sufficiently copious induction. We are reasoning from what a man does in one situation, to what he will do in another. Sometimes we may be quite justified in reasoning thus. When we have no means of acquiring information about the particular case before us, we are compelled to resort to cases which bear some resemblance to it. But the most satisfactory course is to obtain information about the particular case; and whenever this can be obtained, it ought to be obtained. When first the yellow fever broke out, a physician might be justified in treating it as he had been accustomed to treat those complaints which, on the whole, had the most symptoms in common with it. But what should we think of a physician who should now tell us that he deduced his treatment of yellow fever from the general theory of pathology? Surely we should ask him, Whether, in constructing his theory of pathology, he had, or had not, taken into the account the facts which had been ascertained respecting the yellow fever? If he had, then it would be more correct to say, that he had arrived at the principles of pathology partly by his experience of cases of yellow fever, than that he had deduced his treatment of yellow fever from the principles of pathology. If he had not, he should not prescribe for us. If we had the yellow fever, we should prefer a man who had never treated any cases but cases of yellow fever, to a man who had walked the hospitals of London and Paris for years, but who knew nothing of our particular disease.

Let Lord Bacon speak for us: 'Inductionem censemus eam esse demonstrandi formam, quae sensum tuetur, et naturam premit, et operibus imminet, ac fere immiscetur. Itaque ordo quoque demonstrandi plane invertitur. Adhuc enim res ita geri consuevit, ut a sensu et particularibus primo loco ad maxime generalia advoletur, tanquam ad polos fixos, circa quos disputationes vertantur; ab illis coetera, per media, deriventur; viâ certe compendiariâ, sed praecipiti, ed ad naturam imperviâ, ad disputationes proclivi et accommodatâ. At, secundum nos, axiomata continenter et gradatim excitantur, ut non, nisi postremo loco, ad maxime generalia veniatur.'[1] Can any words more exactly describe the political reasonings of Mr Mill than those in which Lord Bacon thus describes the logomachies of the schoolmen? Mr Mill springs at once to a general principle of the widest extent, and from that general principle deduces syllogistically every thing which is included in it. We say with Bacon—'non, nisi postremo loco, ad maxime generalia veniatur.' In the present enquiry, the science of human nature is the 'maxime generale.' To this the Utilitarian rushes at once, and from this he deduces a hundred sciences. But the true philosopher, the inductive reasoner, travels up to it slowly, through those hundred sciences, of which the science of government is one.

As we have lying before us that incomparable volume, the noblest and most useful of all the works of the human reason, the Novum Organum, we will transcribe a few lines, in which the Utilitarian philosophy is pourtrayed to the life.

Syllogismus ad *principia* scientiarum non adhibetur, ad media axiomata frustra adhibetur, cum sit subtilitati naturae longe impar. Assensum itaque constringit, non res. Syllogismus ex propositionibus constat, propositiones ex verbis, verba notionum tesserae sunt. Itaque si notiones ipsae, id quod basis rei est, confusae sint, et temere a rebus abstractae, nihil in iis quae superstruuntur est firmitudinis. Itaque spes est una in Inductione vera. In notionibus nil sani est, nec in Logicis nec in physicis. Non substantia, non qualitas, agere, pati, ipsum esse, bonae notiones sunt; multo minus

---

[1] 'I consider induction to be that form of demonstration which upholds the senses, and closes with nature, and is close to, and almost takes part in, production of results.

'Hence it follows that the order of demonstration is likewise inverted. For hitherto the proceeding has been to fly at once from the senses and particulars up to the most general propositions, as certain fixed poles for the argument to turn upon, and from these to derive the rest by middle terms: a short way, no doubt, but precipitate; and one which will never lead to nature, though it offers an easy and ready way to disputation. Now my plan is to proceed regularly and gradually from one axiom to another, so that the most general are not reached till the last.' Bacon, *Novum Organum,* ed. Fowler (2nd edition, 1889), pp. 172–3.

grave, leve, densum, tenue, humidum, siccum, generatio, corruptio, attrahere, fugare, elementum, materia, forma, et id genus, sed omnes phantasticae et male terminatae.'[2]

Substitute for the 'substantia,' the 'generatio,' the 'corruptio,' the 'elementum,' the 'materia' of the old schoolmen, Mr Mill's pain, pleasure, interest, power, objects of desire,—and the words of Bacon will seem to suit the current year as well as the beginning of the seventeenth century.

We have now gone through the objections that Mr Bentham makes to our article; and we submit ourselves on all the charges to the judgment of the public.

The rest of Mr Bentham's article consists of an exposition of the Utilitarian principle, or, as he decrees that it shall be called, the 'greatest happiness principle.' He seems to think that we have been assailing it. We never said a syllable against it. We spoke slightingly of the Utilitarian sect, as we thought of them, and think of them; but it was not for holding this doctrine that we blamed them. In attacking them we no more meant to attack the 'greatest happiness principle,' than when we say that Mahometanism is a false religion, we mean to deny the unity of God, which is the first article of the Mahometan creed;—no more than Mr Bentham, when he sneers at the Whigs, means to blame them for denying the divine right of kings. We reasoned throughout our article on the supposition, that the end of government was to produce the greatest happiness to mankind.

Mr Bentham gives an account of the manner in which he arrived at the discovery of the 'greatest happiness principle.' He then proceeds to describe the effects which, as he conceives, that discovery is producing, in language so rhetorical and ardent, that, if it had been written by any other person, a genuine

---

[2] 'The syllogism is not applied to the first principles of sciences, and is applied in vain to intermediate axioms; being no match for the subtlety of nature. It commands assent therefore to the proposition, but does not take hold of the thing. The syllogism consists of propositions, propositions consist of words, words are symbols of notions. Therefore if the notions themselves (which is the root of the matter) are confused and over-hastily abstracted from the facts, there can be no firmness in the superstructure. Our only hope therefore lies in a true induction.

'There is no soundness in our notions whether logical or physical. Substance, Quality, Action, Passion, Existence itself, are not sound notions: much less are Heavy, Light, Dense, Rare, Moist, Dry, Generation, Corruption, Attraction, Repulsion, Element, Matter, Form, and the like; but all are fantastical and ill defined.' Fowler ed., pp. 198–9.

Utilitarian would certainly have thrown down the book in disgust . . . ['The only rivals . . . gift of common sense.' pp. 141–3]

Mr Bentham's discovery does not, as we think we shall be able to show, approach in importance to that of gravitation, to which he compares it. At all events, Mr Bentham seems to us to act much as Sir Isaac Newton would have done, if he had gone about boasting that he was the first person who taught bricklayers not to jump off scaffolds and break their legs.

Does Mr Bentham profess to hold out any new motive which may induce men to promote the happiness of the species to which they belong? Not at all. He distinctly admits that, if he is asked why governments should attempt to produce the greatest possible happiness, he can give no answer. . . . ['The real answer . . . mutton if they can.' pp. 140–1]

The principle of Mr Bentham, if we understand it, is this, that mankind ought to act so as to produce their greatest happiness. The word *ought*, he tells us, has no meaning, unless it be used with reference to some interest. But the interest of a man is synonymous with his greatest happiness:—and therefore to say that a man *ought* to do a thing, is to say that it is for his greatest happiness to do it. And to say that mankind *ought* to act so as to produce their greatest happiness, is to say that the greatest happiness is the greatest happiness—and this is all!

Does Mr Bentham's principle tend to make any man wish for any thing for which he would not have wished, or do any thing which he would not have done, if the principle had never been heard of? If not, it is an utterly useless principle. Now, every man pursues his own happiness or interest—call it which you will. If his happiness coincides with the happiness of the species, then, whether he ever heard of the 'greatest happiness principle' or not, he will, to the best of his knowledge and ability, attempt to produce the greatest happiness of the species. But, if what he thinks his happiness be inconsistent with the greatest happiness of mankind, will this new principle convert him to another frame of mind? Mr Bentham himself allows, as we have seen, that he can give no reason why a man should promote the greatest happiness of others, if their greatest happiness be inconsistent with what he thinks his own. We should very much like to know how the Utilitarian principle would run, when reduced to one plain imperative proposition. Will it run thus—pursue your own happiness? This is superfluous. Every man pursues it, according to his light, and always has pursued it, and always must pursue it. To say that a man has done any thing, is to say that he thought it for his happiness to do it. Will the principle run thus—pursue the greatest happiness of mankind, whether it be your own greatest happiness or not? This is absurd and impossible, and Mr Bentham himself allows it to be so. But if the principle be not stated in one of these two ways, we cannot imagine how it is to be stated at all. Stated in one of these ways, it is an identical proposition,—true, but utterly barren of consequences. Stated in the other way, it is a contradiction in terms. Mr Bentham has distinctly declined the absurdity. Are we then to suppose that he adopts the truism?

There are thus, it seems, two great truths which the Utilitarian philosophy is to communicate to mankind—two truths which are to produce a revolution in morals, in laws, in governments, in literature, in the whole system of life. The first of these is speculative; the second is practical. The speculative truth is, that the greatest happiness is the greatest happiness. The practical rule is very simple, for it imports merely that men should never omit, when they wish for any thing, to wish for it, or when they do any thing, to do it! It is a great comfort to us to think, that we readily assented to the former of these great doctrines as soon as it was stated to us; and that we have long endeavoured, as far as human frailty would permit, to conform to the latter in our practice. We are, however, inclined to suspect, that the calamities of the human race have been owing less to their not knowing that happiness was happiness, than to their not knowing how to obtain it—less to their neglecting to do what they did, than to their not being able to do what they wished, or not wishing to do what they ought.

Thus frivolous, thus useless is this philosophy,—'controversiarum ferax, operum effoeta, ad garriendum prompta, ad generandum invalida.'[3] The humble mechanic who discovers some slight improvement in the construction of safety lamps or steam-vessels, does more for the happiness of mankind than the 'magnificent principle,' as Mr Bentham calls it, will do in ten thousand years. The mechanic teaches us how we may, in a small

---

[3] 'It is fruitful of controversies but barren of works; it can talk but it cannot generate.' Fowler ed., p. 162.

degree, be better off than we were. The Utilitarian advises us, with great pomp, to be as well off as we can.

The doctrine of a moral sense may be very unphilosophical, but we do not think that it can be proved to be pernicious. Men did not entertain certain desires and aversions because they believed in a moral sense, but they gave the name of moral sense to a feeling which they found in their minds, however it came there. If they had given it no name at all, it would still have influenced their actions; and it will not be very easy to demonstrate that it has influenced their actions the more, because they have called it the moral sense. The theory of the original contract is a fiction, and a very absurd fiction; but in practice it meant, what the 'greatest happiness principle,' if ever it becomes a watchword of political warfare, will mean—that is to say, whatever served the turn of those who used it. Both the one expression and the other sound very well in debating clubs; but in the real conflicts of life, our passions and interests bid them stand aside and know their place. The 'greatest happiness principle' has always been latent under the words, social contract, justice, benevolence, patriotism, liberty, and so forth, just as far as it was for the happiness, real or imagined of those who used these words to promote the greatest happiness of mankind. And of this we may be sure, that the words 'greatest happiness' will never, in any man's mouth, mean more than the greatest happiness of others which is consistent with what he thinks his own. The project of mending a bad world, by teaching people to give new names to old things, reminds us of Walter Shandy's scheme for compensating the loss of his son's nose by christening him Trismegistus. What society wants is a new motive— not a new cant. If Mr Bentham can find out any argument yet undiscovered which may induce men to pursue the general happiness, he will indeed be a great benefactor to our species. But those whose happiness is identical with the general happiness, are even now promoting the general happiness to the very best of their power and knowledge; and Mr Bentham himself confesses that he has no means of persuading those whose happiness is not identical with the general happiness, to act upon his principle. Is not this, then, darkening counsel by words without knowledge? If the only fruit of the 'magnificent principle' is to be, that the oppressors and pilferers of the next generation are to talk of seeking the greatest happiness of the greatest number, just as the same class of men have talked in our time of seeking to uphold the Protestant Constitution—just as they talked under Anne of seeking the good of the Church, and under Cromwell of seeking the Lord—where is the gain? Is not every great question already enveloped in a sufficiently dark cloud of unmeaning words? Is it so difficult for a man to cant some one or more of the good old English cants which his father and grandfather canted before him, that he must learn, in the schools of the Utilitarians, a new sleight of tongue, to make fools clap and wise men sneer? Let our countrymen keep their eyes on the neophytes of this sect, and see whether we turn out to be mistaken in the prediction which we now hazard. It will before long be found, we prophesy, that, as the corruption of a dunce is the generation of an Utilitarian, so is the corruption of an Utilitarian the generation of a jobber.

The most elevated station that the 'greatest happiness principle' is ever likely to attain is this, that it may be a fashionable phrase among newspaper writers and members of parliament— that it may succeed to the dignity which has been enjoyed by the 'original contract,' by the 'constitution of 1688,' and other expressions of the same kind. We do not apprehend that it is a less flexible cant than those which have preceded it, or that it will less easily furnish a pretext for any design for which a pretext may be required. The 'original contract' meant in the Convention Parliament the co-ordinate authority of the Three Estates. If there were to be a radical insurrection to-morrow, the 'original contract' would stand just as well for annual parliaments and universal suffrage. The 'Glorious Constitution,' again, has meant every thing in turn: the Habeas Corpus Act, the Suspension of the Habeas Corpus Act, the Test Act, the Repeal of the Test Act. There has not been for many years a single important measure which has not been unconstitutional with its opponents, and which its supporters have not maintained to be agreeable to the true spirit of the constitution. Is it easier to ascertain what is for the greatest happiness of the human race than what is the constitution of England? If not, the 'greatest happiness principle' will be what the 'principles of the constitutution' are, a thing to be appealed to by every body, and understood by every body in the sense which suits him best.

It will mean cheap bread, dear bread, free trade, protecting duties, annual parliaments, septennial parliaments, universal suffrage, Old Sarum, trial by jury, martial law—every thing, in short, good, bad, or indifferent, of which any person, from rapacity or from benevolence, chooses to undertake the defence. It will mean six and eight-pence with the attorney, tithes at the rectory, and game-laws at the manor house. The statute of Uses, in appearance the most sweeping legislative reform in our history, was said to have produced no other effect than that of adding three words to a conveyance. The universal admission of Mr Bentham's great principle would, as far as we can see, produce no other effect than that those orators who, while waiting for a meaning, gain time (like bankers paying in sixpences during a run) by uttering words that mean nothing, would substitute 'the greatest happiness,' or rather, as the longer phrase, 'the greatest happiness of the greatest number,' for, 'under existing circumstances,'—'now that I am on my legs,'—and 'Mr Speaker, I, for one, am free to say.' In fact, principles of this sort resemble those forms which are sold by law-stationers, with blanks for the names of parties, and for the special circumstances of every case—mere customary headings and conclusions, which are equally at the command of the most honest and of the most unrighteous claimant. It is on the filling up that every thing depends.

The 'greatest happiness principle' of Mr Bentham is included in the Christian morality; and, to our thinking, it is there exhibited in an infinitely more sound and philosophical form, than in the Utilitarian speculations. For in the New Testament it is neither an identical proposition, nor a contradiction in terms; and, as laid down by Mr Bentham, it must be either the one or the other. 'Do as you would be done by: Love your neighbour as yourself;' these are the precepts of Jesus Christ. Understood in an enlarged sense, these precepts are, in fact, a direction to every man to promote the greatest happiness of the greatest number. But this direction would be utterly unmeaning, as it actually is in Mr Bentham's philosophy, unless it were accompanied by a sanction. In the Christian scheme, accordingly, it is accompanied by a sanction of immense force. To a man whose greatest happiness in this world is inconsistent with the greatest happiness of the greatest number, is held out the prospect of an infinite happiness hereafter, from which he excludes himself by wronging his fellow-creatures here.

This is practical philosophy, as practical as that on which penal legislation is founded. A man is told to do something which otherwise he would not do, and is furnished with a new motive for doing it. Mr Bentham has no new motive to furnish his disciples with. He has talents sufficient to effect any thing that can be effected. But to induce men to act without an inducement is too much, even for him. He should reflect that the whole vast world of morals cannot be moved, unless the mover can obtain some stand for his engines beyond it. He acts as Archimedes would have done, if he had attempted to move the earth by a lever fixed on the earth. The action and reaction neutralize each other. The artist labours, and the world remains at rest. Mr Bentham can only tell us to do something which we have always been doing, and should still have continued to do, if we had never heard of the 'greatest happiness principle'— or else to do something which we have no conceivable motive for doing, and therefore shall not do. Mr Bentham's principle is at best no more than the golden rule of the Gospel without its sanction. Whatever evils, therefore, have existed in societies in which the authority of the Gospel is recognized, may, *à fortiori*, as it appears to us, exist in societies in which the Utilitarian principle is recognised. We do not apprehend that it is more difficult for a tyrant or a persecutor to persuade himself and others, that in putting to death those who oppose his power, or differ from his opinions, he is pursuing 'the greatest happiness,' than that he is doing as he would be done by. But religion gives him a motive for doing as he would be done by: And Mr Bentham furnishes him with no motive to induce him to promote the general happiness. If, on the other hand, Mr Bentham's principle means only that every man should pursue his own greatest happiness, he merely asserts what every body knows, and recommends what every body does.

It is not upon this 'greatest happiness principle' that the fame of Mr Bentham will rest. He has not taught people to pursue their own happiness; for that they always did. He has not taught them to promote the happiness of others, at the expense of their own; for that they will not and cannot do. But he has taught them *how*, in some most important points, to promote their own happiness; and if his school had emulated him as successfully in this respect, as in the trick of passing off truisms for discoveries, the name of Benthamite would have been no word for the scoffer. But few of those who consider themselves as in a more especial manner his followers, have any thing in common with him but his faults. The whole science of Juris-prudence is his. He has done much for Political Economy; but we are not aware, that in either department any improvement has been made by members of his sect. He discovered truths; all that *they* have done has been to make those truths unpopular. He investigated the philosophy of law; he could teach them only to snarl at lawyers.

We entertain no apprehensions of danger to the institutions of this country from the Utilitarians. Our fears are of a different kind. We dread the odium and discredit of their alliance. We wish to see a broad and clear line drawn between the judicious friends of practical reform, and a sect which, having derived all its influence from the countenance which they have im-prudently bestowed upon it, hates them with the deadly hatred of ingratitude. There is not, and we firmly believe that there never was, in this country, a party so unpopular. They have already made the science of Political Economy—a science of vast importance to the welfare of nations,—an object of disgust to the majority of the community. The question of Parliamen-tary Reform will share the same fate, if once an association be formed in the public mind between Reform and Utilitarianism.

We bear no enmity to any member of the sect: and for Mr Bentham, we entertain very high admiration. We know, that among his followers there are some well-intentioned men, and some men of talents: But we cannot say that we think the logic on which they pride themselves likely to improve their heads, or the scheme of morality which they have adopted likely to improve their hearts. Their theory of morals, however, well de-serves an article to itself; and perhaps, on some future occasion, we may discuss it more fully than time and space at present allow.

The preceding article was written, and was actually in types, when a letter from Mr Bentham appeared in the newspapers, importing, that 'though he had furnished the Westminster Review with some *memoranda* respecting "the greatest happiness principle," he had nothing to do with the remarks on our former article.' We are truly happy to find that this illustrious man had so small a share in a performance which, for his sake, we have treated with far greater lenity than it deserved. The mistake, however, does not in the least affect any part of our arguments; and we have therefore thought it unnecessary to cancel or cast anew any of the foregoing pages. Indeed, we are not sorry that the world should see how respectfully we were disposed to treat a great man, even when we considered him as the author of a very weak and very unfair attack on ourselves. We wish, however, to intimate to the actual writer of that attack, that our civilities were intended for the author of the 'Preuves Judiciaires,' and the 'Defence of Usury'—and not for him. We cannot conclude, indeed, without expressing a wish—though we fear it has but little chance of reaching Mr Bentham—that he would endeavour to find better editors for his compositions. If M. Dumont had not been a *rédacteur* of a different description from some of his successors, Mr Bentham would never have attained the distinction of even giving his name to a sect.

VI

Edinburgh Review and the 'Greatest Happiness Principle'

Westminster Review, vol. xxii (October 1829), Article xvi.

WHEN a thoughtless little boy makes an unadvised assault upon the venerable father of the flock, and is rolled in the dust for his reward, he runs to his mamma and complains of a 'very unfair attack upon ourselves.' Of this kind has been the deportment of the Edinburgh Reviewers, in pursuance of their inconsiderate molestation of Mr. Bentham and his followers. Nor does their ill-humour seem to have been diminished by discovering, that there had been no occasion for the principal to appear at all,— that he can do things of this kind by his journeymen.* They took for granted that the prophet must come forth, and curse them by his gods; instead of which, one of his disciples poured out the prophetic wash-pot on the heads of the assailants. As is usual on such occasions, they give more voice to their irritation than is politic or wise. They stand pointing to the unlucky inverter of earthen-ware, and call the neighbourhood to witness that 'their civilities were not meant for *him*.' It is quite a mistake of their own, if they think they have been civil to any body. They began with being petulant, and ended with being silly. They walked out of the common path of courtesy, to mock at an individual whom it now suits them to allow to be 'illustrious' and 'great;' and if they have received a rebutter for their pains, they must ascribe it to the fatality which prompted them to folly, taking advantage of the absence of their good genius in the person of their *bonne*.

It matters very little whether the blue rag or the 'whity-brown' is last upon the field; but it matters very much that an opportunity should not be lost of exposing the sleights of the *aristocrats en carmagnole*, who pretend to court the people when they have any thing to gain by it, and spurn them as 'the ranks and the rabble'† when they have not. To make this exposure

* If by 'puffs and placards' the Edinburgh reviewers meant the advertisement in the newspapers and the booksellers bills into which it was copied, the description of the Article they allude to ran as follows, which certainly announces nothing like what they have assumed.
'XVI. GREATEST HAPPINESS PRINCIPLE DEVELOPED.—With MR. BENTHAM's latest improvements, now published for the first time: and an Answer to the attacks of the Edinburgh Review.'
† —'as we have no heroes and statesmen chosen from the ranks and the rabble,'— *Edinburgh Review, No. XCVIII*, p. 333.
These are the men who profess to do everything '*for* the people,' nothing '*by* the people;' and who are at this moment pushing a not over-wise government into persecution of the press. If Tories are to be put down for speaking their minds, there

was the object of the rebutter; and not to determine whether the Essay on Government was perfect. In fact it was expressly said, that it contained much that was right, and something that was wrong; and that the reviewers had attacked the first, and let alone the other. The design was not to prove the original a master-piece of demonstration, but the comment a master-piece of insincerity.

The first extract given by the Edinburgh Reviewers from the Essay was an insulated passage, purposely despoiled of what had preceded and what followed. The author had been observing, that 'some profound and benevolent investigators of human affairs had adopted the conclusion, that of all the possible forms of government, absolute monarchy is the best.' This is what the reviewers have omitted at the beginning. He then adds, as in the extract, that 'Experience, *if we look only at the outside of the facts*, appears to be divided on this subject;' there are Caligulas in one place, and kings of Denmark in another. 'As the surface of history affords, therefore, no certain principle of decision, *we must go beyond the surface*, and penetrate to the springs within.' This is what the reviewers have omitted at the end. The author's argument was, that when facts are not such that the causes are determinable by simple inspection, it is necessary to go deeper, and look for some more complex causes that may account for the whole. And the conclusion to which the author came was the very reasonable one, that there was a general principle, and when it appeared not to act, it was because it was overpowered by some force in an opposite direction. To take an instance in natural phenomena, there are many bodies that fall towards the earth, but there are some that ascend and go from it. From simple inspection of these facts, therefore, no conclusion can be derived. But by looking a little deeper into the experience of mankind it is discoverable, that all bodies have a tendency to fall, and when they do not it is because this tendency is over-

---

is an end of the liberty of speech for all and every body. There have been great soldiers in England, who scorned to flinch at paper bullets thus. If somebody has said the Guards marched three deep upon the pavement and we have a military government, why is not the corporal called to prove that they did not? No government prosecutes, except under the impression of there being something it cannot confute;—with the single further reservation, of being put upon it by somebody who wants to take the opportunity of depressing those he is not a match for in fair debate.

powered by another force. The conclusion which the author in like manner deduced from experience was, that absolute monarchy tends to misgovernment, and would always arrive at it, *'if checks did not operate in the way of prevention.'** What the reviewers object to, is the going beyond the surface. Because an inference cannot be derived from the outside of the facts, they desire to have no inference at all. They have a wish that the thing should be unsettled; because they see no prospect of a settlement that accords with their interests. Whether the inference deduced is right, is a matter for after consideration; what is plain in the present stage is, that the objections of the reviewers are without foundation. *'Mr. Mill gave it as a reason for deducing the theory of government from the general laws of human nature, that the king of Denmark was not Caligula.'* A natural philosopher gave it as a reason for deducing the theory of moving bodies from the general laws of external nature, that some move upwards and some downwards. 'This,' say the Edinburgh reviewers, 'we said, and still say, was absurd.'

When it was said by Mr. Mill that the people of Denmark resolved that their king should be 'absolute,' it clearly meant, that he should be absolute in form. When it was said by the Westminster Review that the king of Denmark 'is not a despot,' it as clearly meant, that though absolute in form, there was a virtual check on his being despotic in practice. It would be a foolish difficulty to insist upon referring to Mr. Bentham.

When it was said that there was in Denmark a balanced contest between the king and the nobility, what was said was, that there was a balanced contest but it did not last. It was balanced till something put an end to the balance; and so is every thing else. That such a balance will not last, is precisely what Mr. Mill had demonstrated.

When Mr. Mill asserted that it cannot be for the interest of either the monarchy or the aristocracy to combine with the democracy, it is plain he did not assert that if the monarchy and aristocracy were in doubtful contest with each other, they would not either of them accept of the assistance of the democracy. He spoke of their taking the side of the democracy; not of their allowing the democracy to take side with themselves.

Mr. Mill never asserted *'that under no despotic government does*

* Essay on Government. Supp. to Encycl. Brit. Vol. IV, p. 496. [Above p. 68].

any human being, except the tools of the sovereign, possess more than the necessaries of life, and that the most intense degree of terror is kept up by constant cruelty.' He said that absolute power leads to such results, 'by infallible sequence, where power over a community is attained, *and nothing checks.*'* The critic on the Mount never made a more palpable misquotation.

The spirit of this misquotation runs through every part of the reply of the Edinburgh Review that relates to the Essay on Government; and is repeated in as many shapes as the Roman pork. The whole description of 'Mr. Mill's argument against despotism,'—including the illustration from right-angled triangles and the square of the hypothenuse,—is founded on this invention of saying what an author has not said, and leaving unsaid what he has.

The reply to the argument against 'saturation,' supplies its own answer. The reason why it is of no use to try to 'saturate,' is precisely what the Edinburgh reviewers have suggested,—'*that there is no limit to the number of thieves.*' There are the thieves, and the thieves cousins,—with their men-servants, their maid-servants, and their little ones, to the fortieth generation. It is true that 'a man cannot become a king or a member of the aristocracy whenever he chuses;' but if there is to be no limit to the depredators except their own inclination to increase and multiply, the situation of those who are to suffer is as wretched as it needs be. It is impossible to define what *are* 'corporal pleasures.' A duchess of Cleveland was a 'corporal pleasure.' The most disgraceful period in the history of any nation,—that of the Restoration,—presents an instance of the length to which it is possible to go in an attempt to 'saturate' with pleasures of this kind.†

When the Edinburgh reviewers declare that though 'they said there is a *certain* check to the rapacity and cruelty of men in their desire of the good opinion of others, they never said it was *sufficient,*'—it may be left to the public opinion whether this is not simple quibbling. What is a *certain* check, but a check that is sufficient to a certain extent for a certain purpose?

---

* Essay on Government. Supp. to Encycl. Brit. Vol. IV. p. 495. [Above p. 67].

† It was found on one occasion, that nearly half the money that had been voted for the Dutch war, had gone to the 'corporal pleasures' of the most religious and gracious king.—*See Pepys's Diary*, A.D. 1666, *Sept.* 23 *and Oct.* 10.

'*The argument in favour of kings and nobles is this:—they will not wrong the people, because they care for the good opinion of the people.*' A man will not beat his wife, because he cares for the good opinion of his wife.—But a man who beats his wife, cares nothing for her good opinion. Let experience determine, whether there are men who beat their wives or not.

Nobody ever said that 'men will necessarily prefer the pleasures of oppression to those of popularity.' What was said was, that the desire of popularity is no sufficient security against oppression.

That no man cares for the good opinion of those he has been accustomed to wrong, instead of being a 'too sweeping position', is almost a truism;—for if he cared for their good opinion, it is plain he would cease to wrong.

'*That some men will plunder their neighbours if they can, is a sufficient reason for the existence of governments. But it is not demonstrated that kings and aristocracies will plunder the people, unless it be true that all men will plunder their neighbours if they can.* And thence it is inferred, that if it is held proved that kings and aristocracies will plunder the people, it follows that in a democracy men will plunder their neighbours. The argument is, that because the aristocracy will plunder the people, the *people* will plunder the people. There is no congruity between the things produced as similar.

'*They never alluded to the French Revolution for the purpose of proving that the poor were inclined to rob the rich.*'—They only said, 'as soon as the poor *again* began to compare their cottages and salads with the hotels and banquets of the rich, there would have been another scramble for property, another general confiscation,' &c. It is denied as before, that they *ever* compared, —that there *ever* was either a general confiscation or a scramble for property at all.

The fallacy that '*if Mr. Mill's reasoning à priori be sound, the people in a democracy will plunder the rich,*' depends on omitting the qualifying clause '*if nothing checks.*' History and experience prove that the love of individuals for property is always sufficient to unite a sufficient number of individuals to prevent the pillage of the rich. History and experience prove, that the love of individuals for property is very generally insufficient to prevent the pillage of the poor.

The assertion—or intimation—or inclination to think,—that 'it would on the whole be for the interest of the majority to plunder the rich,' was never met by a *'simple assertion.'* It was met by the argument, that such an act would amount to a declaration that nobody should be rich, and that as all men desire to be rich, it would involve the destruction of their own hopes, and therefore would not be attempted. It may be referred to the common judgment of mankind, whether this is not the principle which makes ninety-nine men out of a hundred abstain from picking pockets, and discountenance it in others. Some perplexity is attempted to be got up, between the interest of the existing generation and the interest of future ones. Men do not set themselves against picking pockets for the love of future generations, but of their own.

What was said in the Westminster Review on the subject of 'levelling,' does not appear to have been understood. It was not stated that 'the wish has been put forward as a blind,' on the part of the people, to conceal some other design; but that 'levelling is brought forward as the blind' by the accusers of the people, to conceal the fact that the real cause of the commotion was the desire to escape from oppression.

It was never said, that there was no difference between the practical quantity of theft in different places; but 'that numbers of men had a propensity to thieving, and the business of the officers was to catch them.' The mis-statement is a branch of the suppression of all mention of the check. By putting the extract from the Edinburgh Review into the mouth of the Whiggery of Bow-street, it was intended to show that all this *verbiage* was nothing but what every body knew, and every body acted upon;—that it was precisely by the operations described, that men knew there were thieves, and to watch them was the way to hinder them;—and that the wordy enumeration was brought there only to puzzle the question, and make a diversion from the truth. The aim and object of the Edinburgh reviewers was to prove, 'that the theory of government is to be deduced from experience,' which is exactly the quarter where Mr. Mill had looked for it. They will perhaps blush at the idea of having meant so much; but, with characteristic policy, they have inserted their meaning in their postscript.*

* Ed. Rev. No. XCVIII. Index p. 542; at the end of the article *Mill.*

The quotations from Lord Bacon are misapplications, such as any body may make to any thing he dislikes. There is no more resemblance between pain, pleasure, motives &c., and *substantia, generatio, corruptio, elementum, materia,*—than between lines, angles, magnitudes &c., and the same.

The Edinburgh reviewers *'never said a syllable against the "greatest happiness principle;"*—only they say that it is good for nothing. They never meant to deny it, any more than *'to deny the unity of God;'* only the unity is a truism of which nobody can make any use. All that they have established is, that they do not understand it. Instead of the truism of the Whigs, 'that the greatest happiness is the greatest happiness,'—what Mr. Bentham had demonstrated, or at all events had laid such foundations that there was no trouble in demonstrating, was that the greatest happiness of the individual was in the long run to be obtained by pursuing the greatest happiness of the aggregate.* It was an extension of the ancient proverb, that honesty is the best policy. There are men who think honesty is *not* the best policy in private life, and who think in the same way with relation to politics and international law; and the corollary from Mr. Bentham's principles demonstrated that these are the fools, and the others are the wise. The inefficient attempts which had been made for the explanation of moral and political phenomena, were superseded by a clearer clue, in the same manner as the epicycles and *abhorret vacuum* of the early ages were swept away by the discovery of the principle of gravitation. The comparison to gravitation is therefore accurate and just.†

'Does Mr. Bentham profess to hold out any new motive which may induce men to promote the happiness of the species to which they belong?

---

* See 'Introduction to the Principles of Morals and Legislation.' Chap. XVII. Sect. VI and VII.

† 'Some, indeed, may imagine, that there was no such extraordinary merit as is generally supposed even in the grand conjecture of Newton, and that it amounted, after all, merely to the application of a law to the movements of the heavenly bodies, which was already known to affect at least every body in the immediate neighbourhood of the earth. But these things are only simple after they are explained. Slight and transparent as we may think the veil to have been which covered the truths alluded to, and others of a similar nature, immediately before they were detected, it is yet an unquestionable fact, that this veil had been sufficient to conceal them, for thousands of years, from the observation of all the world.'— *Library of Entertaining Knowledge,* Vol. iii. Part I. p. 9.

Not at all.'—The motive which Mr. Bentham's principle holds
out, is the same as the motive to personal honesty; namely, that
the conduct which leads to the greatest happiness of the
aggregate, is in the end the soundest policy for the individual.
To those who have not found this out, such a motive is a 'new
motive.'

'*He distinctly admits that, if he is asked why governments should
attempt to produce the greatest possible happiness, he can give no answer.*'
—Nothing of the kind will be admitted at all. In the passage
thus selected to be tacked to the other, the question started was
concerning 'the object of government;' in which government
was spoken of as an operation, not as any thing that is capable of
feeling pleasure or pain. In this sense it is true enough, that
ought is not predicable of governments. *Other men*, only meant
men who are suffering from the operation, in contradistinction
to those who are conducting it. At the same time the double
meaning of the word government was not got clear of without
confusion. It is certain that the individual operators in any
government, if they were thoroughly intelligent and entered into
a perfect calculation of all existing chances, would seek for their
own happiness in the promotion of the general; which brings
them, if they knew it, under Mr. Bentham's rule. The mistake
of supposing the contrary, lies in confounding criminals who
have had the luck to escape punishment, with those who have
the risk still before them. Suppose, for instance, a member of
the House of Commons were at this moment to debate within
himself, whether it would be for his ultimate happiness to begin,
according to his ability, to misgovern. If he could be sure of
being as lucky as some that are dead and gone, there might be
difficulty in finding him an answer. But he is *not* sure; and never
can be, till he is dead. He does not know that he is not close
upon the moment, when misgovernment such as he is tempted
to contemplate, will be made a terrible example of. It is not fair
to pick out the instance of the thief that has died unhanged.
The question is whether thieving is at this moment an advisable
trade to begin, with all the possibilities of hanging not got over.
This is the spirit of Mr. Bentham's principle; and if there is any
thing opposed to it in any former statement, it may be corrected
by the present. But all this only proves that the members of a
government would do well if they were all-wise, or had that

perfect apprehension of all the risks they run, which is lacking in the thief. But the whole of human experience proves, that they are *not* all-wise; but on the contrary do invariably sacrifice a certain portion of contingent safety to the prospect of present gain, in the hope that punishment will not fall personally upon themselves. The punishment comes down every now and then on some luckless set of governors, in the shape of resistance or a revolution. It is not equally divided among all the sinners; but all the sinners run the chance, and it is the existence of this chance at any given moment which makes the misconduct veritably unwise. At the same time the proving the misconduct to be veritably unwise, is in no shape in opposition with the fact, that experiment demonstrates that all governments *do* run into such misconduct, except so far as they see very prompt and immediate symptoms of danger. They all steal, till they can see the noose with their bodily eyes; and the practical and substantial interest of the public is to take care, that this most salutary vision shall in a more or less remote form be ever present to their sight.

'*The principle of Mr. Bentham, if we understand it, is this, that mankind ought to act so as to produce their greatest happiness.*' It is plain that 'we' do *not* understand it; and 'the ranks and the rabble' do. The *vis* of Mr. Bentham's principle was, that individuals, societies, nations, would in the end increase their particular stock of happiness, by taking the road which leads to the happiness of the aggregate, instead of the road which appears to lead to their own at the expense of the aggregate,—and therefore ought to take this road, though they do not.

'*But, if what a man thinks his happiness be inconsistent with the greatest happiness of mankind, will this new principle convert him to another frame of mind?*'—It will, if it persuades him that he is a fool to think so.

It is undeniably true, that every thing is capable of being applied to a bad use. It is possible to imagine a heretic burnt on pretence of 'the greatest happiness principle,' as well as on pretence of the love of God. The planter and the military flogger avow boldly, that flogging is the greatest happiness. But their misfortune is, that notwithstanding their attempt to misapply, the principle on the whole has made it vastly more difficult either to burn or to flog than before. For one man that has been taken in by the misapplication, fifty have been strengthened in their conviction of the truth.

'*We should very much like to know how the Utilitarian principle would run, when reduced to one plain imperative proposition.*'—It would run thus—'Pursue the rule which is best for the general happiness; because, in the long run and taking all the chances that are before you together, it is the most likely to increase your own.'

'*Will it run thus—pursue your own happiness? This is superfluous. Every man pursues it, according to his light, and always has pursued it, and always must pursue it. To say that a man has done any thing, is to say that he thought it for his happiness to do it.*'—It will run thus— Pursue your own happiness *aright*. The precept is not 'Do what you may *think* for your happiness;' but 'Do thus and thus, and it will *be* for your happiness.' The man who steals, does what he thinks for his happiness. The object of the precept and its accompaniment, is to persuade him that he is mistaken.

Will the principle run thus—pursue the greatest happiness of mankind, whether it be your own greatest happiness or not? This is absurd and impossible.—Present greatest happiness is here confounded with ultimate; which in fact constitutes the error of all immorality. The man who takes a purse, pursues his greatest happiness in the sense of the Edinburgh reviewers. The precept says, 'Pursue the rule which tends to the greatest general happiness, in pre-ference to *this* greatest happiness; and the chances are, you will be the better for it in the end.' There is a momentary interest and a final one; an apparent interest and a real one; and what is desired is to persuade men to take the one and not the other.

'*The "greatest happiness principle" has always been latent under the words, social contract, justice, benevolence, patriotism, liberty, and so forth, just as far as it was for the happiness, real or imagined, of those who used these words to promote the greatest happiness of mankind. And of this we may be sure, that the words "greatest happiness" will never, in any man's mouth, mean more than the greatest happiness of others which is consistent with what he thinks his own.*'—The question was not what would be in any man's mouth. There are people every where, into whose mouths there is no putting any good. But the question was, whether a dangerous light was not thrown upon the way for men to promote their interest in concert; and whether the good would not on the whole be assisted by it, and the bad depressed and kept in check, in the same manner that has been the consequence of the demonstration of the individual policy of honesty.

'*What society wants is a new motive—not a new cant.*'—Society has got the motive; and those that fear it, find the cant.

The next objection is, considering the quarter from which it comes, a remarkable one. It is no less than that Mr. Bentham's principle 'is included in the Christian morality.' Nobody ever thought of denying, that the author of Christianity was the first of Utilitarians. But the world at large is not so decided in its submission to the sanctions of theology, as to make it a trifling service to have demonstrated the grounds on which any given precept is recommended by men's present interests. The holy alliance may profess to govern by the rules of Christianity; but large portions of mankind think it quite as well to inquire whether the interpretation agrees with their temporal interests besides. If the discoveries of worldly philosophy agree with the precepts of Christianity, it is a triumph for the latter. The precept had been uttered of 'Thou shalt not steal;' and Christianity had given it the sanction of its hopes and fears. But nobody ever conceived there was any harm in demonstrating to individuals in all manner of earthly ways besides, that it was much the best for them on the whole that they should not steal. In the same manner Mr. Bentham has demonstrated that for individuals, societies, nations, to 'do as they would be done by,' is sound earthly policy. The bigots keep a close lock on their Elysium; but whenever the time comes for the *second* Utilitarian to present himself at the gate, it is presumable the *first* will not wait for their leave, to greet him with 'Well done.'

Where so much real service has been derived from the agitation of a question, it would be ingratitude to conclude with any thing approaching to the ill humour of the little codicillular appendage of the Edinburgh reviewers. Another time, they are entreated not to do any thing like checking their thunder in mid volley; but freely pour out the vials of their wrath, that all men may be convinced that there was something in the bottle.

VII

Utilitarian Theory of Government, and the 'Great Happiness' Principle

Edinburgh Review, no. xcix (October 1829), Article vi.

WE have long been of opinion that the Utilitarians have owed all their influence to a mere delusion—that, while professing to have submitted their minds to an intellectual discipline of peculiar severity, to have discarded all sentimentality, and to have acquired consummate skill in the art of reasoning, they are decidedly inferior to the mass of educated men in the very qualities in which they conceive themselves to excel. They have undoubtedly freed themselves from the dominion of some absurd notions. But their struggle for intellectual emancipation has ended, as injudicious and violent struggles for political emancipation too often end, in a mere change of tyrants. Indeed, we are not sure that we do not prefer the venerable nonsense which holds prescriptive sway over the Ultra-Tory, to the upstart dynasty of prejudices and sophisms, by which the revolutionists of the moral world have suffered themselves to be enslaved.

The Utilitarians have sometimes been abused as intolerant, arrogant, irreligious,—as enemies of literature, of the fine arts, and of the domestic charities. They have been reviled for some things of which they were guilty, and for some of which they were innocent. But scarcely any body seems to have perceived, that almost all their peculiar faults arise from the utter want both of comprehensiveness and of precision in their mode of reasoning. We have, for some time past, been convinced that this was really the case; and that, whenever their philosophy should be boldly and unsparingly scrutinized, the world would see that it had been under a mistake respecting them.

We have made the experiment, and it has succeeded far beyond our most sanguine expectations. A chosen champion of the School has come forth against us. A specimen of his logical abilities now lies before us; and we pledge ourselves to show, that no Prebendary at an Anti-Catholic meeting, no true-blue Baronet after the third bottle at a Pitt Club, ever displayed such utter incapacity of comprehending or answering an argument, as appears in the speculations of this Utilitarian apostle; that he does not understand our meaning, or Mr Mill's meaning, or Mr Bentham's meaning, or his own meaning; and that the various parts of his system—if the name of system can be so misapplied—directly contradict each other.

Having shown this, we intend to leave him in undisputed possession of whatever advantage he may derive from the last word. We propose only to convince the public that there is nothing in the far-famed logic of the Utilitarians, of which any plain man has reason to be afraid;—that this logic will impose on no man who dares to look it in the face.

The Westminster Reviewer begins by charging us with having misrepresented an important part of Mr Mill's argument . . .

['The first extract . . . omitted at the end.' p. 182]

It is perfectly true, that our quotation from Mr Mill's Essay was, like most other quotations, preceded and followed by something which we did not quote. But if the Westminster Reviewer means to say, that either what preceded, or what followed, would, if quoted, have shown that we put a wrong interpretation on the passage which was extracted, he does not understand Mr Mill rightly.

Mr Mill undoubtedly says that, 'as the surface of history affords no certain principle of decision, we must go beyond the surface, and penetrate to the springs within.' But these expressions will admit of several interpretations. In what sense, then, does Mr Mill use them? If he means that we ought to inspect the facts with close attention, he means what is rational. But if he means that we ought to leave the facts, with all their apparent inconsistencies, unexplained—to lay down a general principle of the widest extent, and to deduce doctrines from that principle by syllogistic argument, without pausing to consider whether those doctrines be, or be not, consistent with the facts,—then he means what is irrational; and this is clearly what he does mean: For he immediately begins, without offering the least explanation of the contradictory appearances which he has himself described, to go beyond the surface in the following manner:— 'That one human being will desire to render the person and property of another subservient to his pleasures, notwithstanding the pain or loss of pleasure which it may occasion to that other individual, is the foundation of government. The desire of the object implies the desire of the power necessary to accomplish the object.' And thus he proceeds to deduce consequences directly inconsistent with what he has himself stated respecting the situation of the Danish people.

If we assume that the object of government is the preservation of the persons and property of men, then we must hold that, wherever that object is attained, there the principle of good government exists. If that object be attained both in Denmark and in the United States of America, then that which makes government good must exist, under whatever disguise of title or name, both in Denmark and in the United States. If men lived in fear for their lives and their possessions under Nero and under the National Convention, it follows that the causes from which misgovernment proceeds, existed both in the despotism of Rome, and in the democracy of France. What, then, is that which, being found in Denmark and in the United States, and not being found in the Roman Empire, or under the administration of Robespierre, renders governments, widely differing in their external form, practically good? Be it what it may, it certainly is not that which Mr Mill proves *a priori* that it must be,—a democratic representative assembly. For the Danes have no such assembly.

The latent principle of good government ought to be tracked, as it appears to us, in the same manner in which Lord Bacon proposed to track the principle of Heat. Make as large a list as possible, said that great man, of those bodies in which, however widely they differ from each other in appearance, we perceive heat; and as large a list as possible of those which, while they bear a general resemblance to hot bodies, are nevertheless not hot. Observe the different degrees of heat in different hot bodies; and then, if there be something which is found in all hot bodies, and of which the increase or diminution is always accompanied by an increase or diminution of heat, we may hope that we have really discovered the object of our search. In the same manner, we ought to examine the constitution of all those communities in which, under whatever form, the blessings of good government are enjoyed; and to discover, if possible, in what they resemble each other, and in what they all differ from those societies in which the object of government is not attained. By proceeding thus we shall arrive, not indeed at a perfect theory of government, but at a theory which will be of great practical use, and which the experience of every successive generation will probably bring nearer and nearer to perfection.

The inconsistences into which Mr Mill has been betrayed, by taking a different course, ought to serve as a warning to all speculators. Because Denmark is well governed by a monarch who, in appearance at least, is absolute, Mr Mill thinks, that the only mode of arriving at the true principles of government, is to deduce them *a priori* from the laws of human nature. And what conclusion does he bring out by this deduction? We will give it in his own words:—'In the grand discovery of modern times, the system of representation, the solution of all the difficulties, both speculative and practical, will perhaps be found. If it cannot, we seem to be forced upon the extraordinary conclusion, that good government is impossible.' That the Danes are well governed without a representation, is a reason for deducing the theory of government from a general principle, from which it necessarily follows, that good government is impossible without a representation! We have done our best to put this question plainly; and we think, that if the Westminster Reviewer will read over what we have written twice or thrice with patience and attention, some glimpse of our meaning will break in, even on his mind.

Some objections follow, so frivolous and unfair, that we are almost ashamed to notice them.

When it was said that there was in Denmark a balanced contest between the king and the nobility, what was said was, that there was a balanced contest, but it did not last. It was balanced till something put an end to the balance; and so is every thing else. That such a balance will not last, is precisely what Mr Mill had demonstrated.

Mr Mill, we positively affirm, pretends to demonstrate, not merely that a balanced contest between the king and the aristocracy will not last, but that the chances are as infinity to one against the existence of such a balanced contest. This is a mere question of fact: We quote the words of the Essay, and defy the Westminster Reviewer to impeach our accuracy:—

It seems impossible that such equality should ever exist. How is it to be established? Or by what criterion is it to be ascertained? If there is no such criterion, it must, in all cases, be the result of chance. If so, the chances against it are as infinity to one.

The Reviewer has confounded the division of power with the balance or equal division of power. Mr Mill says, that the division of power can never exist long, because it is next to impossible that the equal division of power should ever exist at all.

When Mr Mill asserted that it cannot be for the interest of either the monarchy or the aristocracy to combine with the democracy, it is plain he did not assert that if the monarchy and aristocracy were in doubtful contest with each other, they would not, either of them, accept of the assistance of the democracy. He spoke of their taking the side of the democracy; not of their allowing the democracy to take side with themselves.

If Mr Mill meant any thing, he must have meant this—that the monarchy and the aristocracy will never forget their enmity to the democracy, in their enmity to each other.

'The monarchy and aristocracy,' says he, 'have all possible motives for endeavouring to obtain unlimited power over the persons and property of the community. The consequence is inevitable. They have all possible motives for combining to obtain that power, and unless the people have power enough to be a match for both, they have no protection. The balance, therefore, is a thing, the existence of which, upon the best possible evidence, is to be regarded as impossible.'

If Mr Mill meant only what the Westminster Reviewer conceives him to have meant, his argument would leave the popular theory of the balance quite untouched. For it is the very theory of the balance, that the help of the people will be solicited by the nobles when hard pressed by the king, and by the king when hard pressed by the nobles; and that, as the price of giving alternate support to the crown and the aristocracy, they will obtain something for themselves, as the Reviewer admits that they have done in Denmark. If Mr Mill admits this, he admits the only theory of the balance of which we ever heard—that very theory which he has declared to be wild and chimerical. If he denies it, he is at issue with the Westminster Reviewer as to the phenomena of the Danish government.

We now come to a more important passage. Our opponent has discovered, as he conceives, a radical error which runs through our whole argument, and vitiates every part of it. We suspect that we shall spoil his triumph.

Mr Mill never asserted '*that under no despotic government does any human being, except the tools of the sovereign, possess more than the necessaries of life, and that the most intense degree of terror is kept up by constant cruelty.*' He said that absolute power leads to such results, 'by infallible sequence, where power over a community is attained, *and nothing checks.*' The critic on the Mount never made a more palpable misquotation.

The spirit of this misquotation runs through every part of the reply of the Edinburgh Review that relates to the Essay on Government; and is repeated in as many shapes as the Roman pork. The whole description of 'Mr Mill's argument against despotism',—including the illustration from right-angled triangles and the square of the hypothenuse,—is founded on this invention of saying what an author has not said, and leaving unsaid what he has.

We thought, and still think, for reasons which our readers will soon understand, that we represented Mr Mill's principle quite fairly, and according to the rule of law and common sense, *ut res magis valeat quam pereat*. Let us, however, give him all the advantage of the explanation tendered by his advocate, and see what he will gain by it.

The Utilitarian doctrine then is, not that despots and aristocracies will always plunder and oppress the people to the last point, but that they will do so if nothing checks them.

In the first place, it is quite clear that the doctrine thus stated, is of no use at all, unless the force of the checks be estimated. The first law of motion is, that a ball once projected will fly on to all eternity with undiminished velocity, unless something checks. The fact is, that a ball stops in a few seconds after proceeding a few yards with very variable motion. Every man would wring his child's neck, and pick his friend's pocket, if nothing checked him. In fact, the principle thus stated, means only that governments will oppress, unless they abstain from oppressing. This is quite true, we own. But we might with equal propriety turn the maxim round, and lay it down as the fundamental principle of government, that all rulers will govern well, unless some motive interferes to keep them from doing so.

If there be, as the Westminster Reviewer acknowledges, certain checks which, under political institutions the most arbitrary in seeming, sometimes produce good government, and almost always place some restraint on the rapacity and cruelty of the powerful; surely the knowledge of those checks, of their nature, and of their effect, must be a most important part of the science of government. Does Mr Mill say any thing upon this part of the subject? Not one word.

The line of defence now taken by the Utilitarians, evidently degrades Mr Mill's theory of government from the rank which, till within the last few months, was claimed for it by the whole sect. It is no longer a practical system, fit to guide statesmen, but merely a barren exercise of the intellect, like those propositions in mechanics in which the effect of friction and of the resistance of the air is left out of the question; and which, therefore, though correctly deduced from the premises, are in practice utterly false. For if Mr Mill professes to prove only that absolute monarchy and aristocracy are pernicious without checks,—if he allows that there are checks which produce good government, even under absolute monarchs and aristocracies,—and if he omits to tell us what those checks are, and what effects they produce under different circumstances, he surely gives us no information which can be of real utility.

But the fact is,—and it is most extraordinary that the Westminster Reviewer should not have perceived it,—that if once the existence of checks on the abuse of power in monarchies and aristocracies be admitted, the whole of Mr Mill's theory falls to the ground at once. This is so palpable, that, in spite of the opinion of the Westminster Reviewer, we must acquit Mr Mill of having intended to make such an admission. We still think that the words, 'where power over a community is attained, and nothing checks,' must not be understood to mean, that under a monarchical or aristocratical form of government, there can really be any check which can in any degree mitigate the wretchedness of the people.

For, all possible checks may be classed under two general heads,—want of will, and want of power. Now, if a king or an aristocracy, having the power to plunder and oppress the people, can want the will, all Mr Mill's principles of human nature must be pronounced unsound. He tells us, 'that the desire to possess unlimited power of inflicting pain upon others, is an inseparable part of human nature;' and that 'a chain of inference, close and strong to a most unusual degree,' leads to the conclusion, that those who possess this power will always desire to use it. It is plain, therefore, that, if Mr Mill's principles be sound, the check on a monarchical or an aristocratical government will not be the want of will to oppress.

If a king or an aristocracy, having, as Mr Mill tells us that they always must have, the will to oppress the people with the utmost severity, want the power, then the government, by whatever name it may be called, must be virtually a mixed government, or a pure democracy: for it is quite clear that the people possess some power in the state—some means of influencing the nominal rulers. But Mr Mill has demonstrated that no mixed government can possibly exist, or at least that such a government must come to a very speedy end: therefore, every country in which people not in the service of the government have, for any length of time, been permitted to accumulate more than the bare means of subsistence, must be a pure democracy. That is to say, France before the Revolution, and Ireland during the last century, were pure democracies. Prussia, Austria, Russia, all the governments of the civilized world, are pure democracies. If this be not a *reductio ad absurdum*, we do not know what is.

The errors of Mr Mill proceed principally from that radical vice in his reasoning, which, in our last number, we described in the words of Lord Bacon. The Westminster Reviewer is unable to discover the meaning of our extracts from the *Novum Organum*, and expresses himself as follows:

The quotations from Lord Bacon are misapplications, such as any body may make to any thing he dislikes. There is no more resemblance between pain, pleasure, motives, &c., and *substantia, generatio, corruptio, elementum, materia*,—than between lines, angles, magnitudes, &c., and the same.

It would perhaps be unreasonable to expect that a writer who cannot understand his own English, should understand Lord Bacon's Latin. We will, therefore, attempt to make our meaning clearer.

What Lord Bacon blames in the schoolmen of his time, is this,—that they reasoned syllogistically on words which had not been defined with precision; such as moist, dry, generation, corruption, and so forth. Mr Mill's error is exactly of the same kind. He reasons syllogistically about power, pleasure, and pain, without attaching any definite notion to any one of those words. There is no more resemblance, says the Westminster Reviewer, between pain and *substantia*, than between pain and a line or an angle. By his permission, in the very point to which Lord Bacon's observation applies, Mr Mill's subjects do resemble the *substantia* and *elementum* of the schoolmen, and differ from the lines and magnitudes of Euclid. We can reason *a priori* on mathematics, because we can define with an exactitude which precludes all possibility of confusion. If a mathematician were to admit the least laxity into his notions; if he were to allow himself to be deluded by the vague sense which words bear in popular use, or by the aspect of an ill-drawn diagram; if he were to forget in his reasonings that a point was indivisible, or that the definition of a line excluded breadth, there would be no end to his blunders. The schoolmen tried to reason mathematically about things which had not been, and perhaps could not be, defined with mathematical accuracy. We know the result. Mr Mill has in our time attempted to do the same. He talks of power, for example, as if the meaning of the word power were as determinate as the meaning of the word circle. But when we analyze his speculations, we find that his notion of power is, in the words of Bacon, '*phantastica et male terminata.*'

There are two senses in which we may use the word *power*, and those words which denote the various distributions of power, as, for example, *monarchy*;—the one sense popular and superficial,—the other more scientific and accurate. Mr Mill, since he chose to reason *a priori*, ought to have clearly pointed out in which sense he intended to use words of this kind, and to have adhered inflexibly to the sense on which he fixed. Instead of doing this, he flies backwards and forwards from the one sense to the other, and brings out conclusions at last which suit neither.

The state of those two communities to which he has himself referred—the kingdom of Denmark and the empire of Rome—may serve to illustrate our meaning. Looking merely at the surface of things, we should call Denmark a despotic monarchy, and the Roman world, in the first century after Christ, an aristocratical republic. Caligula was, in theory, nothing more than a magistrate elected by the Senate, and subject to the Senate. That irresponsible dignity which, in the most limited monarchies of our time, is ascribed to the person of the sovereign, never belonged to the earlier Caesars. The sentence of death which the great council of the commonwealth passed on Nero, was strictly according to the theory of the constitution. Yet, in fact, the power of the Roman Emperors approached nearer to absolute dominion than that of any prince in modern Europe. On the other hand, the King of Denmark, in theory the most despotic of princes, would, in practice, find it most perilous to indulge in cruelty and licentiousness. Nor is there, we believe, at the present moment, a single sovereign in our part of the world, who has so much real power over the lives of his sub-jects, as Robespierre, while he lodged at a chandler's and dined at a restaurateur's, exercised over the lives of those whom he called his fellow-citizens.

Mr Mill and the Westminster Reviewer seem to agree, that there cannot long exist, in any society, a division of power between a monarch, an aristocracy, and the people; or between any two of them. However the power be distributed, one of the three parties will, according to them, inevitably monopolize the whole. Now, what is here meant by power? If Mr Mill speaks of the external semblance of power,—of power recognized by the theory of the constitution,—he is palpably wrong. In England, for example, we have had for ages the name and form of a mixed government, if nothing more. Indeed, Mr Mill himself owns, that there are appearances which have given colour to the theory of the balance, though he maintains that these appearances are delusive. But if he uses the word power in a deeper and philosophical sense, he is, if possible, still more in the wrong than on the former supposition. For if he had considered in what the power of one human being over other human beings must ultimately consist, he would have perceived, not only that there are mixed governments in the world, but that all the governments in the world, and all the governments which can even be conceived as existing in the world, are virtually mixed.

If a king possessed the lamp of Aladdin,—if he governed by the help of a genius, who carried away the daughters and wives of his subjects through the air to the royal *Parc-aux-cerfs*, and turned into stone every man who wagged a finger against his majesty's government, there would indeed be an unmixed despotism. But, fortunately, a ruler can be gratified only by means of his subjects. His power depends on their obedience; and, as any three or four of them are more than a match for him by himself, he can only enforce the unwilling obedience of some, by means of the willing obedience of others. Take any of those who are popularly called absolute princes—Napoleon for example. Could Napoleon have walked through Paris, cutting off the head of one person in every house which he passed?

Certainly not without the assistance of an army. If not, why not? Because the people had sufficient physical power to resist him, and would have put forth that power in defence of their lives and of the lives of their children. In other words, there was a portion of power in the democracy under Napoleon. Napoleon might probably have indulged himself in such an atrocious freak of power if his army would have seconded him. But if his army had taken part with the people, he would have found himself utterly helpless; and even if they had obeyed his orders against the people, they would not have suffered him to decimate their own body. In other words, there was a portion of power in the hands of a minority of the people, that is to say, in the hands of an aristocracy, under the reign of Napoleon.

To come nearer home,—Mr Mill tells us that it is a mistake to imagine that the English government is mixed. He holds, we suppose, with all the politicians of the Utilitarian school, that it is purely aristocratical. There certainly is an aristocracy in England, and we are afraid that their power is greater than it ought to be. They have power enough to keep up the game-laws and corn-laws; but they have not power enough to subject the bodies of men of the lowest class to wanton outrage at their pleasure. Suppose that they were to make a law, that any gentleman of two thousand a-year might have a day-labourer or a pauper flogged with a cat-of-nine-tails whenever the whim might take him. It is quite clear, that the first day on which such flagellation should be administered, would be the last day of the English aristocracy. In this point, and in many other points which might be named, the commonalty in our island enjoy a security quite as complete as if they exercised the right of universal suffrage. We say, therefore, that the English people have in their own hands a sufficient guarantee that in some points the aristocracy will conform to their wishes;—in other words, they have a certain portion of power over the aristocracy. Therefore the English government is mixed.

Wherever a king or an oligarchy refrains from the last extremity of rapacity and tyranny, through fear of the resistance of the people, there, the constitution, whatever it may be called, is in some measure democratical. The admixture of democratic power may be slight. It may be much slighter than it ought to be; but some admixture there is. Wherever a numerical minority, by means of superior wealth or intelligence, of political concert, or of military discipline, exercises a greater influence on the society than any other equal number of persons,—there, whatever the form of government may be called, a mixture of aristocracy does in fact exist. And wherever a single man, from whatever cause, is so necessary to the community, or to any portion of it, that he possesses more power than any other man, there is a mixture of monarchy. This is the philosophical classification of governments; and if we use this classification we shall find, not only that there are mixed governments, but that all governments are, and must always be, mixed. But we may safely challenge Mr Mill to give any definition of power, or to make any classification of governments, which shall bear him out in his assertion, that a lasting division of authority is impracticable.

It is evidently on the real distribution of power, and not on names and badges, that the happiness of nations must depend. The representative system, though doubtless a great and precious discovery in politics, is only one of the many modes in which the democratic part of the community can efficiently check the governing few. That certain men have been chosen as deputies of the people,—that there is a piece of paper stating such deputies to possess certain powers,—these circumstances in themselves constitute no security for good government. Such a constitution nominally existed in France; while, in fact, an oligarchy of committees and clubs trampled at once on the electors and the elected. Representation is a very happy contrivance for enabling large bodies of men to exert their power, with less risk of disorder than there would otherwise be. But, assuredly, it does not of itself give power. Unless a representative assembly is sure of being supported, in the last resort, by the physical strength of large masses, who have spirit to defend the constitution, and sense to defend it in concert, the mob of the town in which it meets may overawe it;—the howls of the listeners in its gallery may silence its deliberations;—an able and daring individual may dissolve it. And if that sense and that spirit of which we speak be diffused through a society, then, even without a representative assembly, that society will enjoy many of the blessings of good government.

Which is the better able to defend himself;—a strong man

with nothing but his fists, or a paralytic cripple encumbered with a sword which he cannot lift? Such, we believe, is the difference between Denmark and some new republics in which the constitutional forms of the United States have been most sedulously imitated.

Look at the Long Parliament, on the day on which Charles came to seize the five members, and look at it again on the day when Cromwell stamped with his foot on its floor. On which day was its apparent power the greater? On which day was its real power the less? Nominally subject, it was able to defy the sovereign. Nominally sovereign, it was turned out of doors by its servant.

Constitutions are in politics what paper money is in commerce. They afford great facilities and conveniences. But we must not attribute to them that value which really belongs to what they represent. They are not power, but symbols of power, and will, in an emergency, prove altogether useless, unless the power for which they stand be forthcoming. The real power by which the community is governed, is made up of all the means which all its members possess of giving pleasure or pain to each other.

Great light may be thrown on the nature of a circulating medium by the phenomena of a state of barter. And in the same manner it may be useful to those who wish to comprehend the nature and operation of the outward signs of power, to look at communities in which no such signs exist; for example, at the great community of nations. There we find nothing analogous to a constitution: But do we not find a government? We do in fact find government in its purest, and simplest, and most intelligible form. We see one portion of power acting directly on another portion of power. We see a certain police kept up; the weak to a certain degree protected; the strong to a certain degree restrained. We see the principle of the balance in constant operation. We see the whole system sometimes undisturbed by any attempt at encroachment for twenty or thirty years at a time; and all this is produced without a legislative assembly, or an executive magistracy—without tribunals,—without any code which deserves the name; solely by the mutual hopes and fears of the various members of the federation. In the community of nations, the first appeal is to physical force.

In communities of men, forms of government serve to put off that appeal, and often render it unnecessary. But it is still open to the oppressed or the ambitious.

Of course, we do not mean to deny that a form of government will, after it has existed for a long time, materially affect the real distribution of power throughout the community. This is because those who administer a government, with their dependents, form a compact and disciplined body, which, acting methodically and in concert, is more powerful than any other equally numerous body which is inferior in organization. The power of rulers is not, as superficial observers sometimes seem to think, a thing *sui generis*. It is exactly similar in kind, though generally superior in amount, to that of any set of conspirators who plot to overthrow it. We have seen in our time the most extensive and the best organized conspiracy that ever existed—a conspiracy which possessed all the elements of real power in so great a degree, that it was able to cope with a strong government, and to triumph over it—the Catholic Association. An Utilitarian would tell us, we suppose, that the Irish Catholics had no portion of political power whatever on the first day of the late Session of Parliament.

Let us really go beyond the surface of facts: Let us, in the sound sense of the words, penetrate to the springs within; and the deeper we go, the more reason shall we find to smile at those theorists who hold that the sole hope of the human race is in a rule-of-three sum and a ballot-box.

We must now return to the Westminster Reviewer. The following paragraph is an excellent specimen of his peculiar mode of understanding and answering arguments.

The reply to the argument against 'saturation', supplies its own answer. The reason why it is of no use to try to 'saturate', is precisely what the Edinburgh Reviewers have suggested,—'*that there is no limit to the number of thieves.*' There are the thieves, and the thieves' cousins,—with their men-servants, their maid-servants, and their little ones, to the fortieth generation. It is true, that 'a man cannot become a king or a member of the aristocracy whenever he chooses;' but if there is to be no limit to the depredators except their own inclination to increase and multiply, the situation of those who are to suffer is as wretched as it needs be. It is impossible to define what *are* 'corporal pleasures'. A Duchess of Cleveland was a 'corporal pleasure'. The most disgraceful period in the history of any nation, —that of the Restoration,—presents an instance of the length to which it is possible to go in an attempt to 'saturate' with pleasures of this kind.

To reason with such a writer is like talking to a deaf man, who catches at a stray word, makes answer beside the mark, and is led further and further into error by every attempt to explain. Yet, that our readers may fully appreciate the abilities of the new philosophers, we shall take the trouble to go over some of our ground again.

Mr Mill attempts to prove, that there is no point of saturation with the objects of human desire. He then takes it for granted that men have no objects of desire but those which can be obtained only at the expense of the happiness of others. Hence he infers that absolute monarchs and aristocracies will necessarily oppress and pillage the people to a frightful extent.

We answered in substance thus: There are two kinds of objects of desire; those which give mere bodily pleasure, and those which please through the medium of associations. Objects of the former class, it is true, a man cannot obtain without depriving somebody else of a share: But then with these every man is soon satisfied. A king or an aristocracy cannot spend any very large portion of the national wealth on the mere pleasures of sense. With the pleasures which belong to us as reasoning and imaginative beings we are never satiated, it is true: But then, on the other hand, many of those pleasures can be obtained without injury to any person, and some of them can be obtained only by doing good to others.

The Westminster Reviewer, in his former attack on us, laughed at us for saying, that a king or an aristocracy could not be easily satiated with the pleasures of sense, and asked why the same course was not tried with thieves. We were not a little surprised at so silly an objection from the pen, as we imagined, of Mr Bentham. We returned, however, a very simple answer. There is no limit to the number of thieves. Any man who chooses can steal: But a man cannot become a member of the aristocracy, or a king, whenever he chooses. To satiate one thief, is to tempt twenty other people to steal. But by satiating one king or five hundred nobles with bodily pleasures, we do not produce more kings or more nobles. The answer of the Westminster

Reviewer we have quoted above; and it will amply repay our readers for the trouble of examining it. We never read any passage which indicated notions so vague and confused. The number of the thieves, says our Utilitarian, is not limited. For there are the dependents and friends of the king and of the nobles. Is it possible that he should not perceive that this comes under a different head? The bodily pleasures which a man in power dispenses among his creatures, are bodily pleasures as respects his creatures, no doubt. But the pleasure which he derives from bestowing them is not a bodily pleasure. It is one of those pleasures which belong to him as a reasoning and imaginative being. No man of common understanding can have failed to perceive, that when we said that a king or an aristocracy might easily be supplied to satiety with sensual pleasures, we were speaking of sensual pleasures directly enjoyed by themselves. But 'it is impossible,' says the Reviewer, 'to define what are corporal pleasures.' Our brother would indeed, we suspect, find it a difficult task; nor, if we are to judge of his genius for classification from the specimen which immediately follows, would we advise him to make the attempt. 'A Duchess of Cleveland was a corporal pleasure.' And to this wise remark is appended a note, setting forth that Charles the Second gave to the Duchess of Cleveland the money which he ought to have spent on the war with Holland. We scarcely know how to answer a man who unites so much pretension to so much ignorance. There are among the many Utilitarians who talk about Hume, Condillac, and Hartley, a few who have read those writers. Let the Reviewer ask one of these what he thinks on the subject. We shall not undertake to whip a pupil of so little promise through his first course of metaphysics. We shall, therefore, only say—leaving him to guess and wonder what we can mean—that in our opinion, the Duchess of Cleveland was not a merely corporal pleasure,—that the feeling which leads a prince to prefer one woman to all others, and to lavish the wealth of kingdoms on her, is a feeling which can only be explained by the law of association.

But we are tired, and even more ashamed than tired, of exposing these blunders. The whole article is of a piece. One passage, however, we must select, because it contains a very gross misrepresentation.

'*They never alluded to the French Revolution for the purpose of proving that the poor were inclined to rob the rich.*'—They only said, 'as soon as the poor *again* began to compare their cottages and salads with the hotels and banquets of the rich, there would have been another scramble for property, another general confiscation,' &c.

We said, that, *if Mr Mill's principles of human nature were correct*, there would have been another scramble for property, and another confiscation. We particularly pointed this out in our last article. We showed the Westminster Reviewer that he had misunderstood us. We dwelt particularly on the condition which was introduced into our statement. We said that we had not given, and did not mean to give, any opinion of our own. And after this, the Westminster Reviewer thinks proper to repeat his former misrepresentation, without taking the least notice of that qualification to which we, in the most marked manner, called his attention.

We hasten on to the most curious part of the article under our consideration—the defence of the 'greatest happiness principle.' The Reviewer charges us with having quite mistaken its nature.

All that they have established is, that they do not understand it. Instead of the truism of the Whigs, 'that the greatest happiness is the greatest happiness,' what Mr Bentham had demonstrated, or at all events had laid such foundations that there was no trouble in demonstrating, was, that the greatest happiness of the individual was, in the long run, to be obtained by pursuing the greatest happiness of the aggregate.

It was distinctly admitted by the Westminster Reviewer, as we remarked in our last article, that he could give no answer to the question,—why governments should attempt to produce the greatest possible happiness? The Reviewer replies thus:—

Nothing of the kind will be admitted at all. In the passage thus selected to be tacked to the other, the question started was, concerning 'the object of government;' in which government was spoken of as an operation, not as any thing that is capable of feeling pleasure or pain. In this sense it is true enough, that *ought* is not predicable of governments.

We will quote, once again, the passage which we quoted in our last Number, and we really hope that our brother critic will feel something like shame while he peruses it.

The real answer appeared to be, that men at large *ought* not to allow a government to afflict them with more evil or less good, than they can help. What a *government* ought to do, is a mysterious and searching question, which those may answer who know what it means; but what other men ought to do, is a question of no mystery at all. The word *ought*, if it means any thing, must have reference to some kind of interest or motives; and what interest a government has in doing right, when it happens to be interested in doing wrong, is a question for the school-men. The fact appears to be, that *ought* is not predicable of governments. The question is not, why governments are bound not to do this or that, but why other men should let them if they can help it. The point is not to determine why the lion should not eat sheep, but why men should not eat their own mutton if they can.

We defy the Westminster Reviewer to reconcile this passage with the 'general happiness principle,' as he now states it. He tells us, that he meant by government, not the people invested with the powers of government, but a mere *operation* incapable of feeling pleasure or pain. We say, that he meant the people invested with the powers of government, and nothing else. It is true, that *ought* is not predicable of an operation. But who would ever dream of raising any question about the *duties* of an operation? What did the Reviewer mean by saying, that a government could not be interested in doing right because it was interested in doing wrong? Can an operation be interested in either? And what did he mean by his comparison about the lion? Is a lion an operation incapable of pain or pleasure? And what did he mean by the expression, 'other men,' so obviously opposed to the word 'government?' But let the public judge between us. It is superfluous to argue a point so clear.

The Reviewer does indeed seem to feel that his expressions cannot be explained away, and attempts to shuffle out of the difficulty by owning, that 'the double meaning of the word government was not got clear of without confusion.' He has now, at all events, he assures us, made himself master of Mr Bentham's philosophy. The real and genuine 'greatest happiness principle' is, that the greatest happiness of every individual is identical with the greatest happiness of society; and all other 'greatest happiness principles' whatever, are counterfeits. 'This,' says he, 'is the spirit of Mr Bentham's principle; and if there is any thing opposed to it in any former statement, it may be corrected by the present.'

Assuredly, if a fair and honourable opponent had, in discussing a question so abstruse as that concerning the origin of moral obligation, made some unguarded admission inconsistent with the spirit of his doctrines, we should not be inclined to triumph over him. But no tenderness is due to a writer, who, in the very act of confessing his blunders, insults those by whom his blunders have been detected, and accuses them of misunderstanding what, in fact, he has himself mis-stated.

The whole of this transaction illustrates excellently the real character of this sect. A paper comes forth, professing to contain a full developement of the 'greatest happiness principle,' with the latest improvements of Mr Bentham. The writer boasts, that his article has the honour of being the announcement and the organ of this wonderful discovery, which is to make 'the bones of sages and patriots stir within thier tombs.' This 'magnificent principle' is then stated thus: Mankind ought to pursue their greatest happiness. But there are persons whose interest is opposed to the greatest happiness of mankind. *Ought* is not predicable of such persons. For the word *ought* has no meaning, unless it be used with reference to some interest.

We answered, with much more lenity than we should have shown to such nonsense, had it not proceeded, as we supposed, from Mr Bentham, that interest was synonymous with greatest happiness; and that, therefore, if the word *ought* has no meaning, unless used with reference to interest, then, to say that mankind ought to pursue their greatest happiness, is simply to say, that the greatest happiness is the greatest happiness; that every individual pursue his own happiness; that either what he thinks his happiness must coincide with the greatest happiness of society, or not; that if what he thinks his happiness coincides with the greatest happiness of society, he will attempt to promote the greatest happiness of society, whether he ever heard of the 'greatest happiness principle' or not; and that, by the admission of the Westminster Reviewer, if his happiness is inconsistent with the greatest happiness of society, there is no reason why he should promote the greatest happiness of society. Now, that there are individuals who think that for their happiness which is not for the greatest happiness of society, is evident.

The Westminster Reviewer allowed that some of these individuals were in the right; and did not pretend to give any reason which could induce any one of them to think himself in the wrong. So that the 'magnificent principle' turned out to be, either a truism or a contradiction in terms; either this maxim—'Do what you do;' or this maxim, 'Do what you cannot do.'

The Westminster Reviewer had the wit to see that he could not defend this palpable nonsense; but, instead of manfully owning that he had misunderstood the whole nature of the 'greatest happiness principle' in the summer, and had obtained new light during the autumn, he attempts to withdraw the former principle unobserved, and to substitute another, directly opposed to it, in its place; clamouring all the time against our unfairness, like one who, while changing the cards, diverts the attention of the table from his sleight of hand, by vociferating charges of foul play against other people.

The 'greatest happiness principle' for the present quarter is then this,—that every individual will best promote his own happiness in this world, religious considerations being left out of the question, by promoting the greatest happiness of the whole species. And this principle, we are told, holds good with respect to kings and aristocracies, as well as with other people . . .

['It is certain . . . corrected by the present.' p. 188]

We hope that we have now at last got to the real 'magnificent principle,'—to the principle which is really to make 'the bones of the sages and patriots stir.' What effect it may produce on the bones of the dead we shall not pretend to decide; but we are sure that it will do very little for the happiness of the living.

In the first place, nothing is more certain than this, that the Utilitarian theory of government, as developed in Mr Mill's Essay, and in all the other works on the subject which have been put forth by the sect, rests on these two principles,—that men follow their interest, and that the interest of individuals may be, and in fact perpetually is, opposed to the interest of society. Unless these two principles be granted, Mr Mill's Essay does not contain one sound sentence. All his arguments against monarchy and aristocracy, all his arguments in favour of democracy, nay, the very argument by which he shows that there is any necessity for having government at all, must be rejected as utterly worthless.

This is so palpable, that even the Westminster Reviewer, though not the most clear-sighted of men, could not help seeing it. Accordingly, he attempts to guard himself against the objection, after the manner of such reasoners, by committing two blunders instead of one. 'All this,' says he, 'only shows that the members of a government would do well if they were all-wise;' and he proceeds to tell us, that as rulers are not all-wise, they will invariably act against this principle wherever they can, so that the democratical checks will still be necessary to produce good government.

No form which human folly takes is so richly and exquisitely laughable as the spectacle of an Utilitarian in a dilemma. What earthly good can there be in a principle upon which no man will act until he is all-wise? A certain most important doctrine, we are told, has been demonstrated so clearly, that it ought to be the foundation of the science of government. And yet the whole frame of government is to be constituted, exactly as if this fundamental doctrine were false, and on the supposition that no human being will ever act as if he believed it to be true!

The whole argument of the Utilitarians, in favour of universal suffrage, proceeds on the supposition that even the rudest and most uneducated men cannot, for any length of time, be deluded into acting against their own true interest. Yet now they tell us that, in all aristocratical communities, the higher and more educated class will, not occasionally, but invariably, act against its own interest. Now, the only use of proving any thing, as far as we can see, is that people may believe it. To say that a man does what he believes to be against his happiness, is a contradiction in terms. If, therefore, government and laws are to be constituted on the supposition on which Mr Mill's Essay is founded, that all individuals will, whenever they have power over others put into their hands, act in opposition to the general happiness, then government and laws must be constituted on the supposition that no individual believes, or ever will believe, his own happiness to be identical with the happiness of society. That is to say, government and laws are to be constituted on the supposition that no human being will ever be satisfied by Mr Bentham's proof of his 'greatest happiness principle,'—a supposition which may be true enough, but which says little, we think, for the principle in question.

But where has this principle been demonstrated? We are curious, we confess, to see this demonstration which is to change the face of the world, and yet is to convince nobody. The most amusing circumstance is, that the Westminster Reviewer himself does not seem to know whether the principle has been demonstrated or not. 'Mr Bentham,' he says, 'has demonstrated it, or at all events has laid such foundations that there is no trouble in demonstrating it.' Surely it is rather strange that such a matter should be left in doubt. The Reviewer proposed, in his former article, a slight verbal emendation in the statement of the principle; he then announced that the principle had received its last improvement; and gloried in the circumstance that the Westminster Review had been selected as the organ of that improvement. Did it never occur to him that one slight improvement to a doctrine is to prove it?

Mr Bentham has not demonstrated the 'greatest happiness principle,' as now stated. He is far too wise a man to think of demonstrating any such thing. In those sections of his *Introduction to the Principles of Morals and Legislation,* to which the Reviewer refers us in his note, there is not a word of the kind. Mr Bentham says, most truly, that there are no occasions in which a man has not *some* motives for consulting the happiness of other men; and he proceeds to set forth what those motives are—sympathy on all occasions, and the love of reputation on most occasions. This is the very doctrine which we have been maintaining against Mr Mill and the Westminster Reviewer. The principal charge which we brought against Mr Mill was, that those motives to which Mr Bentham ascribes so much influence, were quite left out of consideration in his theory. The Westminster Reviewer, in the very article now before us, abuses us for saying, in the spirit and almost in the words of Mr Bentham, that 'there is a certain check to the rapacity and cruelty of men in their desire of the good opinion of others.' But does this principle, in which we fully agree with Mr Bentham, go the length of the new 'greatest happiness principle?' The question is not whether men have *some* motives for promoting the greatest happiness, but whether the *stronger* motives be those which impel them to promote the greatest happiness. That this would always be the case, if men knew their own worldly interests, is the assertion of the Reviewer. As he expresses some doubt whether Mr Bentham has demonstrated this or not, we would advise him to set the point at rest by giving his own demonstration.

The Reviewer has not attempted to give a general composition of the 'greatest happiness principle;' but he has tried to prove that it holds good in one or two particular cases. And even in those particular cases he has utterly failed. A man, says he, who calculated the chances fairly, would perceive that it would be for his greatest happiness to abstain from stealing; for a thief runs a greater risk of being hanged than an honest man.

It would have been wise, we think, in the Westminster Reviewer, before he entered on a discussion of this sort, to settle in what human happiness consists. Each of the ancient sects of philosophy held some tenet on this subject which served for a distinguishing badge. The *summum bonum* of the Utilitarians, as far as we can judge from the passage which we are now considering, is the not being hanged.

That it is an unpleasant thing to be hanged, we most willingly concede to our brother. But that the whole question of happiness or misery resolves itself into this single point, we cannot so easily admit. We must look at the thing purchased, as well as the price paid for it. A thief, assuredly, runs a greater risk of being hanged than a labourer; and so an officer in the army runs a greater risk of being shot than a banker's clerk; and a governor of India runs a greater risk of dying of cholera than a lord of the bedchamber. But does it therefore follow that every man, whatever his habits or feelings may be, would, if he knew his own happiness, become a clerk rather than a cornet, or goldstick in waiting rather than governor of India?

Nothing can be more absurd than to suppose, like the Westminster Reviewer, that thieves steal only because they do not calculate the chances of being hanged as correctly as honest men. It never seems to have occurred to him as possible, that a man may so greatly prefer the life of a thief to the life of a labourer, that he may determine to brave the risk of detection and punishment, though he may even think that risk greater than it really is. And how, on Utilitarian principles, is such a man to be convinced that he is in the wrong? 'You will be found out.'—'Undoubtedly.'—'You will be hanged within two years.'—'I expect to be hanged within one year.'—'Then why do you pursue this lawless mode of life?'—'Because I would rather live for one year with plenty of money, dressed like a gentleman, eating and drinking of the best, frequenting public places, and visiting a dashing mistress, than break stones on the road, or sit down to the loom, with the certainty of attaining a good old age. It is my humour. Are you answered?'

A king, says the Reviewer again, would govern well if he were wise, for fear of provoking his subjects to insurrection. Therefore, the true happiness of a king is identical with the greatest happiness of society. Tell Charles II that if he will be constant to his queen, sober at table, regular at prayers, frugal in his expenses, active in the transaction of business; if he will drive the herd of slaves, buffoons, and procurers from Whitehall, and make the happiness of his people the rule of his conduct, he will have a much greater chance of reigning in comfort to an advanced age; that his profusion and tyranny have exasperated his subjects, and may, perhaps, bring him to an end as terrible as his father's. He might answer, that he saw the danger, but that life was not worth having without ease and vicious pleasures. And what has our philosopher to say? Does he not see that it is no more possible to reason a man out of liking a short life and a merry one more than a long life and a dull one, than to reason a Greenlander out of his train oil? We may say that the tastes of the thief and the tyrant differ from ours; but what right have we to say, looking at this world alone, that they do not pursue their greatest happiness very judiciously?

It is the grossest ignorance of human nature to suppose that another man calculates the chances differently from us, merely because he does what, in his place, we should not do. Every man has tastes and propensities, which he is disposed to gratify at a risk and expense, which people of different temperaments and habits think extravagant. 'Why,' says Horace, 'does one brother like to lounge in the forum, to play in the Campus, and to anoint himself in the baths, so well, that he would not put himself out of his way for all the wealth of the richest plantations of the East; while the other toils from sunrise to sunset for the purpose of increasing his fortune?' Horace attributes the diversity to the influence of the Genius and the natal star: and eighteen hundred years have taught us only to disguise our ignorance beneath a more philosophical language.

We think, therefore, that the Westminster Reviewer, even if we admit his calculation of the chances to be right, does not make out his case. But he appears to us to miscalculate chances more grossly than any person who ever acted or speculated in this world. 'It is for the happiness,' says he, 'of a member of the House of Commons to govern well; for he never can tell that he is not close on the moment when misgovernment will be terribly punished: if he was sure that he should be as lucky as his predecessors, it might be for his happiness to misgovern; but he is not sure.' Certainly a member of Parliament is not sure that he shall not be torn in pieces by a mob, or guillotined by a revolutionary tribunal, for his opposition to reform. Nor is the Westminster Reviewer sure that he shall not be hanged for writing in favour of universal suffrage. We may have democratical massacres. We may also have aristocratical proscriptions. It is not very likely, thank God, that we should see either. But the radical, we think, runs as much danger as the aristocrat. As to our friend, the Westminster Reviewer, he, it must be owned, has as good a right as any man on his side, *'Antoni gladios contemnere.'* But take the man whose votes, ever since he has sate in Parliament, have been the most uniformly bad, and oppose him to the man whose votes have been the most uniformly good. The Westminster Reviewer would probably select Mr Sadler and Mr Hume. Now, does any rational man think,—will the Westminster Reviewer himself say,—that Mr Sadler runs more risk of coming to a miserable end, on account of his public conduct, than Mr Hume? Mr Sadler does not know that he is not close on the moment when he will be made an example of; for Mr Sadler knows, if possible, less about the future than about the past. But he has no more reason to expect that he shall be made an example of, than to expect that London will be swallowed up by an earthquake next spring; and it would be as foolish in him to act on the former supposition as on the latter. There is a risk; for there is a risk of every thing which does not involve a contradiction; but it is a risk from which no man in his wits would give a shilling to be insured. Yet our Westminster Reviewer tells us, that this risk alone, apart from all considerations of religion, honour, or benevolence, would, as a matter of mere calculation, induce a wise member of the House of Commons to refuse any emoluments which might be offered him as the price of his support to pernicious measures.

We have hitherto been examining cases proposed by our opponent. It is now our turn to propose one, and we beg that he will spare no wisdom in solving it.

A thief is condemned to be hanged. On the eve of the day fixed for the execution, a turnkey enters his cell, and tells him that all is safe, that he has only to slip out, that his friends are waiting in the neighbourhood with disguises, and that a passage is taken for him in an American packet. Now, it is clearly for the greatest happiness of society that the thief should be hanged, and the corrupt turnkey exposed and punished. Will the Westminster Reviewer tell us, that it is for the greatest happiness of the thief to summon the head jailer, and tell the whole story? Now, either it is for the greatest happiness of a thief to be hanged, or it is not. If it is, then the argument, by which the Westminster Reviewer attempts to prove, that men do not promote their own happiness by thieving, falls to the ground. If it is not, then there are men whose greatest happiness is at variance with the greatest happiness of the community.

To sum up our arguments shortly, we say, that the 'greatest happiness principle,' as now stated, is diametrically opposed to the principle stated in the Westminster Review three months ago.

We say, that if the 'greatest happiness principle,' as now stated, be sound, Mr Mill's Essay, and all other works concerning Government, which, like that Essay, proceed on the supposition, that individuals may have an interest opposed to the greatest happiness of society, are fundamentally erroneous.

We say, that those who hold this principle to be sound, must be prepared to maintain, either that monarchs and aristocracies may be trusted to govern the community, or else that men cannot be trusted to follow their own interest, when that interest is demonstrated to them.

We say, that if men cannot be trusted to follow their own interest, when that interest has been demonstrated to them, then the Utilitarian arguments, in favour of universal suffrage, are good for nothing.

We say, that the 'greatest happiness principle' has not been proved; that it cannot be generally proved; that even in the particular cases selected by the Reviewer it is not clear that the principle is true; and that many cases might be stated in which the common sense of mankind would at once pronounce it to be false.

We now leave the Westminster Reviewer to alter and amend his 'magnificent principle' as he thinks best. Unlimited, it is false. Properly limited, it will be barren. The 'greatest happiness principle' of the 1st of July, as far as we could discern its meaning through a cloud of rodomontade, was an idle truism. The 'greatest happiness principle' of the 1st of October is, in the phrase of the American newspapers, 'important if true.' But unhappily it is not true. It is not our business to conjecture what new maxim is to make the bones of sages and patriots stir on the 1st of December. We can only say, that, unless it be something infinitely more ingenious than its two predecessors, we shall leave it unmolested. The Westminster Reviewer may, if he pleases, indulge himself like Sultan Schahriar, with espousing a rapid succession of virgin theories. But we must beg to be excused from playing the part of the vizier, who regularly attended on the day after the wedding to strangle the new Sultana.

The Westminster Reviewer charges us with urging it as an objection to the 'greatest happiness principle,' that, 'it is included in the Christian morality.' This is a mere fiction of his own. We never attacked the morality of the Gospel. We blamed the Utilitarians for claiming the credit of a discovery, when they had merely stolen that morality, and spoiled it in the stealing. They have taken the precept of Christ, and left the motive; and they demand the praise of a most wonderful and beneficial invention, when all that they have done has been to make a most useful maxim useless by separating it from its sanction. On religious principles, it is true that every individual will best promote his own happiness by promoting the happiness of others. But if religious considerations be left out of the question, it is not true. If we do not reason on the supposition of a future state, where is the motive? If we do reason on that supposition, where is the discovery?

The Westminster Reviewer tells us, that 'we wish to see the science of Government unsettled, because we see no prospect of a settlement which accords with our interests.' His angry eager-ness to have questions settled resembles that of a judge in one of Dryden's plays—the Amphitryon, we think—who wishes to decide a cause after hearing only one party, and when he has been at last compelled to listen to the statement of the defen-dant, flies into a passion, and exclaims, 'There now, sir! See what you have done. The case was quite clear a minute ago; and you must come and puzzle it!' He is the zealot of a sect. We are searchers after truth. He wishes to have the question settled. We wish to have it sifted first. The querulous manner in which we have been blamed for attacking Mr Mill's system, and pro-pounding no system of our own, reminds us of the horror with which that shallow dogmatist, Epicurus, the worst parts of whose nonsense the Utilitarians have attempted to revive, shrank from the keen and searching scepticism of the second Academy.

It is not our fault that an experimental science of vast extent does not admit of being settled by a short demonstration;—that the subtilty of nature, in the moral as in the physical world, triumphs over the subtilty of syllogism. The quack who declares on affidavit that, by using his pills, and attending to his printed directions, hundreds who had been dismissed incurable from the hospitals, have renewed their youth like the eagles, may, per-haps, think that Sir Henry Halford, when he feels the pulses of patients, enquires about their symptoms, and prescribes a different remedy to each, is unsettling the science of medicine for the sake of a fee.

If, in the course of this controversy, we have refrained from expressing any opinion respecting the political institutions of England, it is not because we have not an opinion, or because we shrink from avowing it. The Utilitarians, indeed, conscious that their boasted theory of government would not bear in-vestigation, were desirous to turn the dispute about Mr Mill's Essay into a dispute about the Whig party, rotten boroughs, unpaid magistrates, and ex-officio informations. When we blamed them for talking nonsense, they cried out that they were insulted for being reformers,—just as poor Ancient Pistol swore that the scars which he had received from the cudgel of Fluellen were got in the Gallia wars. We, however, did not think it desirable to mix up political questions, about which the public mind is violently agitated, with a great problem in moral philosophy.

Our notions about Government are not, however, altogether unsettled. We have an opinion about parliamentary reform, though we have not arrived at that opinion by the royal road which Mr Mill has opened for the explorers of political science. As we are taking leave, probably for the last time, of this controversy, we will state very concisely what our doctrines are. On some future occasion we may, perhaps, explain and defend them at length.

Our fervent wish, and, we will add, our sanguine hope, is, that we may see such a reform of the House of Commons as may render its votes the express image of the opinion of the middle orders of Britain. A pecuniary qualification we think absolutely necessary; and in settling its amount, our object would be to draw the line in such a manner, that every decent farmer and shopkeeper might possess the elective franchise. We should wish to see an end put to all the advantages which particular forms of property possess over other forms, and particular portions of property over other equal portions. And this would content us. Such a reform would, according to Mr Mill, establish an aristocracy of wealth, and leave the community without protection, and exposed to all the evils of unbridled power. Most willingly would we stake the whole controversy between us on the success of the experiment which we propose.

VIII

Edinburgh Review and the 'Greatest Happiness Principle'

Westminster Review, vol. xxiii (January 1830), Article xiv.

THE conductors of the Westminster Review were desirous of an opportunity of making some additional remarks upon the principle they have in two preceding numbers had the good fortune to defend. A controversy, whatever may be its effects in approving the defensibleness of particular branches of a system, is not always the best adapted for the orderly statement of its substance. It is possible therefore that their design may have its use; though at some risk of incurring the scandal of repetition, and the disgrace of presenting what every body knows. The article in the last number of the Edinburgh Review has afforded them the opportunity desired; without materially altering the execution of their plan.

They therefore state,—for the edification of those who may be disposed to be edified by it, and without the slightest desire to interfere with the right of any body to prefer 'the keen and searching scepticism of the second Academy,'—that the substance of what they have endeavoured to maintain, when presented with more attention to order than a controversy would admit, is as follows.

First, That Morality, as applied to the conduct of individuals, is reducible to being the rule, the general observation of which would produce the greatest sum or aggregate of happiness among those who are to be affected by the consequences. That though moral precepts may have been uttered without any reference made to this principle, and many of them may have been right,—it is a reference to this principle which in disputed cases distinguishes the true from the pseudo-morality;—which establishes, for example, that it is not a meritorious action for a man to eat his father, as in some countries has been inculcated as a duty, and that it is not criminal *per se* to drink wine, which in others has been accounted an offence. If they are asked how they know that morality is reducible to this rule, they reply, Because on comparison with any of the systems of morality which have attained to extensive acceptance among mankind, it is palpable that in by far the largest portion of their extent the rules coincide; and that in respect of that portion in which they do not, the contest, with one solitary species of exception, has always been rested upon the effects in some shape of suffering or the contrary, on the sentient creatures that were concerned. If, for example, it was ever contended that it was a moral act for

a man to kill and eat his father, it was supported on the ground
that it was for the happiness of society and of themselves, that
men on arriving at a certain stage of decrepitude should be put
out of pain, and that it was a mark of respect for their sons to eat
them. There may be doubt whether the reasoning was good;
but there is none that this was the reasoning. And the same in
other cases. The solitary exception remarked, is where on the
ground of some asserted supernatural sanction or authority,
actions have been defended as consonant with the moral rule,
which have been hostile to the increase of the temporal happiness of men in the aggregate. On which peculiar description of
cases it is sufficient to reply, that to make them of any weight it
is requisite that it should be proved, not only that the authority
referred to is unimpeachable, but that the interpretation of
those who make the reference is unimpeachable also; and that
none of those who have at any time brought forward a precept
of the nature described, have established their title upon both
these points. The Vedas, for example, may be considered as
having failed upon the first point, and the Inquisition on the
other. And further, that even in these cases, there has always
been a virtual reference to some final advantage, which either
through the influence of a supernatural power or otherwise, was
to be the result of obedience.

Secondly, That though for any thing they have to say to the
contrary there may be a hundred different reasons why men
should be moral, one reason which to a certain extent may dis-
pense with the production of the other ninety-nine, is that the
circumstances in which man is placed are such, that the habitual
observance of the rule asserted to be the rule of morality, is in
the long run and taking all chances together, the safest and most
likely guide to the happiness of the individual. It may not be
accordant with experience that in every individual case the man
who lives in the breach of moral rules shall, in exteriors at least,
be less happy than some other;—any more than it is accordant
with experience that every man of eighty will die before every
man of twenty-five. On the contrary it may be allowed to be
certain, that in some instances the contrary will happen. But
what is urged is, that in the same way as it is proveable by
experience that a man would be a simpleton, who with all the
chances before him, should chuse an annuity on the life of an

average man of eighty in preference to one of twenty-five,—so it is proveable that a man commits an error and a folly, who with all the chances to encounter, chuses the quantity of happiness which shall be consequent on a course of immorality, in preference to the quantity he might have obtained by another course. The way in which each of these propositions must be established, is by individual attention to the evidence, that though now and then a man of eighty sees the funeral of a man of twenty-five, and a man of immoral conduct is (in outward appearance at least) more fortunate and happy than some one of opposite character, this does not destroy the general inference that nine times out of ten the event is of a contrary description, and that the man is a blockhead who makes his election the wrong way. If indeed any body says he sees reason to believe, that men of eighty are on the whole better lives than those of twenty-five, or that immoral men do upon the whole lead happier lives than moral ones, he is at perfect liberty to retain his own opinion. All that is insisted on is, that there are reasons sufficient to induce the greatest part of mankind to come to a contrary conclusion.

Thirdly, That the principle after being elucidated and established in the simpler case of individuals, is transferable to the operations of masses or combinations of men,—as for example, notably, to the conduct of those collections of influential persons who regulate the affairs of others under the title of governments, and to the conduct of independent nations in their behaviour towards each other. The interest of those who are in these cases to be acted upon, in receiving the greatest happiness, it seems unnecessary to go about to prove; the point in question relates to the happiness of the actors. And here the object is to establish as in accordance with the dictates of a sound and enlightened experience, that though there is no certainty that in any individual case the rule which would produce the greatest aggregate of happiness will be attended with the greatest happiness to the party whose mode of action is in question, there is a certainty that the habitual observance of the rule will on the whole be the most likely guide to the happiness of this very party. It may not be absolutely certain that a particular government or nation which conducts itself according to the rule of the general happiness shall not be unfortunate;—but it is absolutely certain, that if all the instances in which governments or nations have acted according to the rule be compared with those in which they have not, the comparative result will be found vastly in favour of the former. This may not be as much as some could have found in their hearts to wish;—they may think it would have been very useful if it had been regulated, that every man who stole should die of an apoplexy the next week. But it is as much as Providence has chosen to give; and quite enough for wise men to act upon.

An important fact connected with these propositions is, that as men advance in civilization and improvement, the closeness of the connection between morality and particular happiness increases. In such a progressive state of general society, the actual proportion of cases in which immorality (personal, governmental, or national) is not attended with greater suffering in the end, may be viewed as continually decreasing, in the same manner that the number of men of eighty who mourn at the funerals of their grand-children is likely to be diminished. As the accidents by which men are exposed to be hurried to a premature death are on the decrease, and the appliances by which they are assisted to attain old age are on the increase,—so in the moral case, the combinations of society to connect suffering with guilt are continually gaining strength, and the power and opportunities of those who would oppose it are declining. Cacus had but one Hercules to guard against; but a robber of the diligence between Paris and Turin, has two legions of gendarmerie. In the same manner with respect to the crimes of nations, the feeling of community of interest with the sufferers is every where augmented, and the conviction of any real interest in the participation of the crime, among the citizens of the aggressive state, is every where diminished. The zeal for retribution, and the knowledge of the means, combine in all directions to increase the force of God's natural check upon iniquity and wrong.

After having laid down the motives which should induce all individuals without exception to concur in promoting the greatest happiness, it was an easy inference that if the happiness of men is to be the object of government, the object is to be obtained by their being governed with a view to their own interest, and not to the interest of somebody else; and that the way to effect this is, that they should govern themselves, or at all events hold an effectual check over those to whom the reins of government are committed. And this led to those conclusions on the subject of modes of government, which it is unnecessary to repeat.

Whether all this is right, is known perhaps to beings in a higher state of existence than our own; and is certainly not known to every man who has attained to the faculty of writing in a quarterly Review. But if it is not right, it has very much the air of leading to what is right. Whenever it is found capable of improvement, the degradation of amendment shall be submitted to. To gain with labour and hold fast with pains, is the way in which men are doomed to come by knowledge; with the exception of that peculiar class, who come from the hands of the maker as perfect as they ever are.

The remainder of the paper will consist of replies to objections from the Edinburgh Review and other quarters; beginning with such as relate to the general principle.

What earthly good can there be in a principle upon which no man will act until he is all-wise? A certain most important doctrine, we are told, has been demonstrated so clearly, that it ought to be the foundation of the science of government. And yet the whole frame of government is to be constituted, exactly as if this fundamental doctrine were false, and on the supposition that no human being will ever act as if he believed it to be true!'[1]

The substitution of one proposition for another. It was never stated that no man will act upon the principle till he is all-wise; but that if he was all-wise he would act upon it. If men were all-wise, they would be honest. But it does not follow that nobody will be honest, but one that is all-wise. The truth that if men were all-wise they would be honest, may be demonstrated ever so clearly upon paper; and yet form no reason why government should not be constituted upon the supposition that men will not be honest after all.

To say that a man does what he believes to be against his happiness, is a contradiction in terms. If, therefore, government and laws are to be constituted on the supposition on which Mr. Mill's Essay is founded, that all individuals will, whenever they have power over others put into their hands, act in opposition to the general

[1] [p. 215]

happiness, then government and laws must be constituted on the supposition that no individual believes, or ever will believe, his own happiness to be identical with the happiness of society. That is to say, government and laws are to be constituted on the supposition that no human being will ever be satisfied by Mr. Bentham's proof of his 'greatest happiness principle,'—a supposition which may be true enough, but which says little, we think, for the principle in question.[2]

Mr. Mill's proposition was, that all men will abuse power *when nothing checks*; and therefore it is the interest of the community to multiply checks. It may be quite true that men would be honest if they were wise; and yet form no reason why the prevention of dishonesty should be taken out of the hands of law and government, and trusted to the operation of the precept of morality. The real object is to check dishonesty by the exertions of the law, and to check it by the dissemination of the principle that dishonesty is bad policy besides.

Nothing can be more absurd than to suppose, like the Westminster Reviewer, that thieves steal only because they do not calculate the chances of being hanged as correctly as honest men.[3]

It never was supposed that they steal *only* for that reason. *'Only'* is an insertion.

It never seems to have occurred to him as possible, that a man may so greatly prefer the life of a thief to the life of a labourer, that he may determine to brave the risk of detection and punishment, though he may even think that risk greater than it really is. And how, on Utilitarian principles, is such a man to be convinced that he is in the wrong? 'You will be found out.'—'Undoubtedly.'—'You will be hanged within two years.'—'I expect to be hanged within one year.'—'Then why do you pursue this lawless mode of life?'—'Because I would rather live for one year with plenty of money, dressed like a gentleman, eating and drinking of the best, frequenting public places, and visiting a dashing mistress, than break stones on the road, or sit down to the loom, with the certainty of attaining a good old age. It is my humour. Are you answered?'[4]

The sophism is in stating, that it is his humour therefore it is wise. The question was, whether it is not capable of being demonstrated to the satisfaction of men in general, and with a manifest tendency to dissuade from the vocation of a thief,—that if all the pleasures and pains of the thief be put together,

[2] [pp. 215–16]   [3] [p. 217]   [4] [pp. 217–18]

he has a worse balance on winding up the account than an honest man. It is no answer to this to say, that the thief voluntarily prefers the enjoyment of the credit side of the account at the present moment, and shuts his eyes to the other. The spendthrift tradesman does the same; but it does not follow that the balance is finally in his favour. It is very possible for a man to do a foolish act; and it is not the less foolish because he *chose* to do it. To say that the man chuses which he likes best, and must therefore always have his greatest happiness, is a mere evasion. The question was, whether of two things set before him, an individual may not chuse the worst. The answer given is, that the fact of his chusing necessarily makes it the best. The caution of the nurse is, 'Avoid green gooseberries, or you will have cause to rue.' The answer of the baby is, 'I like to have green gooseberries; and therefore I can never have cause to rue.' The immoral man, like the baby, acts under a most imperfect consciousness of the real comparative value of the two sides of the account. He sees the one under the favouring aspect of immediate certainty of enjoyment; and the other under a false estimate, or an almost total ignorance, both of its actual magnitude and of the chances of escape. The baby runs all risks for the present gratification of a very paltry appetite; but vastly altered is its estimate of things, when the gripes come upon it like an armed man. According to the Edinburgh Review, the gripes are its greatest happiness. In the same manner the thief who steals to the amount of twenty shillings and gets hanged for it, would assuredly never have done it if he had made a sober estimate of the pleasures of twenty shillings and the actual unpleasantness of hanging by the neck, together with a correct judgment of the probabilities that one would be consequent upon the other. The fact is, that he makes no estimate at all, or none that approaches to correctness. He opens his eyes wide to the twenty shillings, and winks and runs his head into the disgraceful noose; and because he chuses to do this, he is to be held to have obtained his greatest happiness. Hogarth's 'Idle Apprentice' is a representation of the greatest happiness of the Edinburgh Review.

But it is practicable to go further. It is possible to borrow from theology, and ask, why the man who is supposed to do amiss and incur perpetual punishment in another world in return, is not to be allowed to have got his greatest happiness.

He has had his choice,—he has taken that which he preferred to take,—as well as any of the rest. It follows, therefore, by evident connection, that this man also has had his greatest happiness.

'A king, says the Reviewer again, would govern well if he were wise, for fear of provoking his subjects to insurrection. Therefore, the true happiness of a king is identical with the greatest happiness of society. Tell Charles II. that if he will be constant to his queen, sober at table, regular at prayers, frugal in his expenses, active in the transaction of business; if he will drive the herd of slaves, buffoons, and procurers from Whitehall, and make the happiness of his people the rule of his conduct, he will have a much greater chance of reigning in comfort to an advanced age; that his profusion and tyranny have exasperated his subjects, and may, perhaps, bring him to an end as terrible as his father's. He might answer, that he saw the danger, but that life was not worth having without ease and vicious pleasures. And what has our philosopher to say? Does he not see that it is no more possible to reason a man out of liking a short life and a merry one more than a long life and a dull one, than to reason a Greenlander out of his train oil? We may say that the tastes of the thief and the tyrant differ from ours; but what right have we to say, looking at this world alone, that they do not pursue their greatest happiness very judiciously?'[5]

The question was not whether the argument should produce a certain effect on a given thief or tyrant, but whether it may not produce the effect of dissuading some men somewhere from theft and tyranny. If it does this, it produces good, whether it proves effectual upon a given individual or not. The demonstration of the perils attendant on profusion and tyranny might not be effectual on Charles II.; but it does not follow that it may not be effectual on somebody else. A given Greenlander may not be to be persuaded out of his train oil; but it might be possible to lay the foundations for persuading some future Greenlander, that claret is the better of the two.

It is the grossest ignorance of human nature to suppose that another man calculates the chances differently from us, merely because he does what, in his place, we should not do. Every man has tastes and propensities, which he is disposed to gratify at a risk and expense, which people of different temperaments and habits think extravagant.[6]

Men have sufficient community of feeling to enable them to pronounce with considerable certainty on the comparative value of different pains and pleasures, whoever may be the subject. The theory of the Edinburgh Review is, that the thief may possess a peculiar gust in the joys of profligacy, and an idiosyncrasy for diminishing the pains of hanging, the torment of perpetual fear, and the sufferings of remorse,—of which the man who is not a thief has no right to form any apprehension. To which it may be replied, that not only there is no proof that any thing of this kind exists, but that there is proof to the opposite effect, of as strong a nature as to the fact that fire burns one man as well as another, or to any other community of feeling, though it cannot be established by an absolute exchange of personal consciousness.

—take the man whose votes, ever since he has sate in Parliament, have been the most uniformly bad, and oppose him to the man whose votes have been the most uniformly good.—Now, does any rational man think, that the one runs more risk of coming to a miserable end, on account of his public conduct, than the other? The first does not know that he is not close on the moment when he will be made an example of. But he has no more reason to expect that he shall be made an example of, than to expect that London will be swallowed up by an earthquake next spring; and it would be as foolish in him to act on the former supposition as on the latter.[7]

So said the sinners that were before the flood;—and before its great political parallel, the French Revolution. All this might have been said to any active member of the French government for the century that preceded; and still the Revolution came at last, and vindicated the soundness of the principle in question. Take the happiness of the members of the American government during the fifty years it has existed,—take also the happiness of the Stuarts and their courtiers, or any other race who have governed notoriously ill, and make a proper allowance for the misery which has come upon them in those seasons when they were brought to a reckoning for their misconduct;—divide the resulting masses fairly among the individuals concerned;— and let any thinking man decide for himself, on which side he

[7] [p. 219]

should wish his lot to be cast, if the whole, with all its chances and uncertainties, was to come over again. If he decides for the Americans, it is proof that *he* at least, is of opinion that conduct like that of the Stuarts is unwise.

A thief is condemned to be hanged. On the eve of the day fixed for the execution, a turnkey enters his cell, and tells him that all is safe, that he has only to slip out, that his friends are waiting in the neighbourhood with disguises, and that a passage is taken for him in an American packet. Now, it is clearly for the greatest happiness of society that the thief should be hanged, and the corrupt turnkey exposed and punished. Will the Westminster Reviewer tell us, that it is for the greatestest happiness of the thief to summon the head jailer, and tell the whole story? Now, either it is for the greatest happiness of a thief to be hanged, or it is not. If it is, then the argument, by which the Westminster Reviewer attempts to prove, that men do not promote their own happiness by thieving, falls to the ground. If it is not, then there are men whose greatest happiness is at variance with the greatest happiness of the community.[8]

The case produced in opposition, is itself the most awful exemplification of the rule. The proposition is, that men risk suffering, by breaches of the law of general happiness. And the objection offered is, that a man may bring himself to such a state, that he shall have no means to escape a shameful death but by a further infraction of the law. Suppose the rule supported was, that men risk their health by dram-drinking. But, says the opponent, there are men who have brought themselves to such a state by dram-drinking, that they could not survive a day without taking a quantity of drams; is it possible to maintain in this case, that dram-drinking is unwholesome? The answer to which is, that the state to which the man is reduced, is itself the most powerful proof of the verity of the rule. In the same manner the argument with the novice who is thinking of putting on the vocation of a thief, should be, that he will have made an awfully bad choice if he comes to be sentenced to be hanged, with no chance but that of allowing the turnkey to take him a passage to America.

We say, that if the 'greatest happiness principle,' as now stated, be sound, Mr. Mill's Essay, and all other works concerning Government, which, like that Essay, proceed on the supposition, that indivi-

[8] [p. 220]

duals may have an interest opposed to the greatest happiness of society, are fundamentally erroneous.[9]

A confusion between temporary or apparent interest, and ultimate or real.

We say, that those who hold this principle to be sound, must be prepared to maintain, either that monarchs and aristocracies may be trusted to govern the community, or else that men cannot be trusted to follow their own interest, when that interest is demonstrated to them.[10]

Nothing is more undeniable, than that men cannot be trusted to follow their own interest, merely because pains have been taken to demonstrate it to them. The fallacy is in the word 'demonstrated;' which may mean either 'impressed on the mind so as to produce perfect conviction and belief,' or 'laid down in a printed demonstration in a book.' The last of these meanings makes no dilemma; it is intended therefore that the proposition should be granted in this sense, and interpreted in the other.

We say, that if men cannot be trusted to follow their own interest, when that interest has been demonstrated to them, then the Utilitarian arguments, in favour of universal suffrage, are good for nothing.[11]

The same fallacy as before. Men *may* be trusted to follow their own interest, if they have an intimate persuasion of what their interest is, and are persuaded right. Men have already attained to so much knowledge of their true interest, as to lead the Utilitarians to maintain, that for them to have the power also, would be the most likely way to cause their true interest to be enforced.

We say, that the 'greatest happiness principle' has not been proved; that it cannot be generally proved; that even in the particular cases selected by the Reviewer it is not clear that the principle is true; and that many cases might be stated in which the common sense of mankind would at once pronounce it to be false.[12]

Every thing depends upon opinion. Some men look through the world, and come to the conclusion that honesty is the best policy; others do the same, and come to the conclusion that it is not. There is a wide and increasing schism between these two

[9] [p. 220]   [10] [p. 220]   [11] [p. 220]   [12] [p. 221]

parties; and nothing that has been said in the Edinburgh Review is likely to end it.

The Westminster Reviewer charges us with urging it as an objection to the 'greatest happiness principle,' that, 'it is included in the Christian morality.' This is a mere fiction of his own. We never attacked the morality of the Gospel. We blamed the Utilitarians for claiming the credit of a discovery, when they had merely stolen that morality, and spoiled it in the stealing. They have taken the precept of Christ, and left the motive; and they demand the praise of a most wonderful and beneficial invention, when all that they have done has been to make a most useful maxim useless by separating it from its sanction. On religious principles, it is true that every individual will best promote his own happiness by promoting the happiness of others. But if religious considerations be left out of the question, it is not true. If we do not reason on the supposition of a future state, where is the motive? If we do reason on that supposition, where is the discovery?[13]

The assertion was not that the being included in the Christian morality was urged as an 'objection to the greatest happiness principle;' but that it was urged as an 'objection'—manifestly not to the principle, but to the use there was in bringing it into notice. The Edinburgh Review is too fond of interpolation. The answer to the objection has been given before. But if it is necessary to dilate upon the subject, it must be stated, that since after nearly two thousand years, only one sixth of the population of the world have adopted the precepts of Christianity as their rule of conduct, there is some utility in deducing both a rule and a motive, which shall be applicable to the service of the other five. Either there is a possibility of doing this, or the Creator has left on the lowest possible computation more than nineteen-twentieths of the human beings that have existed, without the possibility of having either. There is no reason in supposing the last; nor does it accord with the authority to which the Edinburgh Reviewers profess to refer every thing. The scriptures to which they refer, contain numerous admissions that the nations who never heard of Christianity had the means of ascertaining a moral rule. Large portions of those who profess Christianity make no scruple of avowing, that they believe it because its precepts agree with a sound morality; in fact Christians with

[13] [p. 221]

scarcely an exception, appeal to the pureness of its morality as evidence of truth. The teachers of Christianity, in determining what *is* their morality, continually appeal to some other rule, which on being examined will be found to be the rule of the general happiness. For example, the command when smitten on one cheek to turn the other, has by none been interpreted literally. It has always been assumed to be limited by a rational regard to the consequences of obedience. Even the great precept of 'doing to others as we would they should do to us,' is limited in the same manner. It is possible that if the experiment was made on a beggar, he might find in his heart to desire his rich neighbour to give him half his property, and marry him to his daughter. But no person has ever contended that this ought to be the interpretation; and for no reason that can be assigned, but that it would be contrary to the well-being of mankind. Again, if men professing Christianity in these latter times are much less disposed to commit atrocious actions on the plea of religious duty than in former ages,—if massacres and burnings for the love of heaven have been rarer,—it seems to be mainly attributable to the influence which what may be termed natural morality has obtained over the interpreters. The men who massacred and burnt, had the precepts of the gospel in their mouths, as much as any who live in the present day. The precepts of the gospel, therefore, have received from natural morality a most beneficial aid. All these considerations go to prove, that the Creator has given men the natural means of ascertaining a moral rule, and that the rule is no other than the general happiness. But if they have the power of finding a rule, it appears to be almost a contradiction in terms to suppose that they have not the power of finding a motive. A rule without a motive, is no rule at all. The rule of the greatest happiness evidently includes the motive; and wants nothing but the expansion of the process by which the happinesss of the individual is involved in that of the species.

Another reason why the importance of the 'greatest happiness principle' is not absorbed in the coincidence of the Christian precepts, is that it applies to combinations of men in their aggregate capacity. Granting that the religious sanction applies to the conduct of individuals,—it by no means applies with equal vigour to the conduct of communities. It may be urged, that it applies to the individuals that compose the community, and this is enough. But the 'greatest happiness principle' applies to individuals, and to communities besides. In addition to the motives held out to individuals by both principles, the earthly principle says to nations, that it is for their ultimate interest to deal justly towards each other. It would be difficult to say what motive the religious principle holds out to nations in their corporate capacity; for it certainly does not threaten them *en masse*, with the 'sanction' alluded to by the Edinburgh Reviewers. And the consequence has been, that if Christian men have had small morality, Christian states have had less. It is notorious that many of the worst acts of Christian nations, have been committed under the direction of men who as individuals had not the least idea of missing heaven. It would be thought hard and severe in any man, who should threaten a bad administration with sending them individually to the devil. The true check on bad administrations, is in setting before them the risk of present ruin, and of future if not present disgrace. Will the reputation of the conductors of the American and anti-revolutionary wars, be any prize in a lottery a century hence? Will the fame of Pitt be *'bella?'* It seems established therefore, that the principle contended for is at all events capable of doing good service in the political department, and has the field almost entirely to itself.

After this it may be useful to go back to the objections which relate peculiarly to the propositions of Mr. Mill on government. . . . ['If we assume that . . . different degrees of heat' pp. 196–7.]

There is no need for going through all that has been said by the great man. The latent principle had been tracked by Mr. Mill long ago, and uttered in one word, 'check.' It consists in the possession of the virtual power of interference, on the part of the governed. The Danes and Americans had this power; and the Romans and French had not. The Danish people had it by virtue of their accidental position, which enabled them to keep two other forces in a state of balance, by the power of acting with either against the other; and they had it in spite of the absence of the forms of popular representation. The French people had the forms of representation, but not the effective power. In defiance of both these anomalies, it is perfectly possible that the forms of popular representation, combined with the power, may constitute the rational and practical mode of promoting good government. The rational and practical way of causing an individual to be taken care of, is to allow him to take care of himself. There have been individuals who have not been allowed to take care of themselves, and have yet been taken good care of. There have been individuals who have been allowed to take care of themselves, and have not been taken good care of after all. Both these are anomalies; but neither of them destroy the general rule. The general rule is that which is alone applicable to the simple case; the cases where it is not applicable, are complicated by the intervention of some fortuitous circumstance. It would be unreasonable to say to nations in general 'If you want to enjoy good government, make yourselves a balanced monarchy and aristocracy, as there was in Denmark;'—just as it would be unreasonable to say to men in general 'If you want to take care of yourselves, get somebody else to take care of you,' because in a single case it answered.

The Utilitarian doctrine then is, not that despots and aristocracies will always plunder and oppress the people to the last point, but that they will do so if nothing checks them.

In the first place, it is quite clear that the doctrine thus stated is of no use at all, unless the force of the checks be estimated. The first law of motion is, that a ball once projected will fly on to all eternity with undiminished velocity, unless something checks. The fact is, that a ball stops in a few seconds after proceeding a few yards with very variable motion. Every man would wring his child's neck, and pick his friend's pocket, if nothing checked him. In fact, the principle thus stated, means only that governments will oppress, unless they abstain from oppressing.[14]

It no more means so, than a ball's moving till something checks, means only that it will move unless it abstains from moving.

It is evidently on the real distribution of power, and not on names and badges, that the happiness of nations must depend. The representative system, though doubtless a great and precious discovery in politics, is only one of the many modes in which the democratic part of the community can efficiently check the governing few. That certain men have been chosen as deputies of the people,—that there

[14] [p. 200]

is a piece of paper stating such deputies to possess certain powers,—these circumstances in themselves constitute no security for good government. Such a constitution nominally existed in France; while, in fact, an oligarchy of committees and clubs trampled at once on the electors and the elected. Representation is a very happy contrivance for enabling large bodies of men to exert their power, with less risk of disorder than there would otherwise be. But, assuredly, it does not of itself give power.[15]

The answer to all this appears to be, that Mr. Mill undoubtedly spoke of representation accompanied by power, and not of representation deprived of it. At the same time it is not true that the connection between representation and power is one of simple accident. There may have been cases where they have been separated; but the general and natural tendency of possessing the representation is to give the power. There may have been men who had a sword and still could not defend themselves. But it does not follow, that to have a sword, is not a considerable step towards defence.

The special pleading of the Reviewers on the subject of 'sensual pleasures,' is only an effort to lead off from the point in question. If by the 'sensual pleasures' of a king or an aristocracy, they meant to define such pleasures cut off from all wherewith kings and aristocracies necessarily accompany them, they might as well have stated that it costs comparatively little to find a king or an aristocracy in small beer. What they really intended was, to reduce and cut down the estimate of the cost of sensual pleasures, and huddle up the reckoning of the remainder by hastening to descant on the appetite for good opinion. The sensual pleasures of a king differ from those of a cobbler, as much as their liquors. The Reviewers desire to reckon only for the water that is in the king's Tokay; and to represent every thing that makes it a kingly draught, as referable to another account.

Objections will next be noticed from other sources. It has been stated in a quarter entitled to the most friendly attention, that the principle of Mr. Bentham ought to be limited to its operation on governments, and that its application to individual morality is a burthensome addition. To this it may be replied, that in the first place, the application is true, and for the reasons

[15] [p. 206]

already stated is not without considerable value in itself; and secondly, that the application to the simpler case is the best method of introducing and illustrating its application to the more complex. Men have already made considerable progress in the comprehension and practical use of the principle in the first form; it is therefore politic to enter the wedge by this end, with a view to the introduction of the remainder.

It has been objected from another quarter, that 'the magnificent law that was declared to be of such positive utility, is reduced to the working of a *probable* good.' This is a confusion between uncertainty in individual cases, and uncertainty in the aggregate. There may be uncertainty in one individual of twenty-five surviving another of eighty; but there is no uncertainty in the fact that men of twenty-five are on the whole the better lives. To say that the law which tells a man to prefer an annuity on a life of twenty-five to one of eighty, is only the enunciation of a *probable* good, would present the same mistake as in the objection. If every man of twenty-five had been certain of surviving every man of eighty, and every immoral act had been certain of being punished without the possibility of escape, there could have been no disinclination to note the fact. But as nature has willed otherwise, the next thing to be done is to note the *average* certainty which she has chosen to decree.

Another objection has consisted in 'begging to be informed what is the rule that is best for the general happiness;' and subjoining, that 'if it is to be left to the private judgment of individuals to decide upon what is best for the general happiness, the principle is useless, because mankind will never agree upon the mode of carrying it into effect.' This is only quarrelling with a principle that goes a certain length, because it does not go farther. It is perfectly true that there remains the question of what *is* for the general happiness. But the virtue of the previous proposition consisted in having reduced the question from a state of greater difficulty to a state of less. It is much easier to judge with some accuracy whether a given practice tends to the promotion of the general happiness, than to determine whether it is moral or immoral without the intervention of any such clue. For the palpable fact is, that men have an exceeding aptitude for judging of what is for the general happiness. They are all capable of forming a very tolerable theory—for

244 Utilitarian Logic and Politics

their neighbours. Men may fight shy of the truth for some particular purpose; but the practical reality is, that on most points
their knowledge is nearly as perfect as can be desired. There
may be some debateable ground after all; but the extent of that
on which there can be no general debate is incomparably
greater.

In all that has preceded, reference has been made to habits,
and not to insulated acts. The differences between single acts of
immorality and their habitual repetition have been exhausted
by writers to whom it is unnecessary to refer.

The final inference impressed by the whole case is, that the
friends of the 'greatest happiness' have only to persevere, to
arrive at the firmest establishment of their principle. They are
wrong if they think all that is necessary has been done somewhere to their hands already; the battle is still to finish, though
the good position is their own. What is wanted, is the laborious
and extensive illustration of the various ways in which national
and political invasions of the law of the greatest happiness work
to produce their own punishment. The world has been deluged
with illustrations of the corresponding truth in personal morality.
All dying speeches are portions of it; not a father that places his
son as an apprentice, but adds his fragment to the testimony.
There wants a collection of dying speeches of nefarious governments. It would not be difficult to make something of this kind
out of the history of the Stuarts. France could supply something
like it from periods of her history. The kingdoms of the Penin-
sula may be considered as in that state where the dying speech
is in every body's hands before the man is dead. The antiquary
might go back to Rome, and the orientalist to Babylon. One of
the first consequences of this resolute prosecution of the principle, would be the abandonment of the theological argument
against it, as happened in the case of the geologists. Every body
knows the kind of persecution a geologist was exposed to a few
years ago, if he ventured to make any portion of the world more
ancient than ultra theologians thought proper. The geologists
persevered; and now all rational theologians are glad to support
their own system by such facts as they can collect from the
observations of the geologists. In the same manner let the friends
of the greatest happiness persevere; and they will soon find
theologians anxious only to have the benefit of such support as

they may derive from the establishment of a coincidence between their rules. There is no war between Christianity and philosophy. Pure and undefiled Christianity is sound philosophy. If there ever has been war, it has been against the temporal abuses which pretences of religion were brought forward to protect. This was at the bottom of the outcry made against philosophy during the French Revolution. The real struggle was against arbitrary power sheltering itself under the influence of religious establishments. Religion was assailed because it was made an engine in the hands of the common enemy; the animosity was against the enemy, not against the abstract instrument that was in his hands. Those times are past. It is all too late now, to get up a religious opposition to the exercise of reason on any subject connected with the welfare of mankind.

IX

Of the Geometrical, or Abstract Method

[J. S. Mill: *System of Logic*, Book VI, chapter viii]

IX

Of the Economical, or Abstract Method

The extract which follows, apart from very minor deletions, constitutes chapter viii of Book VI of J. S. Mill's *System of Logic* (8th edition, 1872). Earlier in the *Logic* Mill is concerned with scientific generalizations and what justifies their acceptance. In his introduction to the work he says: 'All science consists of data and conclusions from those data, of proofs and what they prove: now logic points out what relations must subsist between data and whatever can be concluded from them, between proof and everything which it can prove.' Central to his inquiry is the process of 'induction' which he defines as, 'the operation of discovering and proving general propositions'. There is, he states, an underlying assumption, a fundamental principle, involved in all inductive reasoning, namely, that 'the course of nature is uniform' or 'that the universe is governed by general laws'. In Book VI he discusses the application of the principles of procedure which he claims are characteristic of the natural sciences to human individuals and social life.

At the outset Mill is faced with the question 'whether the law of causality applies in the same strict sense to human actions as to other phenomena,' and he goes on to argue that it does so apply, but with the crucial proviso that among the circumstances which determine a person's conduct can be the desire to shape his own character. Having thus established that man himself can be the subject of science, Mill seeks to identify the methods appropriate to this study and concludes that social science must rest on the laws of individual psychology which are themselves discoverable by direct observation and experiment. Unless generalizations about social phenomena can be connected with, and shown to be derived from, these laws they lack a scientific basis and thus attain the status only of *empirical*, as opposed to *causal*, laws.

Mill set great store by 'ethology', his term for knowledge of the formation of individual, group, and national character, whose laws would be derived from those of psychology and obtained by deducing what sort of character would be produced given the laws of mind and a specific set of circumstances. But sociology could not proceed by simply deducing the phenomena to be explained directly from psychological and ethological laws, since many factors contribute to a particular effect and the special circumstances of the society concerned must be taken into account. The propositions of sociology are therefore hypothetical and relate to tendencies. The main aim of sociology must be to discover laws of social development having the character of empirical generalizations but to be connected with the laws of human nature.

It is in the light of this general strategy for social science that we should place Mill's analysis of the errors in two methods of approach current in his day, what he calls the 'chemical' or 'experimental' method, of which Macaulay was an exponent, and the 'geometrical' method employed by the 'Bentham school'. What Mill found wrong with the latter is set out in the chapter we reprint here; his criticism of the 'chemical' method takes up chapter vii of Book VI, the main points of which we shall attempt to summarize.

The chapter opens with Mill insisting that 'men in a state of society are still men; their actions and passions are obedient to the laws of individual human nature.' Instead of appealing to the principles of human nature the advocates of the chemical method rely on 'specific experience', 'treating political facts in as directly experimental a method as chemical facts . . . [thereby] showing themselves true Baconians, and proving their adversaries to be mere syllogisers and schoolmen'. But, Mill objects, the conditions for experimental investigation are not present in the study of man; artificial experiments, for instance, are impossible. More important, however, is the fact that 'the causes of every phenomenon which we are particularly interested about, security, wealth, freedom, good government, public virtue . . . are infinitely numerous, especially the external or remote causes, which alone are, for the most part, accessible to direct observation. No one cause suffices of itself to produce any of these phenomena . . .' So he concludes: 'In an age in which chemistry itself . . . has found it necessary to become . . . a Deductive Science, it is not to be apprehended that any person of scientific habits, who has kept pace with the general progress of the knowledge of nature, can be in danger of applying the methods of elementary chemistry to explore the sequences of the most complex order of phenomena in existence.'

Of the Geometrical, or Abstract Method

The erroneous method of which we are now to treat, is . . . peculiar to thinking and studious minds. It never could have suggested itself but to persons of some familiarity with the nature of scientific research; who—being aware of the impossibility of establishing, by casual observation or direct experimentation, a true theory of sequences so complex as are those of the social phenomena—have recourse to the simpler laws which are immediately operative in those phenomena, and which are no other than the laws of the nature of the human beings therein concerned. These thinkers perceive (what the partisans of the chemical or experimental theory do not) that the science of society must necessarily be deductive. But, from an insufficient consideration of the specific nature of the subject-matter—and often because (their own scientific education having stopped short in too early a stage) geometry stands in their minds as the type of all deductive science—it is to geometry, rather than to astronomy and natural philosophy, that they unconsciously assimilate the deductive science of society.

Among the differences between geometry (a science of co-existent facts, altogether independent of the laws of the succession of phenomena) and those physical Sciences of Causation which have been rendered deductive, the following is one of the most conspicuous: That geometry affords no room for what so constantly occurs in mechanics and its applications, the case of conflicting forces; of causes which counteract or modify one another. In mechanics we continually find two or more moving forces producing, not motion, but rest; or motion in a different direction from that which would have been produced by either of the generating forces. It is true that the effect of the joint forces is the same when they act simultaneously, as if they had acted one after another, or by turns; and it is in this that the difference between mechanical and chemical law consists. But still the effects, whether produced by successive or by simultaneous action, do, wholly or in part, cancel one another: what the one force does the other, partly or altogether, undoes. There is no similar state of things in geometry. The result which follows from one geometrical principle has nothing that conflicts with the result which follows from another. What is proved true from one geometrical theorem, what would be true if no other geometrical principles existed, cannot be altered and made no longer true by reason of some other geometrical principle. What is once proved true is true in all cases, whatever supposition may be made in regard to any other matter.

Now a conception, similar to this last, would appear to have been formed of the social science, in the minds of the earlier of those who have attempted to cultivate it by a deductive method. Mechanics would be a science very similar to geometry if every motion resulted from one force alone, and not from a conflict of forces. In the geometrical theory of society, it seems to be supposed that this is really the case with the social phenomena; that each of them results always from only one force, one single property of human nature.

At the point which we have now reached, it cannot be necessary to say anything either in proof or in illustration of the assertion that such is not the true character of the social phenmena. There is not, among these most complex and (for that reason) most modifiable of all phenomena, any one over which innumerable forces do not exercise influence; which does not depend on a conjunction of very many causes. We have not, therefore, to prove the notion in question to be an error, but to prove that the error has been committed; that so mistaken a conception of the mode in which the phenomena of society are produced has actually been entertained.

One numerous division of the reasoners who have treated social facts according to geometrical methods, not admitting any modification of one law by another, must for the present be left out of consideration; because in them this error is complicated with, and is the effect of another fundamental misconception, of which we have already taken some notice, and which will be further treated of before we conclude. I speak of those who deduce political conclusions not from laws of nature, not from sequences of phenomena, real or imaginary, but from unbending practical maxims. Such, for example, are all who found their theory of politics on what is called abstract right, that is to say, on universal precepts; a pretension of which we have already noticed the chimerical nature. Such, in like manner, are those who make the assumption of a social contract, or any other kind of original obligation, and apply it to particular cases by mere interpretation. But in this the fundamental error is the attempt to treat an art like a science, and to have a deductive art; the irrationality of which will be shown in a future chapter. It will be proper to take our exemplification of the geometrical theory from those thinkers who have avoided this additional error, and who entertain, so far, a juster idea of the nature of political inquiry.

We may cite, in the first instance, those who assume as the principle of their political philosophy that government is founded on fear; that the dread of each other is the one motive by which human beings were originally brought into a state of society, and are still held in it. Some of the earlier scientific inquirers into politics, in particular Hobbes, assumed this proposition, not by implication, but avowedly, as the foundation of their doctrine, and attempted to build a complete philosophy of politics thereupon. It is true that Hobbes did not find this one maxim sufficient to carry him through the whole of his subject, but was obliged to eke it out by the double sophism of an original contract. I call this a double sophism; first, as passing off a fiction for a fact, and, secondly, assuming a practical principle or precept as the basis of a theory; which is a *petitio principii*, since (as we noticed in treating of that Fallacy) every rule of conduct, even though it be so binding a one as the observance of a promise, must rest its own foundations on the theory of the subject, and the theory, therefore, cannot rest upon it.

Passing over less important instances, I shall come at once to the most remarkable example afforded by our own times of the geometrical method in politics; emanating from persons who are well aware of the distinction between science and art; who knew that rules of conduct must follow, not precede, the ascertainment of laws of nature, and that the latter, not the former, is the legitimate field for the application of the deductive method. I allude to the interest-philosophy of the Bentham school.

The profound and original thinkers who are commonly known under this description, founded their general theory of government on one comprehensive premise, namely, that men's actions are always determined by their interests. There is an ambiguity in this last expression; for, as the same philosophers, especially Bentham, gave the name of an interest to anything which a person likes, the proposition may be understood to mean only this, that men's actions are always determined by their wishes. In this sense, however, it would not bear out any of the consequences which these writers drew from it; and the word, therefore, in their political reasonings, must be understood to mean (which is also the explanation they themselves, on such occasions, gave of it) what is commonly termed private or worldly interest.

Taking the doctrine, then, in this sense, an objection presents itself *in limine* which might be deemed a fatal one, namely, that so sweeping a proposition is far from being universally true. Human beings are not governed in all their actions by their worldly interests. This, however, is by no means so conclusive an objection as it at first appears; because in politics we are for the most part concerned with the conduct, not of individual persons, but either of a series of persons (as a succession of kings), or a body or mass of persons, as a nation, an aristocracy, or a representative assembly. And whatever is true of a large majority of mankind, may without much error be taken for true of any succession of persons, considered as a whole, or of any collection of persons in which the act of the majority becomes the act of the whole body. Although, therefore, the maxim is sometimes expressed in a manner unnecessarily paradoxical, the consequences drawn from it will hold equally good if the assertion be limited as follows: Any succession of persons, or the majority of any body of persons, will be governed in the bulk of their conduct by their personal interests. We are bound to allow to this school of thinkers the benefit of this more rational statement of their fundamental maxim, which is also in strict conformity to the explanations which, when considered to be called for, have been given by themselves.

The theory goes on to infer, quite correctly, that if the actions of mankind are determined in the main by their selfish interests, the only rulers who will govern according to the interest of the governed are those whose selfish interests are in accordance with it. And to this is added a third proposition, namely, that no rulers have their selfish interest identical with that of the governed, unless it be rendered so by accountability, that is, by dependence on the will of the governed. In other words (and as the result of the whole), that the desire of retaining or the fear of losing their power, and whatever is thereon consequent, is the sole motive which can be relied on for producing on the part of rulers a course of conduct in accordance with the general interest.

We have thus a fundamental theorem of political science, consisting of three syllogisms, and depending chiefly on two general premises, in each of which a certain effect is considered as determined only by one cause, not by a concurrence of causes. In the one, it is assumed that the actions of average rulers are determined solely by self-interest; in the other, that the sense of identity of interest with the governed, is produced and producible by no other cause than responsibility.

Neither of these propositions is by any means true; the last is extremely wide of the truth.

It is not true that the actions even of average rulers are wholly, or anything approaching to wholly, determined by their personal interest, or even by their own opinion of their personal interest. I do not speak of the influence of a sense of duty, or feelings of philanthropy, motives never to be mainly relied on, though (except in countries or during periods of great moral debasement) they influence almost all rulers in some degree, and some rulers in a very great degree. But I insist only on what is true of all rulers, viz. that the character and course of their actions is largely influenced (independently of personal calculation) by the habitual sentiments and feelings, the general modes of thinking and acting, which prevail throughout the community of which they are members, as well as by the feelings, habits and modes of thought which characterise the particular class in that community to which they themselves belong. And no one will understand or be able to decipher their system of conduct who does not take all these things into account. They are also much influenced by the maxims and traditions which have descended to them from other rulers, their predecessors; which maxims and traditions have been known to retain an ascendancy during long periods, even in opposition to the private interests of the rulers for the time being. I put aside the influence of other less general causes. Although, therefore, the private interest of the rulers or of the ruling class is a very powerful force, constantly in action, and exercising the most important influence upon their conduct, there is also in what they do a large portion which that private interest by no means affords a sufficient explanation of; and even the particulars which constitute the goodness or badness of their government are in some, and no small degree, influenced by those among the circumstances acting upon them, which cannot, with any propriety, be included in the term self-interest.

Turning now to the other proposition, that responsibility to the governed is the only cause capable of producing in the rulers a sense of identity of interest with the community; this is still less admissible as an universal truth, than even the former. I am not speaking of perfect identity of interest, which is an impracticable chimera, which, most assuredly, responsibility to the people does not give. I speak of identity in essentials; and the essentials are different at different places and times. There are a large number of cases in which those things which it is most for the general interest that the rulers should do, are also those which they are prompted to do by their strongest personal interest, the consolidation of their power. The suppression, for instance, of anarchy and resistance to law—the complete establishment of the authority of the central government, in a state of society like that of Europe in the middle ages—is one of the strongest interests of the people, and also of the rulers simply because they are the rulers: and responsibility on their part could not strengthen, though in many conceivable ways it might weaken, the motives prompting them to pursue this object. During the greater part of the reign of Queen Elizabeth, and of many other monarchs who might be named, the sense of identity of interest between the sovereign and the majority of the people was probably stronger than it usually is in responsible governments: everything that the people had most at heart, the monarch had at heart too. Had Peter the Great, or the rugged savages whom he began to civilize, the truest inclination towards the things which were for the real interest of those savages?

I am not here attempting to establish a theory of government, and am not called upon to determine the proportional weight which ought to be given to the circumstances which this school of geometrical politicians left out of their system, and those which they took into it. I am only concerned to show that their method was unscientific; not to measure the amount of error which may have affected their practical conclusions.

It is but justice to them, however, to remark that their mistake was not so much one of substance as of form; and consisted in presenting in a systematic shape, and as the scientific treatment of a great philosophical question, what should have passed for that which it really was, the mere polemics of the day. Although the actions of rulers are by no means wholly determined by their selfish interests, it is chiefly as a security against those selfish interests that constitutional checks are required; and for that purpose such checks, in England and the other nations of modern Europe, can in no manner be dispensed with. It is likewise true, that in these same nations, and in the present age, responsibility to the governed is the only means practically available to create a feeling of identity of interest, in the cases, and on the points, where that feeling does not sufficiently exist. To all this, and to the arguments which may be founded on it in favour of measures for the correction of our representative system, I have nothing to object; but I confess my regret, that the small though highly important portion of the philosophy of government, which was wanted for the immediate purpose of serving the cause of parliamentary reform, should have been held forth by thinkers of such eminence as a complete theory.

It is not to be imagined possible, nor is it true in point of fact, that these philosophers regarded the few premises of their theory as including all that is required for explaining social phenomena, or for determining the choice of forms of government and measures of legislation and administration. They were too highly instructed, of too comprehensive intellect, and some of them of too sober and practical a character, for such an error. They would have applied, and did apply, their principles with innumerable allowances. But it is not allowances that are wanted. There is little chance of making due amends in the superstructure of a theory for the want of sufficient breadth in its foundations. It is unphilosophical to construct a science out of a few of the agencies by which the phenomena are determined, and leave the rest to the routine of practice or the sagacity of conjecture. We either ought not to pretend to scientific forms, or we ought to study all the determining agencies equally, and endeavour, so far as it can be done, to include all of them within the pale of the science; else we shall infallibly bestow a disproportionate attention upon those which our theory takes into account, while we misestimate the rest, and probably underrate their importance. That the deductions should be from the whole and not from a part only of the laws of nature that are concerned, would be desirable even if those omitted were so insignificant in comparison with the others, that they might, for most purposes and on most occasions, be left out of the account. But this is far indeed from being true in the social science. The phenomena of society do not depend, in essentials, on some one agency or law of human nature, with only inconsiderable modifications from others. The whole of the qualities of human nature influence those phenomena, and there is not one which influences them in a small degree. There is not one, the removal or any great alteration of which would not materially affect the whole aspect of society, and change more or less the sequences of social phenomena generally.

The theory which has been the subject of these remarks is, in this country at least, the principal contemporary example of what I have styled the geometrical method of philosophizing in the social science; and our examination of it has, for this reason, been more detailed than would otherwise have been suitable to a work like the present. Having now sufficiently illustrated the two erroneous methods, we shall pass without further preliminary to the true method; that which proceeds (comformably to the practice of the more complex physical sciences) deductively indeed, but by deduction from many, not from one or a very few, original premises; considering each effect as (what it really is) an aggregate result of many causes, operating sometimes through the same, sometimes through different mental agencies, or laws of human nature.

Appendix: Utilitarian Ethics

THERE are a few passages in Macaulay's articles which raise important questions about Utilitarian ethics. In places Macaulay writes as if he were quite content to go along with the Utilitarian assertion that the end of government is 'to increase to the utmost the pleasures, and diminish to the utmost the pains, which men derive from each other' (p. 56). Indeed, he states emphatically that he has 'never said a syllable' against the 'greatest happiness principle' and contends that, in his original attack on James Mill's essay, 'we reasoned throughout . . . on the supposition that the end of government was to produce the greatest happiness to mankind' (p. 170). Nevertheless Macaulay makes a number of criticisms of the classical Utilitarian position which are clearly related to some of the main issues in the continuing controversy about Utilitarianism as a moral and political philosophy.

We have already referred, in our introduction, to Macaulay's objection to the claim that men always act from self interest; a proposition, he argues, which is either 'identical' (saying no more, in effect, than 'whatever is, is') or, if the meaning of self-interest is narrowed, palpably false. Now, an important issue, both in relation to Bentham and James Mill and to the debate over 'naturalism' in twentieth-century moral philosophy, arises in connection with such *facts* as may be asserted about human behaviour—e.g. that men always *do* act from self-interest (if this is a *factual* assertion)—and any moral judgements which may be thought to follow, in some sense or other, from those facts. The distinction commonly made between 'naturalists' and 'anti-naturalists', and the arguments stemming from Moore's account of the so-called 'naturalistic fallacy', suggest a line of division between those, on the one hand, who contend that 'ethics is autonomous' or that there is a logical gap between 'fact' and 'value' or that no moral conclusions can be derived from purely factual premises and those, on the other hand, who would deny these contentions. We cannot enter into this controversy here but we do want to draw attention to Macaulay's place in the history of the debate, albeit a modest and largely unknown one; and Moore's claim to have exposed the 'naturalistic fallacy' would seem to be an appropriate point of departure.

In his study, *Utilitarian Ethics*, Anthony Quinton writes:

G. E. Moore's *Principia Ethica* of 1903 has been by far the most influential criticism of utilitarian ethics. The purported refutation of ethical naturalism, which is the book's fundamental thesis, dominated moral philosophy for the first half of this century in Britain . . . Its essential claim is that judgements of value, and, in particular, moral judgements, cannot be taken to be, or to be strictly deducible from, statements of ordinary, natural, empirical fact . . . [according to Moore] judgements of value report unordinary, moral facts about an autonomous realm of values.[1]

That Utilitarianism was one of Moore's principal targets is evident from the opening passage of his third chapter:

. . . that pleasure has been so generally held to be the sole good, is almost entirely due to the fact that it has seemed to be somehow involved in the *definition* of 'good'—to be pointed out by the very meaning of the word. If this is so, then the prevalence of Hedonism has been mainly due to what I have called the naturalistic fallacy—the failure to distinguish clearly that unique and indefinable quality which we mean by good.[2]

The fallacy to which Moore refers is constituted by the attempt to define 'good' because, he maintains, it cannot be defined. It may well be the case that all things which we say are good regularly possess some other properties and it is an important task in Ethics to determine what those properties are. But to identify these properties is not to define 'good'. To suppose that these properties are 'simply not "other", but absolutely and entirely the same with goodness' is to commit the 'naturalistic fallacy'.[3]

Commentators have found much that is obscure or question-begging in Moore's account of the naturalistic fallacy[4] but one of the arguments he used in order to establish it as a fallacy has been regarded by some philosophers as a powerful objection to all attempts to identify moral goodness with any empirical property, or set of properties. If someone were to say that 'pleasure is good', Moore contends, it cannot be that he merely means to say that 'pleasure is pleasure' and just that; for 'there is no meaning in saying that pleasure is good, unless good is something different from pleasure.'[5] Whatever state of affairs is asserted to be synonymous or identical with 'good', argues Moore, it always makes sense to ask of that state of affairs whether it is good. Or, to make the point in another way, 'whatever naturalistic value satisfies the variable x, to assert that x is good, right, or obligatory is not to assert a statement that cannot be denied without contradiction.'[6]

Moore concluded, then, that 'good' is indefinable and, he went on to remark, Sidgwick was the only moral philosopher to have shown

[1] op. cit. (1973), pp. 98–9.

[2] G. E. Moore: *Principia Ethica* (1903), p. 59.

[3] ibid.,p. 10.

[4] See W. K. Frankena: 'The Naturalistic Fallacy,' *Mind*, vol. 48 (1939), reprinted in *Theories of Ethics*, ed. by Philippa Foot; A. Prior: *Logic and the Basis of Ethics*, chap. 1; and Mary Warnock: *Ethics since 1900*, chap. 2.

[5] G. E. Moore: op. cit., pp. 12, 14.

[6] Kai Nielsen: 'Problems of Ethics', in *The Encyclopedia of Philosophy*, edited by Paul Edwards, vol. 3, p. 127.

clear recognition of this important fact. A. N. Prior, in an historical survey of the naturalistic fallacy, also singles out Sidgwick as 'the first writer to charge Bentham, in effect, with committing the naturalistic fallacy' and quotes the same passage from Sidgwick's *Methods of Ethics* cited by Moore. The passage, he says, is 'of considerable historical importance, as there is good reason to believe that it inspired Professor Moore's work on the "naturalistic fallacy"'.[7] It runs as follows:

. . . when Bentham explains . . . that his fundamental principle 'states the greatest happiness of all those whose interest is in question as being the right and proper end of human action', we cannot understand him really to *mean* by the word 'right' 'conducive to the general happiness', though his language in other passages of the same chapter . . . would seem to imply this; for the proposition that it is conducive to general happiness to take general happiness as an end of action, though not exactly a tautology, can hardly serve as the fundamental principle of a moral system.[8]

Moreover, adds Prior, Sidgwick's posthumously published work, *The Ethics of Green, Spencer, and Martineau* has some remarks about Herbert Spencer which come 'still closer to the language of Professor Moore':

we must distinguish inquiry into the meaning of words from inquiry into ethical principles. I agree with Mr. Spencer in holding that 'pleasure is the ultimate good', but not in the meaning which he gives to the word 'good'. Indeed, if 'good' (substantive) means 'pleasure', the proposition just stated would be a tautology, and a tautology cannot be an ethical principle.[9]

But, Prior maintains, what Moore identifies as the 'naturalistic fallacy' Sidgwick rightly treats as an element in a larger error, namely 'the denial of the autonomy of ethics'.[10]

What was not known to Prior at the time when he referred to Sidgwick's criticism of Bentham was that Macaulay, replying to the *Westminster Review*'s defence of Mill in the belief that Bentham was its author, makes substantially the same charge later levelled by Sidgwick. Macaulay quotes the passage in the *Westminster Review* in which it is stated that 'the word *ought*, if it means anything, must have reference to some kind of interest or motives'. Macaulay goes on:

---

[7] A. Prior: *Logic and the Basis of Ethics*, pp. 104–5.

[8] Henry Sidgwick: *The Methods of Ethics*, p. 26, footnote. 'It is not "exactly" a tautology,' explains Prior, 'because to aim at some end is not necessarily the best way of actually realising it.' A. Prior: op. cit., p. 105.

[9] Sidgwick, quoted in Prior: op. cit., p. 106.

[10] ibid., p. 107.

The principle of Mr. Bentham, if we understand it, is this, that mankind ought to act so as to produce their greatest happiness. The word *ought*, he tells us, has no meaning, unless it be used with reference to some interest. But the interest of a man is synonymous with his greatest happiness:—and therefore to say that a man ought to do a thing, is to say that it is for his greatest happiness to do it. And to say that mankind *ought* to act so as to produce their greatest happiness, is to say that the greatest happiness is the greatest happiness—and this is all! (p. 171)[11]

But Macaulay does not confine himself to making a purely meta-ethical criticism of the Utilitarian position, for immediately after the passage we have just quoted he goes on to raise an important substantive question about Utilitarian ethics which is still far from being resolved. On the one hand the Utilitarians assert it as a truth about human nature that every man pursues his own happiness or interest. But, on the other hand, they also proclaim the greatest happiness of mankind as their ultimate goal and the true standard of right actions. How, asks Macaulay, are these two assertions to be reconciled? Bentham, he claims, has offered 'no reason why a man should promote the greatest happiness of others if their greatest happiness be inconsistent with what he thinks his own' (p. 171). To which the *Westminster Review* gives the answer that 'the greatest happiness of the individual was in the long run to be obtained by pursuing the greatest happiness of the aggregate . . . an extension of the ancient proverb, that honesty is the best policy . . . "Pursue the rule which tends to the greatest general happiness, in preference to *this* greatest happiness; and the chances are, you will be the better for it in the end." There is a momentary interest and a final one; an apparent interest and a real one; and what is desired is to persuade men to take the one and not the other' (p. 190).

We should note two significant points in this last passage, but only in passing. The precept, 'pursue the *rule* which tends to the greatest general happiness', could well be construed to imply a 'rule' rather than an 'act' type of Utilitarianism. And whilst the distinction between 'apparent' and 'real' interest might seem to close the gap between individual and general happiness it might also generate formidable problems on its own account. Both these matters have figured prominently in subsequent discussions about Utilitarianism. Let us, however, return to the problem of reconciling individual

---

[11] Quinton quotes a remark from James Mill's *Fragment on Mackintosh*: 'The theory of utility makes the utility of an act and the morality of an act two names for the same thing.' Quinton goes on: 'In other words for him the principle of utility is an analytic truth, true in virtue of the meanings of the words of which it is composed. But this is a somewhat parenthetical observation and Mill does not explore its implications. In particular, he does not ask how those who have denied it could have failed to be aware that they were guilty of self-contradiction.' A. Quinton, op. cit., p. 37.

happiness with aggregate happiness, a problem much canvassed since Macaulay's time.

Quinton says, after quoting the well-known opening lines of Bentham's *Principles of Morals and Legislation:* 'Bentham, in effect, asserts both utilitarianism, which states that men ought to aim at the general happiness, and egoism, which states that in actual fact men always aim at their own happiness. His utilitarianism is an ethical theory; his egoism a psychological one.'[12]

He goes on to suggest that the way the two doctrines are presented is meant to imply that there is a significant relationship between them. But, as he points out, it has often been claimed that the two assertions are not compatible with each other; which was, of course, Macaulay's view. How then, might they be reconciled?

The alleged inconsistency between the two assertions is commonly said to derive from the fact that we cannot say of a man that he *ought* to do something unless he *can* do it. If therefore a man is capable only of seeking his own happiness it cannot be the case that he ought to promote the general happiness. However, argues Quinton, what a man *can* do must include what he might be induced to do by a system of sanctions, and if the sanctions are so designed as to promote the general happiness then the inconsistency disappears. We should notice, incidentally, that this argument bears a striking resemblance to James Mill's case for constitutional checks, i.e. that the rulers can be *induced*, through fear of dismissal at elections, to promote the general interest.

Like Halévy and others, Quinton attributes to the Utilitarians the belief that there is a natural harmony of interests and this seems to be the assumption involved in the *Westminster Review*'s claim that the individual's best policy is to act in accordance with the general interest.[13] But the Utilitarians also held, so Quinton maintains (following Halévy again), that the harmony of interests must be secured, in certain areas of social life, by artificial means, through the use of sanctions; because, though a fully rational agent will recognize that his own personal happiness is best achieved by acting to promote the wider happiness, 'men are not all rational and perhaps none are wholly rational'.[14] Here Quinton would seem to be making essentially the same point as the *Westminster Review* in the distinction it drew between real and apparent interests.

Quinton doubts that there is, or could be, an 'ultimate natural harmony of interests', though he thinks there are strong reasons for holding the view that an individual's own happiness requires for its realization that those who constitute his social circle should be happy too or, at least, not miserable. He seems to regard this last consideration enough to show that there is no necessary and direct

[12] Quinton: op. cit., p. 6.
[13] Elie Halévy: *The Growth of Philosophic Radicalism*, pp. 15–17.
[14] A. Quinton: op. cit., p. 7.

incompatibility between the greatest happiness principle and psychological egoism. And to the extent that there is a lack of natural harmony the deficiency can be remedied, to repeat, by inducing men to act in the general interest through a system of carefully devised sanctions.[15]

The reader will notice that in his last article Macaulay signifies his agreement with Bentham 'that there are no occasions in which a man has not *some* motives for consulting the happiness of other men . . . sympathy on all occasions, and the love of reputation on most occasions'. This, he insists, is 'the very doctrine which we have been maintaining against Mr. Mill and the Westminster Reviewer'. It is precisely these motives that Mill 'left out of consideration in his theory' (p. 216). But what Macaulay says here surely falls far short of the position which Quinton defends. And the question he flings at the Westminster Reviewer in the passage we quote below is a strong indication that he did not share Quinton's view of how a fully rational man, out to promote his own interests in our sort of world, would tend to act:

Does he [the Westminster Reviewer] not see that it is no more possible to reason a man out of liking a short life and a merry one than a long life and a dull one than to reason a Greenlander out of his train oil? We may say that the tastes of the thief and the tyrant differ from ours; but what right have we to say, looking at this world alone, that they do not pursue their greatest happiness very judiciously? (p. 218).

[15] Ibid., pp. 6–10. See also the discussion in David Lyons: *In the Interest of the Governed* (1973).

Index

Index